D1715656

Network Reengineering

Network Reengineering

The New Technical Imperative

James T. Geier

McGraw-Hill

New York San Francisco Washington, D.C. Auckland Bogotá
Caracas Lisbon London Madrid Mexico City Milan
Montreal New Delhi San Juan Singapore
Sydney Tokyo Toronto

McGraw-Hill

A Division of The McGraw-Hill Companies

Library of Congress Cataloging-in-Publication Data

Geier, James T.
   Network reengineering: the new technical imperative / by James T.
Geier.
      p.   cm.
   Includes index.
   ISBN 0-07-023034-X
   1. Computer networks—Management.   2. Reengineering (Management)
I. Title
TK5105.5.G45   1996
004.6'068'4—dc20   96-232
                                                                   CIP

1 2 3 4 5 6 7 8 9 0   DOC/DOC   9 0 0 9 8 7 6

ISBN 0-07-023034-X

*The sponsoring editor of this book was John Wyzalek. The book editors
were Michael Christopher and David M. McCandless, the executive
editor was Lori Flaherty, and the indexer was Jennifer M. Secula. The
production supervisor was Katherine G. Brown. This book was set in ITC
Century Light. It was composed in Blue Ridge Summit, PA.*

Printed and bound by R. R. Donnelley & Sons Crawfordsville, Indiana.

McGraw-Hill books are available at special quantity discounts to use as
premiums and sales promotions, or for use in corporate training programs.
For more information, please write to the Director of Special Sales, McGraw-
Hill, 11 West 19th Street, New York, NY 10011. Or contact your local
bookstore.

Product or brand names used in this book may be trade names or
trademarks. Where we believe that there may be proprietary claims to such
trade names or trademarks, the name has been used with an initial capital or
it has been capitalized in the style used by the name claimant. Regardless of
the capitalization used, all such names have been used in an editorial
manner without any intent to convey endorsement of or other affiliation
with the name claimant. Neither the author nor the publisher intends to
express any judgment as to the validity or legal status of any such
proprietary claims.

MH96

Contents

Part 1   Planning

Part 2   Analysis and Design

Part 3 Implementation

Acknowledgments

I would like to express my gratitude to those people who assisted me in writing this book. Many thanks to my wife, Debra Geier, for the many hours she spent reviewing manuscript drafts and editing the list of network vendors. Special thanks to my sons Evan, Brian, Eric, and Jared, for their interest in my book-writing efforts (and allowing Dad to work with very few interruptions!). I also extend my appreciation to Barbara Moore for her consultation on the requirements analysis chapter.

Finally, I would like to dedicate this book to my parents.

Introduction

Over the past decade, computer networks have become a key component for supporting corporate needs of acquiring, storing, and exchanging information. Organizations around the globe have begun to understand the value of utilizing networks to deal economically with an ever-increasing amount of information. The result has been a steady proliferation of networks.

One problem, though, is that many organizations do not have processes in place to direct necessary network alterations that result from the introduction of new technologies and rapid changes in organizational environments. Therefore, existing networks are quickly becoming out-of-date and are not effectively satisfying the needs of the users. The solution to this quandary is to implement a network reengineering process that identifies when to modify the network and specifies how to implement appropriate changes. This allows an organization to proactively control the evolution of its network, which increases user productivity and avoids the creation of a legacy system.

The goal of this book is to introduce you to a network reengineering process that will help organizations ensure that their networks will continue to effectively support their users. The book identifies many factors that may influence an organization to modify its network. It also shows how to determine the feasibility of proposed changes, and explains steps necessary to implement applicable alterations. Thus, the book shows how to keep existing computer networks in line with management plans for the future, application changes, and shifts in technologies.

This book is for both managers and technologists involved in the management, development, implementation, and support of computer networks. By applying the ideas presented here, project managers, MIS directors, network support managers, system administrators, and engineering managers can learn how to develop and maintain a network capable of dealing effectively with factors influencing change. Technologists, such as engineers, analysts, and technicians, can utilize the book to understand principles and methodologies involved in performing requirements analysis, design, installation, and operational support activities.

The book contains the following parts and chapters:

Part 1: Planning

Chapter 1: Introduction to Network Reengineering

This chapter introduces the overall concept of network reengineering by defining a computer network and its life cycle, identifying factors that may sway an organization to reshape its network, and describing a methodology to implement network changes. The chapter also shows how an organization can incorporate a network reengineering process.

Chapter 2: Factors that Influence Network Modifications

To implement network reengineering, an organization must be capable of identifying factors indicating the need for reshaping its network. In addition, to facilitate funding, the organization must determine whether proposed network changes are feasible. This chapter describes factors that may influence an organization to alter its network and shows how to justify the ones dictating changes.

Chapter 3: Planning a Network Modification

Once an organization decides to change its network, a project team should carefully plan a network modification project. A successful modification requires the use of project management principles and knowledge of issues related to the specific network change(s) being undertaken. This chapter covers basic project management concepts and the principles necessary to properly plan a network project.

Part 2: Analysis and Design

Chapter 4: Requirements Analysis

After planning of the project, the next step is requirements analysis . An initial network creation will always demand a complete requirements analysis; however, other types of modifications might need only a review and a possible update of existing requirements. Properly completing a requirements analysis simplifies the design and maximizes the implementation of a modification that effectively satisfies user and organizational needs. This chapter explains the concepts and types of network requirements, general requirements analysis procedures, and how to determine requirements for each factor that may have influenced the network change. These topics explain what is necessary to prepare requirements in a form that eases the design of the network.

Chapter 5: Network Design Concepts

Organizations commonly "design" networks by haphazardly selecting and purchasing components. This often leads to networks full of operational headaches, such as excessive delay, interoperability problems, and missing functionality. A structured, well-planned design will yield much better results. This chapter describes a network design methodology that facilitates the selection of a solution that best satisfies requirements.

Chapter 6: High-Level Design Specifications

Part of the design methodology is to select specifications based on a top-down approach. This includes the need to first define high-level, then lower-level, specifications. The reason for assigning values to high-level specifications first is that they typically satisfy requirements directly. This chapter describes and offers tips on selecting high-level design specifications.

Chapter 7: Low-Level Design Specifications

This chapter continues the presentation of design specifications but emphasizes ones that deal with lower levels of the network architecture. Most of these low-level design specifications directly satisfy other higher-level design attributes, such as signaling and synchronization types.

Part 3: Implementation

Chapter 8: Preparing for Operational Support

The applications and services a network provides will not meet the users' expectations unless the project team fully defines the elements necessary for network operations. Operational support deficiencies equate to decreased user efficiency and higher operating costs. Most modifications will require preparations for operational support; therefore, the project team will need to identify proper network support that maximizes effectiveness of the network. This chapter identifies how to determine and plan for various types of operational support. The emphasis in this chapter is on support preparation; that is, what needs to be in place before turning the modified network over to the users in a production environment.

Chapter 9: Network Installation

After receiving network components, the project team should be ready to install the components and complete the modification. Many organizations install the entire network, then use the "big bang" concept of testing. The problem with this approach is that it is very expensive to correct defects in the design or installation during the final stages of installation. A well-planned installation is completed on time and within budget. This chapter covers applicable preparations and execution procedures for network installations that minimize defects, installation time, and user disturbances.

Chapter 10: Transferring the Network to Operational Mode

After completing the installation and testing of network components, the project team should transfer the network to operational mode. An official transfer avoids common misunderstandings of network functionality and operational responsibilities. This chapter explains how to prepare for the proper transfer of a network to operational mode, how to close the project, and how to evaluate the project outcome.

Part 4: Appendices

Appendix A: Network Component Vendors

This appendix characterizes many network component vendors. For each vendor, a description identifies company contact information, history, and applicable product types.

Appendix B: Network Standards

This appendix lists many common IEEE, EIA, ANSI, and ISO networking standards.

Glossary of Network Terminology

This comprehensive glossary defines numerous computer networking terms. Readers should refer here to find the definition of a phrase or acronym.

Planning

Chapter

1

Introduction to Network Reengineering

Most network managers realize that their current network will not continually satisfy the needs of its users. Factors such as new applications, technology shifts, and organizational resizing can influence an organization to modify the network. Network reengineering is a process for identifying the need to modify the network and implementing the appropriate changes, allowing an organization to proactively control the evolution of its network. This chapter introduces the concept of network reengineering by identifying factors that might influence an organization to modify its network, and by describing a methodology to implement potential network changes. The chapter also shows how an organization can incorporate a network reengineering process.

The Network Life Cycle

It is important to understand the general life cycle of a network before considering network reengineering concepts. This makes it easier to see where network reengineering fits into the network's life. Figure 1.1 identifies each phase of a typical network life cycle. A network is created because of some initial need or reason for the services a network can provide. The decision to establish a network could be based on an in-depth analysis of the benefits of implementing office automation within an organization, or simply the desire to "stay with the times." The latter occurs most often. With enough reason, whether justifiable or not, the network's life then begins with the creation phase and continues on through the operational stage, as described next.

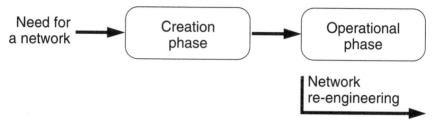

Figure 1.1 The network life cycle

Network Creation Phase

The creation phase consists of a user needs analysis, design, installation, testing, and planning for operational support. During the creation phase, system analysts and engineers specify the network as a set of hardware and software that provides the services the organization desires, such as electronic mail, file transfer, peripheral sharing, and use of groupware applications.

Next, a project team develops and implements the network through various additional phases. Figure 1.2 identifies each major part of the creation phase, which includes requirements analysis, design, preparations for operational support, and installation. A project manager is normally responsible for the network during completion of the creation phase. The following paragraphs give a brief description of each part of the creation phase.

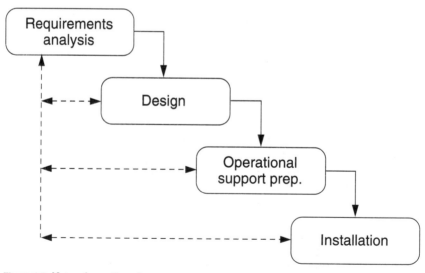

Figure 1.2 Network creation phase

Requirements analysis

The requirements (needs) analysis identifies what the network is supposed to do. It defines the interface between the user and the network, as well as the interface between the network and other systems. This is a step, however, which many organizations overlook or do not adequately accomplish during network creation. The resulting lack of requirements leads to the development and implementation of a network that does not adequately satisfy the needs of its users.

Design

The design determines how the network will do what it is supposed to do. The design identifies necessary technologies, standards, and components necessary to satisfy requirements. The design should specify everything needed to implement the network, such as schematics, cabling drawings, and a materials list.

Preparation for operational support

Soon after (and sometimes during) installation, users will begin utilizing the network. Therefore, the organization must have operational support ready to assist users and maintain the network. Preparations include training development and delivery, and plans for support elements such as maintenance, system administration, and security.

Installation

The installation, often referred to as implementation, begins when an organization installs the network components and runs tests to verify proper operation of the network. This is the "hands-on" part of network creation, and organizations spend most of their time on this stage. However, because many organizations do not emphasize requirements analysis and design, most problems dealing with network creation occur during the network installation.

Network Operational Phase

The final phase in the life of a network is the operational phase, which begins when the network is in production mode and fully capable of supporting user needs. This is when people can utilize the network's services, and mechanisms should be in place to ensure that these services are available. A network manager is responsible for the network during its operational phase. Operational support is critical to the success of the network, and it needs to be planned before installing network components. As shown in

Figure 1.3, an operational support infrastructure consists of many elements. The pieces that provide support are described below:

System administration

A system administrator provides an interface between the system and its users. The system administrator assigns user addresses and log-in passwords, allocates network resources, and performs some network security functions.

Network monitoring

Network monitoring allows network staff members to view the inner workings of the network. Most network monitoring equipment is nonobtrusive and can determine the network's utilization and locate faults. The effective use of communications monitoring equipment can detect most communications problems before they affect the users. Thus, network monitoring can provide proactive maintenance.

Accounting and chargeback

Accounting and chargeback is a mechanism that keeps track of network utilization and determines charges for resources utilized. Users, departments, or divisions can then be charged accordingly. Network managers can use accounting and chargeback to fund network operations and reengineering activities.

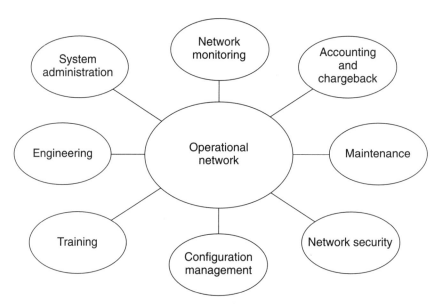

Figure 1.3 Network operational support infrastructure

Maintenance

Maintenance is a mechanism that corrects problems that might occur on the network. Maintenance includes functions such as fault isolation (trouble shooting), repair, and testing. From time to time, a network might fail because of a hard drive crash, a cable break, or unexpected congestion. Network downtime often infuriates users, and rightly so, because they cannot access their work while the network is inoperative. A network manager must have an effective maintenance function that can correct problems quickly and accurately to avoid needless network downtime.

Network security

Network security attempts to protect the network from compromise and destruction, as well as make sure the network will be available when needed. Network security includes elements such as access control, data encryption, and data backup. With proper security, users can depend on the network and its resources to be available when needed.

Configuration management

Configuration management procedures make certain that there is a complete description of the network components, and that proper control exists for making network changes. Configuration management typically requires that anyone wanting to change the network must first request the change by having a technical and managerial review of the recommended change. If the change is approved, then the person requesting the change must not only ensure the change is made but must also update applicable documentation. With proper configuration management, it is much easier to support the network because documentation will accurately reflect the current network configuration.

Training

Training provides users and system administrators with initial and continuous instruction to ensure proper utilization of the network. Users need to know how to log on to the network and how to use network services and run applications. System administrators must know how to manage network peripherals and user accounts. Without training, system administrators will not be able to effectively manage the network, and users will become frustrated because they will probably waste time trying to learn how to perform the network services.

Engineering

During the implementation of the network, project members utilize engineering principles to design the system. This is imperative to the proper operation of the network. Engineering should not stop when the implementation team deems the network operational. As the network becomes older, the needs of the users might change. Therefore, that network might no longer be an effective solution, and the organization would need to reengineer the network.

Network reengineering concepts

Network managers must constantly be aware of and should monitor factors that could influence a decision to modify the existing network. These influencing factors are based on changes in circumstances dealing with the network, the environment, and other systems. As explained in Chapter 2, examples of factors that commonly influence a network change include user needs variations, shifts in technologies, organizational moves and resizing, operational problems, limited network coverage, and funding reductions. As shown in Figure 1.1, network reengineering takes place mainly during the operational phase of the network's life; however, most procedures of this modification process apply to initial network developments as well. For example, someone without an existing network can utilize the modification process this book describes to effectively incorporate a network. In this case, the element influencing changes is the fact that no network exists. Figure 1.4 illustrates the network reengineering process. It consists of continually identifying factors influencing network changes, analyzing the feasibility of countering the factors, and performing modifications as necessary.

Identifying Influencing Factors

An organization should implement network reengineering by continually monitoring the magnitude of influencing factors. When a factor appears to be significant, the organization should analyze the benefits and costs of modifying the network to counter the influencing factor. To identify influencing factors, the network manager should keep abreast of new technologies and applications, company plans, and user problems and comments. New technologies often lead to faster and cheaper ways of networking, and new applications can provide users higher productivity. Company plans can alert the network manager to any facility relocations and company resizing. User problems and com-

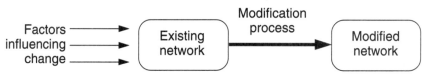

Figure 1.4   Network reengineering process

ments can point to operational problems. Managers should continually monitor influencing factors by utilizing the existing network support infrastructure to the maximum extent. This entails using the experiences gained through system administration, network monitoring, and maintenance.

Analyzing Modification Feasibility

The network manager should determine the feasibility of countering influencing factors that might arise. This provides justification for making network changes. In general, making a network change should result in enough benefits to make it worth funding.

Sometimes, however, such as in the case of a facility relocation, upper management might just tell the network manager, "We're moving!" In many cases, upper management might not have included the costs of relocating the network when considering the overall feasibility of moving the organization. In such cases, the network manager might have to figure the costs of moving the network. These costs might then influence the organization not to move.

Performing Modifications

If it is feasible to modify the network, the organization should establish a team to implement network changes through a carefully planned network modification. As shown in Figure 1.5, the steps involved in implementing network reengineering modifications are similar to the initial network development steps described earlier in this chapter. The next several paragraphs define each step.

Network modification planning

The first step of a network modification is for the network manager to make appropriate plans, including the who, what, when, and where of the modification. The "who" corresponds to a project team, which is a group of individuals with the skill set necessary to carry out the alterations. The "what" refers to the goals of the network modification; that is, what part of the network needs to be changed, for example. The "when" refers to the modification schedule and milestones, and the "where" identifies the facility in which the changes will take place and which users it will affect. Planning the network modification is very important. It increases the probability of finishing the project on time and within budget. Chapter 3 provides details on planning network modifications.

Requirements redetermination

The next step is for the project team to analyze requirements, which identify what the network is supposed to do and provide a basis for the network

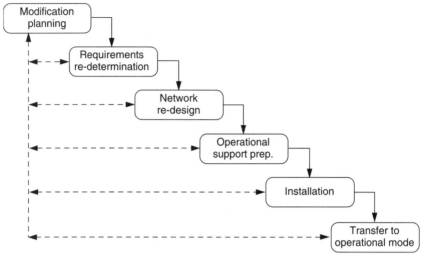

Figure 1.5 Network modification steps

redesign. If existing requirements are accurate, the modification team might just need to review the requirements and begin redesigning the network. If no requirements are available, or if the requirements are outdated or not accurate, then the team should reestablish the requirements. Without accurate requirements the future network will probably not meet the needs of its users. Chapter 4 covers the details of requirements analysis.

Network redesign

The next step for the team is to design the network modification to satisfy network requirements. The network design determines how the network will meet requirements, which involves the selection of technologies, standards, and products that provide a solution. The design is an integral part of the network modification because it highly affects eventual system performance and maintainability. Chapter 5 focuses on the concepts and process of network design.

Operational support preparations

Before implementing the network design changes, it is necessary to plan new levels of operational support. Operational support covers all network elements, such as hardware, software, communications, and users. If the team does not plan adequate support, the network might not provide timely services to its users. Chapter 8 explains how to prepare for network operational support.

Installation

Next, the organization should install the components for the modification based on the outcome of the design. Chapter 9 provides details on installation and testing.

Transfer to operational mode

After the team fully tests the network and fixes any problems that were found, the team should close the project and transfer the responsibility for the network to the appropriate people and organizations. Chapter 10 explains much more about the process of transferring a network to operational support.

It is not always necessary to fully implement each step of the modification process for every type of network change. For instance, the need to upgrade the network's e-mail system from version 2.3 to version 2.4 will probably not require any design changes. However, the incorporation of user mobility will normally require design changes in addition to installation. Table 1.1 identifies the degree of significance for each modification step, based on types of modifications.

TABLE 1.1 Degree of Importance of Each Modification Step in Relation to the Type of Modification

Factor influencing change	Modification steps					
	Planning	Req. analysis	Design	Ops. support preparation	Installation	Turn over
User needs changes	3	3	2	2	2	3
Technology changes	3	2	3	2	2	3
Organizational re-sizing	3	2	2	2	3	3
Organizational moves	3	2	2	2	3	3
Operational problems	3	1	2	1	2	3
Limited network	3	2	2	2	3	3
Non-existent network	3	3	3	3	3	3

1-Low importance
2-Moderate importance
3-High importance

Benefits of Network Reengineering

By following network reengineering principles, an organization can proactively control the evolution of a network. This ensures that the network will always remain finely tuned to the needs of its users, which maximizes user productivity and cost savings. Other benefits include fewer system failures and avoidance of the creation of a legacy system. As a result, network reengineering can provide "just-in-time networking" to an organization.

Higher User Productivity

Network reengineering promotes higher user productivity because the resulting network will closely match the needs of its users. A reengineered network will be utilizing the most effective applications, technologies, and operational support mechanisms. Thus, the network will offer the most efficient services to its users.

Vendors are constantly improving their applications in terms of the human factors, incorporating group functions and integrating voice, video, and data. Users can be more productive by having applications that make more effective use of their time. As a result, though, this often means reengineering the network to support the increasing demands of these applications. As technologies evolve, vendors build networking components that are faster and provide more capabilities. By utilizing network reengineering and incorporating these technologies into the existing network, users are enabled to perform their tasks faster, thus increasing their productivity.

Greater Cost Savings

By incorporating network reengineering concepts, an organization can realize cost savings. Cost savings are based on higher user productivity, lower maintenance costs, and less expensive implementations. With a network providing efficient services, users are able to perform tasks faster and with better quality. As a result, their organizations will save money and increase profits because it will take less time (thus less money) to complete a project.

Even though a network might meet its users' expectations, it might not be easily maintainable. If technologies or components become obsolete, it becomes increasingly difficult to find companies that will sell or support these components. If a vendor is found, the components are often expensive because of very little supply and low demand. Maintaining a system utilizing obsolete technologies is more expensive because of the difficulty in finding people still proficient in these components. Organizations in this position are likely to spend extra money on specialized consultants for network maintenance. Network reengineering can correct this problem by creating a more easily maintainable and less expensive system that still meets user requirements.

Newer technologies often result in systems that are less expensive to implement and operate than systems based on older technologies. For example, it might be less expensive to utilize a distributed LAN versus a centralized mainframe system. By utilizing the network reengineering methodology, organizations will spot the advantages of newer technologies and possibly justify the transition to newer, less expensive technical approaches.

Thus, network reengineering makes certain that users are productive and the network costs are kept to a minimum. This is often the strongest justification for reengineering a network. If an organization chooses not to reengineer, often the network will become inefficient because of the higher costs needed to support components that become obsolete.

Decreased Cost of System Failure

The cost of failure increases exponentially relative to the degree of automation. As more applications are built around a common network infrastructure, and more and more of the company's workflow is supported by those applications, the network becomes an increasingly critical facility. Figure 1.6 illustrates the relationship between the percentage of applications which are networked and the cost of network downtime. A well reengineered network can provide optimum fault-tolerant capabilities, lessening system failures and associated costs.

Legacy System Avoidance

As new components or technologies are brought in they almost never fully replace previous components. The old components are used in less de-

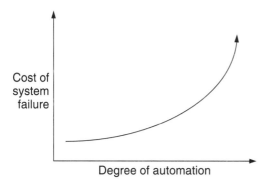

Figure 1.6 Cost of system failure versus degree of automation

manding applications but continue to serve in some capacity. This means the network manager must understand not only the current technology, but the installed-base legacy which might extend back ten years, twenty years, or more. Often, these older parts of the system "slip away;" that is, documentation is not kept up-to-date and support diminishes. As a result, it becomes very difficult to integrate modifications into the existing system. Network reengineering can ensure that a system will not become a needless problem by making certain that modifications are made correctly, documentation is completed and maintained, and all support mechanisms are put in place.

Implementing the Network Reengineering Process

Network reengineering offers many benefits, and it should be an integral part of any organization's network management group. As with other new concepts or methodologies, it might take some time and effort to convince an organization to implement network reengineering principles.

As with any unfamiliar methodology, an organization must make a conscious effort to incorporate different ways of doing things. Network reengineering is not an exception. It might take some education to help organizations establish a network reengineering mindset. Once the mindset it established, though, an organization can utilize network reengineering to keep their network highly effective at satisfying user needs.

An organization should plan the incorporation of network reengineering. To initially implement network reengineering, an organization should accomplish the following steps.

1. Educate upper management.
2. Establish a network reengineering team.
3. Investigate existing influencing factors.
4. Implement necessary modifications.
5. Continually monitor influencing factors.

Educating upper management

Often, an organization's upper management is not aware of the factors that might influence network managers to change a network. Thus, it is very important to educate upper management on network reengineering concepts, such as relevant influencing factors, in order to have adequate corporate support for implementing network reengineering activities. As a result, an organization's information systems management group should prepare and deliver to upper management point papers and presentations on the concepts of network reengineering and possible influencing factors.

Establishing a network reengineering team

The network manager should establish a network reengineering team to implement the network reengineering process of monitoring and assessing influencing factors. If the network reengineering team finds that a network modification is feasible, then the team should either directly participate in or should appoint another team to perform the resulting network modifications. The network reengineering team should consist of people who are capable of discovering factors that might influence a change to the network, and of assessing the feasibility of the network change.

Investigating existing influencing factors

The network reengineering team should start by investigating existing influencing factors. The methodology and techniques of this are the main topics of Chapter 2. Initially, the team might find many influencing factors, which have gone unnoticed without the presence of network reengineering. Thus, it might be necessary to prioritize the factors so that the more important modifications are done first.

Implementing necessary modifications

The next step would be for the team to implement modifications to counter the influencing factors. Again, because a large number of factors could exist, many modifications might be needed initially. However, one modification has the potential to counter several factors at once. After making the changes necessary to counter the first wave of influencing factors, the team might only need to maintain the reengineering process. The methodology and techniques of implementing modifications are covered in the remaining chapters of this book.

Monitoring influencing factors

After making appropriate modifications, the network reengineering team should continually monitor influencing factors. This will keep the reengineering process alive. Technologies and management plans change rapidly; therefore, the reengineering team must always be attentive to factors that might influence network changes. As the future develops, the team should quickly evaluate feasibility and recommend modifications to counter any new factors.

2

Factors that Influence Network Modifications

An organization must be capable of identifying factors indicating the need for network modifications. In addition, the organization must determine whether network alterations are feasible. This chapter describes common influencing factors and shows how to justify the ones dictating changes.

Influencing Factors

Factors that influence an organization to modify its network come in all shapes and sizes. Some are based on user needs or technological shifts; others derive from inadequate documentation or changes in company plans. Strong influential factors might seriously affect the network if network changes are not immediately made. Weaker factors might not presently cause too much trouble, but over time could lead to problems. An organization should analyze each potential influencing factors and determine whether changes should be made to the network. This analysis mainly includes comparing the costs and benefits of modifying the network to counter the influencing factor(s). The following sections define each type of influencing factor.

Changes in User Needs

An implementation team bases most of the original network creation on user needs. But these needs might change as the organizational mission changes, or as the company's employment force changes. The reengineering team should constantly monitor user needs and, if these needs change, should determine whether network modifications are necessary. Reengineering user needs can offer benefits, such as higher user productivity and lower labor costs.

It is easy to comprehend why changes in user needs is an influencing factor. If a user need changes, the network might not be able to support the new need. This might result in poor productivity, which could mean lower company profits. An organization could find user needs change in any of these areas: user interfaces, performance, data processing, databases, mobility/portability, security, or communications.

User interfaces

The user interface need identifies how users access network services. The interface is what the user "sees" and is a crucial part of the network. The effectiveness of an interface depends a great deal on proper human factors engineering, which ensures that the interface provides an efficient method for humans to enter and retrieve information from the network.

The existing interface should be very user-friendly and should provide a seamless mechanism for using the applications, allowing users to concentrate more on the applications they are accessing rather than on how to access them. This makes people more productive. Normally, a graphical user interface (GUI) will provide a good network interface for most people. A GUI is usually simple and easy to use with a minimum of reading.

Most command-line interfaces do not provide an effective way of accessing applications, especially for nontechnical people. Many people who own computers have very little training and experience on how to use them. These people normally find it difficult to learn and remember sets of written commands to control their computers. As a result, command-line interfaces might be difficult to use and might cause users to become frustrated and unable to utilize the network to the fullest extent. In this case, the reengineering team should consider migrating their users to a GUI. Figure 2.1 compares the command-line and GUI attributes.

The frequency with which users operate the interface can provide a basis for the amount of user-friendliness a network interface should have. In general, users tend to forget how to use certain network functions if they do not utilize the network interface often. It is important for the interface to "spoon feed" the user by smoothly stepping the person through the application's functions, and offering plenty of help when necessary. However, users who operate the interface often might become frustrated with a highly detailed and helpful interface. For the heavy users, a striped-down interface that relies on the users' current knowledge might allow them to work more rapidly. Because an organization is normally a mix of users who

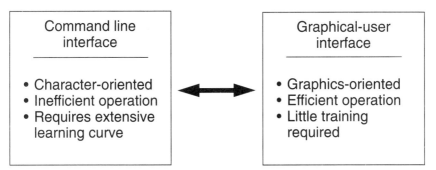

Command line interface	Graphical-user interface
• Character-oriented • Inefficient operation • Requires extensive learning curve	• Graphics-oriented • Efficient operation • Little training required

Figure 2.1 Comparison of command-line and GUI attributes

operate the network with differing frequencies, the interface should allow users to select a skill level the interface will use to set its level of detail.

Performance

Performance identifies how well a network provides its services. Organizations might need to change system performance for various reasons. For example, management might add extra work shifts, which might increase the need for availability. In this case, the organization might need to modify the network to allow more on-line management of the network, because the network will not be able to be shut down for the performance of system management functions. Another example is a company that might start performing a different function that might require the transfer of very large graphics files. Here, the organization might need to modify the network to provide more bandwidth, to decrease the amount of delay expected when transferring the files. For instance, a graphics shop might currently transfer drawing files via modems over phone lines. This method is very time-consuming, and the organization could benefit by utilizing a higher speed internetwork capability, such as frame relay.

Thus, the network reengineering team should ensure that the network meets the needs of its users in terms of performance. If performance is not adequate, the team should determine whether it is advantageous to change the network.

Data processing

Data processing needs include such items as the ability to create, edit, and print documents, and whether these documents should contain just textual or both textual and graphical information. If applications are not implemented to support effective data processing, users might take longer than necessary to complete tasks and might not produce quality products. If organizations have a great need to share information, groupware products could be beneficial to allow groups of people to share information seamlessly in a well-organized manner. Groupware products can disintegrate departmental barriers, allow more effective storage and retrieval of information, and incorporate more organizational flexibility.

Databases

The need for databases on the network might be necessary if groups of users have data elements requiring centralized access. For example, users might currently utilize individual and possibly networked databases. However, users might need to utilize a variety of databases located on different servers. This could require the addition of a standard interface, such as Standard Query Language (SQL). Figure 2.2 illustrates the concept of providing interoperability among databases.

In addition, several database models are available and users might need to migrate to a different model based on certain conditions. For example, a user might need to utilize an object-oriented database rather than a relational database.

Mobility and portability

The mobility need identifies whether the users require mobile access to the network. Mobility allows users to continually move from one location to another. For instance, a person performing an inventory in a warehouse could definitely benefit from a mobile network connection. Another example of the need for mobility occurs within hospital facilities, where doctors and nurses require freedom of movement. Portability defines a network connectivity that can be easily established, used, then dismantled. Thus, porta-

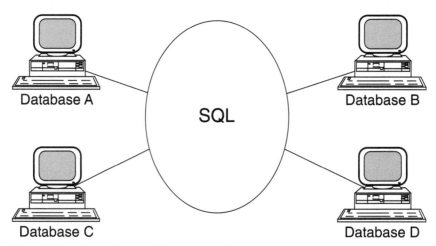

Figure 2.2 Providing interoperability among databases

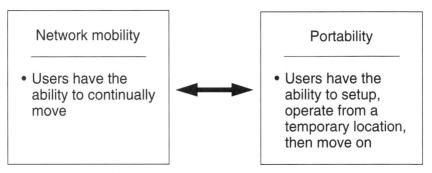

Network mobility	Portability
• Users have the ability to continually move	• Users have the ability to setup, operate from a temporary location, then move on

Figure 2.3 Network mobility versus portability

bility is often good when users need temporary access to network applications. For example, an organization would require portability if it wished to temporarily relocate employees while renovating the primary work space. The organization would need to establish network connections for the employees to use during the renovation, then remove the connections when the employees move back to their primary offices. Figure 2.3 compares mobility versus portability.

In most cases, an organization can reengineer its network to accommodate mobility or portability by incorporating wireless network technologies. Wireless network technologies and products support both local and wide area network environments. The tetherless connectivity between client devices and other network elements allows users to move freely without cabling constraints.

Security

The degree of network security needed depends on an organization's need to protect information, which might change periodically. Not providing a proper level of security can expose sensitive data to unauthorized people, who can mishandle the data and cause much grief over stolen data or corrupted files. Ineffective security can also allow the inadvertent loss of information due to power or system failures. Figure 2.4 identifies weak points in network security.

Security mechanisms include authentication, system access, file backup, and data integrity. Authentication guarantees that only the designated users can log on to the network, and system access specifies what applications and files users can open. Most network operating systems provide some sort of authentication method, such as the use of a password. In most cases, though, these passwords are not encrypted. Encryption techniques can protect the unauthorized disclosure of information. In some cases, such as in electronic banking, it might be necessary to authenticate the transmission of a file. This can be done through the use of an electronic signa-

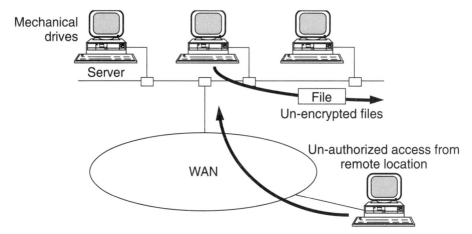

Figure 2.4 Weak points in network security

ture. Access controls should limit users only to what they need to access, which will make the network more secure.

Organizations lacking in effective file backup might wish to add tape backup, disk miring, disk duplexing, or redundant servers. These mechanisms make it possible to restore files if a hard drive crashes. Tape backup systems transfer data from hard drive storage to magnetic tape. Both disk miring and duplexing duplicate the writing of files to a second standby hard drive.

It is very important that precautions be taken if a LAN is connected to a public network, such as the Internet. The Internet could allow millions of users to gain access to the corporate network. This can be avoided by establishing a firewall, which is a device that filters traffic in and out of the local network.

Communications

Communications needs include the ability to access specific network resources and users, typically over great distances. Wide area network technologies, such as point-to-point leased circuits or switched networks, provide most long-haul communications. A change in communications needs could include the need for users to access a data base on a network located in a different city. This would prompt the need to reengineer the network to include a long-haul link between the users and the distant data base. Figure 2.5 illustrates the concept of communications.

Special services

An organization might benefit by incorporating special services in addition to typical office functions (word processing, databases, and electronic mail, for example). Special services include functions and services that might support or go beyond the typical office applications. Examples of special services include access to the World Wide Web, desktop conferencing, telecommuting, and document management. Several of these special services take advantage of newer multimedia technologies, which support the integration of data, imaging, graphics, voice, and video. Much of this demands specialized high-bandwidth network architectures, which usually prompts a substantial network modification.

World Wide Web

The World Wide Web, or Web for short, is an interconnection of privately owned and operated servers. Each server stores a set of hypertext pages that users, or "Web Surfers," can easily search for and view from their workstations through a Web browser, via an Internet connection. Organizations utilize the Webs easy exchange of textual and graphical information. They also maintain Web servers as a means of facilitating electronic marketing and services to millions of Web users. For example, many network vendors have placed descriptions of their products and services on the Web, and banks have started to allow customers to manipulate accounts via Web servers.

Desktop conferencing

Desktop conferencing allows users to have televideo conferences directly from PCs located in their offices. Users who participate in a desktop conference can hear and see a video image of each participant. Desktop conferences also allow participants to jointly edit documents and facilitate electronic white boards. These applications allow users to be more productive by doing more work from their offices and avoiding travel.

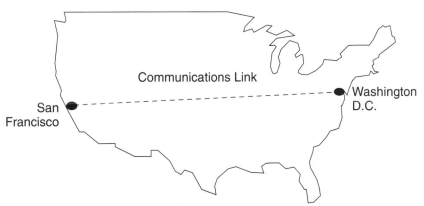

Figure 2.5 Communications between distant sites

Desktop conferencing requires the integration of voice, video, and data. Voice and video signals represent very timely events. Thus, a network must deliver voice and video in real time to ensure that the reception of the signal is understandable. This requires a great deal of bandwidth and a well-synchronized network. Normally, desktop conferencing requires an organization to reengineer its network to include switched-ethernet, FDDI, or ATM to support high-speed synchronous transfer of audio and video signals.

Telecommuting

Another example of a special application is telecommuting, which supports working from home. Telecommuting systems "electronically stretch" the office to the home and save companies money by cutting down on office space. It can also save employees the cost and agony of driving to work every day. By not driving to work, each telecommuter cuts down on pollution. These benefits are fairly significant in certain high-traffic areas, such as Los Angeles, New York, and Chicago.

Most organizations need to reengineer the network to support telecommuting, which requires an effective long-haul connection between the home and the office. High-speed modems and ISDN can provide fairly good connectivity for most data-type telecommuting.

Document management

Document management applications allow users to effectively manage and access information contained within different file types. Most document management software allows users to manipulate both data and images, as well as easily manage files through indexing, search, and query functions. This can minimize the user of paper and save the organization money.

Organizations can benefit from document management applications, especially companies that utilize multiple word processors and graphics applications. Document management software can offer a very effective interface between users and information. In this case, reengineering might only entail adding document management software on each client PC and establishing a database for centralized access of data.

Technological Changes

Technologies are constantly emerging and changing. As a result, some existing technologies have become or might eventually become obsolete. As stated previously, this makes products based on these technologies difficult and expensive to maintain. In addition, newer technologies might offer better performance at lower cost. Therefore, technological changes might greatly influence an organization to migrate from one technology to another. If an organization does not change, it might be more difficult to expand the network later because vendors might not support products based on the older technology.

As an example, decades ago, organizations predominantly utilized large centralized systems to support their information system needs. As personal computers proliferated, though, distributed networking became an effective and efficient method to provide information system functions. Thus, it has become cost-effective for many organizations to migrate their information systems from centralized systems to distributed, client-server environments. Figure 2.6 illustrates both the centralized and distributed environments.

To accommodate the migration to client-server technologies, an organization might employ one of the following approaches. Companies with a mainframe computer could adopt front-end software that enables the mainframe to function effectively as a data server. This is the easiest method to implement, but it might be fairly expensive because of the relatively high cost of maintaining a mainframe computer. Another method would be for the organization to shut down the mainframe immediately and start utilizing a client-server environment. This is not recommended for most cases, because any problems with the migration will affect all users. Another approach is to gradually phase in client-server equipment. This is the preferred method, because a small group of users could be used as a pilot group before the entire organization was switched over to the new system. Once all problems are identified and overcome, then other portions of the organization could be phased in.

Traditionally, organizations have utilized 56 Kbps and T1 point-to-point digital leased circuits to provide connectivity between facilities separated by distances out of reach of local area networks. However, newer connectivity options, such as frame relay, can now provide faster data delivery at less cost. Figure 2.7 shows the concept of using frame relay versus traditional point-to-point connectivity. Typically, point-to-point connectivity requires multiple connections between various network sites, but frame relay requires only one connection per site.

Frame relay can save organizations equipment costs because each site requires only one access line, one router port, and one data service unit. This is especially true for organizations that require a distributed high degree of connectivity (meshness) between sites. Leased lines require more equipment, such as multiplexers, and more expensive routers. Also, with frame relay networks the carrier has the responsibility for maintaining connections between sites. Thus, the organization has less to manage and maintain.

Therefore, if the existing network is based on centralized processing or point-to-point long-haul connectivity, the organization should consider modifying the network to accommodate new technologies.

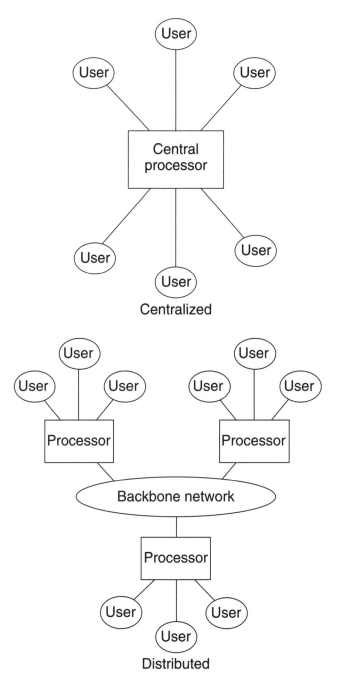

Figure 2.6 Centralized and distributed computing environments

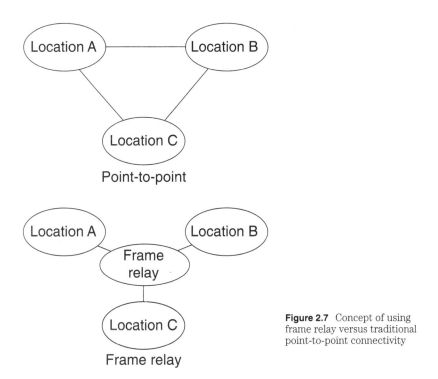

Figure 2.7 Concept of using frame relay versus traditional point-to-point connectivity

Organizational Resizing

Organizations often change size. In some cases, an organization might grow larger, and in other cases it might decrease in size. Any type of organizational growth could give reason for a network manager to change the network. Growth could be based on the hiring of new people, which might result in the addition of users to the existing network. If the network cannot handle the extra load then the network manager will need to modify the network to accommodate the new users. This might mean adding additional network taps, incorporating a higher degree of segmentation, or beefing up the server.

Sometimes companies purchase other companies, which also increases the number of network users. Separate companies often have different network architectures. Thus, this type of expansion can result in the task of integrating multiple systems into a larger network. In this case, solutions need to provide a homogenous environment, which can take a considerable amount of reengineering. Figure 2.8 illustrates this concept of integrating dissimilar networks.

A corporate reorganization can change the distribution of employees from one site to another, which could result in the decrease of network

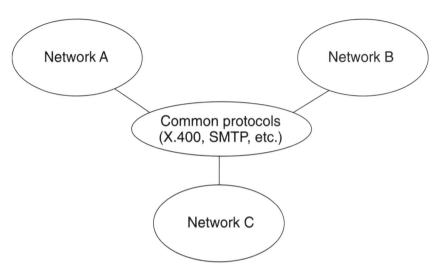

Figure 2.8 Integrating dissimilar networks

users at a particular site. As a result, the network might have more capability than what is needed to support the smaller community of users. With fewer users on the network, the organization might want to reallocate network hardware to other sites that are growing. Or, the extra equipment could be used to support additional features of the network. The redistribution of users will make the data traffic patterns change, which could make the current network architecture inefficient. Reengineering that provides proper resegmentation can help the network match the new performance needs of its users.

Organizational Moves

Most companies will eventually move their people and resources to a different facility. Either the company will outgrow its current building or other areas will offer more opportunities. Moving the network is often a difficult and stressfull event for the network manager and staff. One of the problems is that network users are capable of moving to the new facility much faster than the network can. Yet the same people will need to have the network operational immediately after settling into their new offices. Thus, the network group must very carefully plan the move and really hustle when it is time. This often means relocating network components and computers after hours.

Organizational moves normally do not demand a great deal of reengineering. The engineering needed in a move just includes designing and installing a cable layout for the new facility. However, the network manager must plan many other tasks as part of the move, such as coordinating the reinstallation of cabling and network hardware at the new location.

Operational Problems

Sometimes a network might have operational problems because it was not designed and implemented correctly. It might have been based on faulty information about user requirements, or the implementer might not have had proper experience in designing or installing networks. The network might have become a legacy system, which has been patched up rather than enhanced over the years. It might also have very little documentation. As a result, the network will be difficult to maintain or modify.

Typically, operational problems manifest themselves as poor network performance. This can degrade the effectiveness of the network by causing users to experience unnecessary and unacceptable delays. A carefully planned reengineering effort can make adjustments to the existing network to improve performance.

Another operational problem is what many people refer to as "stovepiping." Stovepiping means that major parts of a company's network are very different, and no mechanism is in place that provides a smooth interface between these parts. Large organizations lacking strategic networking plans and a strong corporate information center are breeding grounds for stovepiping.

Most stovepiping occurs when an organization has divisions that build networks without coordinating the designs and implementations between divisions. These divisions normally have separate funding and build networks based on their own requirements, without regard to other parts of the organization. As the individual networks grow, they can easily become very different from each other. For example, one network might use ethernet, network operating system A, and electronic mail X. Another network might use token ring, network operating system B, and electronic mail Y. These differences make it very difficult to provide interoperability among the stovepipes. To solve this problem an organization might need to do some reengineering to develop a corporate network that allows all the stovepipes to interoperate. For example, an organization could implement a corporate backbone such as FDDI, and deploy X.400 as a common, corporate-wide, electronic mail protocol.

Not having adequate documentation can severely affect the maintenance and modification of the network. When problems occur, it is much easier to locate the problem if accurate schematics and network layout drawings are available. A common example of this occurs when a group of people implement the system and then leave the company without properly documenting the network. This can be a deadly problem, because people unfamiliar with the system will need a great deal of time to troubleshoot or reengineer it. Network documentation might be completely non-existent, partially existent, or inaccurate. In all three cases, problems will eventually arise. Therefore, an organization should consider creating complete documentation if existing documents are inadequate.

Limited Network Coverage

In some cases, an organization might have an existing network that covers some but not all of the organization. As a result, the people in the uncovered part of the facility will not be able to reap the benefits of networking. Thus, the organization should extend the network to cover the remaining portion(s) of its facilities.

The Nonexistent Network

Some organizations might have PCs for some or all of their employees, but they might not have any network in place. Or, the organization could have a very low level of networking in place, such as the use of modems for communication and print-sharing devices. For these scenarios, the organization should seriously consider a network to increase productivity and reduce costs. If the decision is to build a network, then the organization should carefully plan and manage the network implementation, because this represents a prime opportunity for an organization to "do it right" from the beginning.

Benefits of networking

Because of the services that networks provide, an organization can realize many benefits by installing a computer network. These often include tangible benefits, such as higher productivity and lower operating costs. A company can also gain intangible benefits, such as higher employee morale and better company image.

A computer network typically will allow an organization to develop higher productivity because the network provides services that can save user's time. A network supports efficient office functionality because of services and applications such as file transfer, electronic mail, printer sharing, electronic calendaring, and networked fax machines. These items enable users to get their tasks done faster, equating to lower labor costs and higher profits.

If an organization does not network its computers, that organization will probably pay more to maintain the applications and the system. With a network an organization can save money through effective software upgrades, easier management of software licenses, and timely computer help.

With a computer network, software upgrades become much faster because of the centralized storage of applications. Imagine having two hundred nonnetworked, stand-alone, personal computers. Assume someone decides to upgrade an application from version X to version Y. Sure, you could have each user install his own upgrade, but while some will do so others will not, because they do not know how to install software. In this case, an installer would need to install the new version of software on all two hundred PCs. Assuming an average install time of twenty minutes, the job would take one person approximately eight days, at eight hours per day.

Now, assume the same two hundred PCs are connected to a network that provides a centralized access to applications, as shown in Figure 2.9. In this environment, the upgrade from version X to Y becomes much faster. The installer can simply install the new version of software on the server, allowing everyone immediate access. This upgrade takes only twenty minutes, compared to eight days. All users have access to the new version faster, plus the installer can spend his time working on something else. Thus, an organization can save a tremendous amount of time and money by upgrading software on a network versus stand-alone PCs.

It is much easier to manage and maintain software licenses on networks, because an organization can purchase a multiuser software license, which normally includes one set of installation disks. Special software can keep track of how many users are utilizing the software and limit accesses over the license limit. Thus, with a network, there is no need to store and account for multiple copies of the same software. It is normally less expensive to purchase a multiuser license than to buy multiple individual licenses, especially for large numbers of licenses (more than fifty).

A network facilitates help for system users. It is much easier for technicians to set up a help desk and fix many problems from a centralized location on a network. Help desk technicians can assist users with running applications by utilizing utility programs that allow the helper and the user to see the same problem. Thus, the technician can help the users much more easily.

If a company invests in a computer network and the employees have access to up-to-date network applications, then these employees might feel better about both the company and the work they do. The company will also project a better image to other companies, especially its clients.

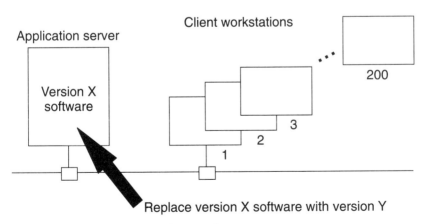

Figure 2.9 Upgrading software via the network

Computer networking pitfalls

There are strong benefits of utilizing a computer network, but there are some pitfalls worth knowing about. The most prominent disadvantages of networking are resistance to change, interoperability problems, potential security weaknesses, and loss of management control. Most organizations, though, can counter these pitfalls with careful planning and control of the network development and operational support.

One issue is the normal resistance of humans to accept change. Such resistance is a common phenomenon in most organizations. If people are accustomed to using stand-alone computers, they often feel overwhelmed when you connect their computer to a network. The same users feel the organization is invading their private workspace. In addition, many people feel more comfortable doing things the way they always have. As an example, someone might be given electronic mail capability, but they might still use only manual methods to send correspondence to other people, even if the other people have electronic mail capability. Also, some people might not know very much about networking, or even computers for that matter. When these people are given network services, they can become highly frustrated. As a result, it might take these people longer to perform their tasks than without a network, which will probably lower productivity. Normally, though, organizations can avoid these problems by providing employees with proper training and preparation.

Organizations often build networks, then later need to interoperate them with other networks having a different architecture. This refers again to the stovepipe syndrome. It is usually not too difficult to provide interoperability between the networks; that is, to enable the smooth transmission of information. The real problem is developing a solution to resolve differences in data formatting and storage. This often causes organizations to reformat data and storage systems, often costing excessive amounts of time and money.

The use of a network weakens security, because there is greater risk of the loss or compromise of information. A network can cover a substantial area, allowing the access of information from remote areas outside the control of the cleared users. Thus, intruders can more easily steal information without being seen, from locations within or even outside the facility. This security risk is extremely important for organizations dealing with sensitive information, such as military and trade secrets, hospital records, and financial records.

In many ways, a network increases the ease of management, by introducing more effective methods of upgrading software and accounting for applications usage. However, a networked organization could experience loss of management control due to creeping escalation of the network. Network growth can occur unnoticed and can cause problems, because the organization might add a couple of users or new applications periodically without planning for any additional support. Eventually, the organization will need to increase operational support and might not have the resources available.

Funding Reduction

Occasionally, organizations might reduce funding available for computer systems, forcing network managers to find methods to cut costs. Generally speaking, the network reengineering methodology can help reduce costs, but it might take some investment to realize the savings. Newer applications and technologies might increase the productivity of users, but the organization will have to purchase the new applications and accept a certain payback period. If no funds are available to invest in new hardware or software, network management could focus on reducing operating costs. For instance, the network reengineering effort could incorporate less expensive communications lines.

Identifying Influencing Factors

To identify the occurrence of the above influencing factors, it is important to continually monitor the system and anything affecting it. You can monitor influencing factors by keeping your eyes open to anything that might affect the ability of the network to satisfy the user's needs.

The best way to monitor influencing factors is to periodically review user needs and match them against the ability of the network to satisfy them. It is also a good idea to utilize any data that the network support infrastructure generates. For example, network monitoring will help identify whether the current network is functioning properly. User complaints can identify network problems as well. It is also a good idea to participate in management meetings to keep up with upcoming reorganizations, renovations, and organizational moves. Table 2.1 is a matrix showing which influencing factors can be monitored by performing periodic user reviews, utilizing the network support infrastructure, and attending management meetings.

Periodic User Needs Review

Over time, the mission of an organization might change. A company might become larger or smaller, or it might take on different types of business. As the company changes, employee requirements for the system might shift. For example, an organization might currently concentrate on the sale of its merchandise within the local vicinity. However, if the company expands its sales area to include the entire United States, then salespeople might need to begin traveling away from the local office. This change in business scope

TABLE 2.1 Methods for Identifying Each Type of Influencing Factor

Factors influencing change	Information sources		
	User reviews	Support infrastructure	Management meetings
User needs changes	3	2	2
Technology changes	1	3	1
Organizational re-sizing	2	1	3
Organizational moves	2	1	3
Operational problems	3	3	1
Limited network	3	3	2
Non-existent network	3	3	2

1-Somewhat useful
2-Moderately useful
3-Very useful

should influence the organization to modify the network to include remote network access, to provide e-mail and other network services to traveling salespeople. This would allow these employees to maintain closer communications with the main office, and clients too. Therefore, an organization should periodically survey the users' needs to determine if changes need to be made. For more details on determining user needs, refer to Chapter 4.

In addition to identifying changes in user needs, user reviews can help identify special application needs, inadequate documentation, and operational problems. The reviews might identify needs that require specialized support, such as wireless networking, integrated voice and video, etc. Comments from the review might also show that documentation is either missing or difficult to understand. The review might uncover facts that users are not able to use certain parts of the system, and further investigation might show that there is an operational problem.

Utilizing the Operational Support Infrastructure

The existing operational support infrastructure is an excellent source for identifying influencing factors. This is because network support systems are in constant close touch with the network and its users. If implemented correctly, the support infrastructure can easily deliver data needed to effectively determine which influencing factors exist. Each element of network support offers a different view for identifying influencing factors. Table 2.2 identifies information available from each operational support element that can aid in discovering influencing factors.

To identify factors that might influence network changes, an organization should review the following network support elements.

System administration

System administrators have a very close relationship with the users, making it easy to spot changes in user needs, special applications needs, inadequate documentation, and operational problems. Users often talk about their needs of the system, and the system administration staff is usually in a position to hear the users' concerns. This is similar to doing a user review, but instead of your going to the users with questions they come to you with immediate concerns. The system administrator can easily track help desk calls and other user complaints, and can then decide whether there is inadequate documentation or operational problems. If a help desk person must

TABLE 2.2 Monitoring Influencing Factors via the Network Support Infrastructure

Operational support elements	Information that can aid in identifying factors influencing changes to the network
System administration	- User complaints - User requests for additional applications - Common user questions
Networking monitoring	- Traffic patterns - Faulty operation of protocols - Interoperability problems
Accounting and chargeback	- Utilization levels of applications - New accounting and chargeback procedures
Maintenance	- Type of operational problems - Occurrence of specific operational problems
Network security	- Audit trails - Security incidents - Security regulations
Configuration management	- Existing systems - Trends with other modifications
Training	- User comments during training classes
Engineering	- New and emerging technologies

explain to the user how to overcome an obstacle, then the documentation might not be clear enough for the user to find the solution himself. More complex user problems might point toward an actual operational problem, such as lack of connectivity or interoperability.

Network monitoring

Network monitoring is very useful in discovering operational problems, by monitoring the utilization on different parts of the network and reporting problem conditions. For instance, monitoring data traffic can identify bottlenecks that might cause unacceptable delays to some users.

Accounting and chargeback

Accounting for the usage of network applications can offer useful data for identifying changes in user needs. If there is very low utilization of Application A, then maybe users do not need that application. Further investigation might show that the organization could be better off by eliminating Application A. On the other hand, heavy usage of Application B might validate the need for Application B.

Maintenance

Preventative maintenance activities, such as cable inspections, connectivity checks, and interoperability tests, can uncover operational problems. For example, if testers cannot utilize certain applications from a user location, then reengineering should take place to provide interoperability. Because maintenance people require system documentation when performing their jobs, these people should be on the lookout for inadequate or missing documentation. For example, a maintenance person might not be able to adequately troubleshoot a segment of the network because documentation of that segment does not exist. This situation should prompt an organization to create the document to better support current and future maintenance, and to review all other documentation as well.

Network security

Network security practices can help identify the need for special applications. As an example, according to most security regulations, the network security manager should be alerted when users need to begin processing highly sensitive or secret information on the network. The existing network might not be secure enough to support the classified information. Thus, the organization would need to implement another stand alone network to support the secret data or utilize some sort of data encryption.

Configuration Management

As discussed in a later chapter, configuration management is a process that maintains a complete and accurate description of the network's hardware, software, and configurations. Configuration management also attempts to control changes to the network. Configuration management reviews focus on discovering inadequate documentation. This makes the configuration management process a good source for locating poor or missing documentation. For example, reviewers might find that documentation is not "user friendly." It might be difficult to read and comprehend. Based on this, the person responsible for the documentation can increase its readability by adding effective graphics and commonly asked questions and answers.

Training

Besides showing people how to use and support the network, training gives an opportunity for users to express their concerns. User concerns could help spot changes in requirements or inadequate documentation. Instructors should realize that users need different features than those provided by the applications they are explaining. When training the users how to do a specific task, the instructor might see that users have difficulties in using certain parts of the network documentation.

Engineering

The engineering staff might be a source for learning about new technological opportunities, because engineers are usually aware of emerging technologies and newly announced products. A good method for monitoring and identifying these technologies is to hold monthly "tech talks" at which engineers and technicians discuss new technologies and products.

The engineering group can also help spot operational problems. Sometimes the help desk might be unable to solve a problem that a user might be experiencing. The engineering staff usually attempts to find a solution, which often results in uncovering an operational problem. For instance, a user might not be able to connect to a distant server. Engineers might look into the problem and discover an improper circuit providing the supposed connection. This problem can be fixed, restoring operations.

Management meetings

Network managers should attend corporate management meetings to keep abreast of future staffing, new business areas, and facilities. This is the best way to get firsthand news of upcoming events that might significantly impact the network. These meetings can provide crucial data for reengineering the network based on changes in user needs, network size, and location.

These future plans, combined with data gathered through existing user reviews, can help the network manager adequately plan reengineering efforts to adjust the network to meet future organizational needs.

As examples, information from a management meeting could reveal these types of changes: The company might desire a new line of business that requires employees to have a high degree of mobility. The existing network infrastructure might not accommodate mobility, causing the organization to reengineer the network to include wireless connectivity. Another important piece of information from a management meeting could be a decision to expand business by purchasing subsidiaries. This type of expansion would normally require a significant amount of network reengineering to provide necessary connectivity and interoperability. For a final example, an organization might wish to move to a different location. This might require the reengineering necessary to fit the network into the new facility.

Analyzing Modification Feasibility

If an organization feels that an influencing factor is significant enough to consider changing the network, they should determine the feasibility of making the change. A change is feasible if the organization will save more than what it costs to develop and implement the change. The savings is calculated over a period of time, typically two to three years. The Return on Investment (ROI) method for judging the feasibility of investment opportunities is most common for network modifications. ROI is an analysis method that assesses annual returns on a business investment.

The outcome of this feasibility study can be the basis for obtaining decisions and funding for the network change. If an organization does not first determine the feasibility before striking out on a major reengineering effort, then very unexpected and costly outcomes could ensue. It is generally appropriate to modify the network after performing a feasibility study, obtaining acceptance and funding approval from upper management, and coordinating the modification with appropriate organizations.

The feasibility study compares costs and benefits of a proposed network modification. The organization should use feasibility studies as a basis for deciding whether to proceed. The approach for performing a feasibility study depends on which influencing factors are present. Usually, the network management division of the organization initiates feasibility studies for influencing factors, such as changes in user needs, inadequate documentation, and incorporation of new technologies. This is because network management should independently discover these types of influencing factors. In this case, network management must prepare a feasibility study that shows both costs and tangible benefits, because upper management will need to see definite cost savings or increases in productivity before funding modifications to an existing network. In another scenario, upper management might direct the network management group to determine the costs associated with moving or resizing the network. For this, upper management might make the decision to initiate network changes by comparing benefits they themselves identify, with costs supplied by the network management group.

The main point to consider when determining the feasibility of making network changes is whether the changes are cost-effective in terms of real dollars saved or increases in productivity. One can determine cost-effectiveness by performing an economic analysis, which compares the costs and benefits of making the changes versus not making the changes. In general, one should implement the modifications if costs related to operating the modified system, in addition to the costs associated to make the modifications, are less than the costs of operating the unchanged system. By carefully identifying the net savings of implementing a network change, one should be able to convince higher-ups to fund any needed modifications.

It is important to compare the cost of operating the existing system versus the modified one. Also, be sure to base current operating costs on current and past data. All costs for the modified system at this point should be termed "preliminary costs," because they are partially based on projections.

The organization should base the feasibility study on a specific operating time period. This is the expected life expectancy of the network or modification, and the organization can base the operational costs and benefits of the network on this time span. Most organizations are satisfied with a two- to three-year recovery of benefits on network purchases. Predicting costs and benefits beyond three years can lead to significant margins of error, mainly because technologies rapidly change, and most business plans are fairly soft beyond two years.

Also, doing a feasibility study requires some design in order to base the costs associated with implementing and operating the modified network. This might mean going forth with part of the network reengineering methodology, especially the requirements determination and design phases. At this point, though, any solutions should only be estimates.

Figure 2.10 illustrates how to analyze the feasibility of changing the network. As discussed before, the decision to make the network change is based on comparisons between costs and the value of benefits. If the value of benefits exceeds all costs involved, then the decision should be to incorporate the change.

Tangible Cost and Benefit Elements

With tangible elements, it is possible to associate very realistic dollar amounts with costs and benefits. General tangible cost and benefits mainly consist of what it takes to implement and support the network modification. Table 2.3 identifies which of these cost/benefit elements to consider.

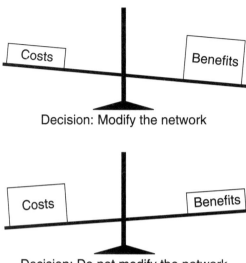

Decision: Modify the network

Decision: Do not modify the network

Figure 2.10 Analyzing modification feasibility

TABLE 2.3 Elements to Consider When Analyzing Feasibility of Each Type of Modification

Factors Influencing change	Feasibility elements to consider			
	Modification costs	Productivity costs/benefits	Electricity costs/benefits	Operational support costs/benefits
User needs changes	2	3	1	2
Technology changes	3	2	2	2
Organizational re-sizing	3	2	3	3
Organizational moves	3	1	1	1
Operational problems	2	1	1	2
Limited network	3	3	3	3
Non-existent network	3	3	3	3

1-Low importance
2-Moderate importance
3-High importance

The following sections identify tangible elements of a network that might result in either direct costs or benefits, depending on the situation.

Modification costs

Most network modification projects include costs of labor and purchases needed to perform the modification. They do not include the costs associated with running the network after it becomes operational. Of course modification actions usually do not result in immediate benefits; they mainly generate immediate costs.

Modification costs fall into these categories:

- Planning
- Requirements analysis
- Network design
- Software development
- Component acquisitions
- Operational support preparations
- Configuration management
- Installation
- Testing
- Documentation
- Training
- User inactivity

All elements of the implementation will entail labor costs, and some will require purchasing hardware, software, and other equipment. Planning includes costs for scheduling the modification, establishing an implementation team, and periodically revising plans. The requirements redetermination and network design will consist primarily of labor costs of both analysts and engineers. Software development, if the modification requires it, will include the costs of programmers and possibly the purchase of compilers or software development kits. Component acquisition consists primarily of hardware and software purchases and applicable taxes, but it will also include labor and fees needed to order, store, and receive the components. Installation and testing will mostly involve the cost of technicians and testers, but the team members might need special tools to accomplish their jobs. Documentation is part of every stage of the modification; therefore, be sure to include the costs to create requirements documents, design specifications, schematics, user manuals, and similar items.

Something to consider when calculating installation and testing costs is that the users are often disturbed during this activity. The users often cannot use the network or their PC during the installation. Thus, it is important to include user inactivity during this time as a modification cost.

Productivity costs/savings

One of the key elements that contribute to cost savings based on the reengineering effort is overall higher user productivity. Increases in productivity equate to lower task completion times, resulting in cost savings based on lower labor hours needed to complete the tasks. This is often the strongest and most clearly defined benefit of a network modification.

You can easily calculate the cost savings based on an increase in user productivity. Just determine the amount of time an individual can save by using the modified network versus the original network, and multiply this time by the person's pay rate. This equals the cost savings for that individual. An aggregate cost savings can be calculated by adding together all individual savings. Initially, user productivity might be less than expected because users normally experience a learning curve when first using the modified network. This sag in productivity should be translated into a cost and subtracted from the overall cost savings.

Environmental costs/savings

The network modification might require a change to the environment on which the network resides. Be sure to consider the possible addition of cooling equipment to provide an adequate operating temperature for network components, such as servers and hubs. Floor space is also something to consider when determining cost savings or expenditures for the modification. Some reengineering efforts might eliminate the need for floor space, while others might require additional room to locate network devices. For example, a migration from a centralized mainframe system to a distributed network normally decreases the need for floor space. The freeing of this floor space can be treated as a cost savings, because the organization can use it for other purposes, thus saving the cost of procuring the floor space from somewhere else. Just be sure to factor in the costs associated with modifying the floor space to fit its new function. Of course, if the modification calls for additional floor space, then determine the cost of providing the necessary floor space.

Electricity costs/savings

If the network modification requires additional active equipment, such as PCs and printers, include the additional cost of electricity needed for these components. The network modification might result in the elimination of active devices as well. In this case, subtract the cost of electricity that is no longer necessary. It is also important to include the cost of electricity needed to support additional cooling equipment.

System administration costs/savings

A network modification might require additional system administration to handle an increase in number of users or network resources. This could increase the labor and equipment needed to provide the system administration function, resulting in a higher operating cost. In some cases, though, the network modification might result in a decrease in system administration costs. For example, the incorporation of a software license and version tracking system would lessen the need for system administration support because it would become much easier to manage software residing on the network and individual PCs.

Network monitoring costs/savings

Network modifications sometimes require or allow greater use of network monitoring. Normally, this equates to an initial implementation expenditure to purchase network monitoring hardware and software. But, the inclusion of network monitoring can help find network problems before they affect the users. This is a cost savings because it maximizes user productivity.

Accounting costs/savings

If network accounting is included as part of the modification, then calculate the initial cost of purchasing the accounting software, as well as the labor necessary to operate the accounting function. In addition, accounting can slightly decrease operating costs. This is because it will assist in the identification of underutilized applications that should be terminated, which decreases the costs of maintaining the software.

Maintenance costs/savings

An effective maintenance organization consists of an adequate set of spare components, documentation, and people, and of a facility for the maintenance staff. The network modification might affect the scope of any of these elements; therefore, associated costs or savings should be factored into the cost-benefit analysis.

Network security costs/savings

If the network modification changes the need for network security, be sure to include costs (or benefits) dealing with an increase or decrease in documentation and people, and a facility for the security staff.

Training costs/savings

Some modifications will require both initial and recurring training for users and support staff. This will result in tuition costs that depend on whether the training is given locally or at some distant location that introduces travel expenses. Training might also reduce the overall cost of the network modification, because users will have less of a learning curve, which lessens the sag in initial productivity.

Intangible Benefits

Intangible benefits are based on elements wherein there is no accurate method to assign a specific dollar amount to the cost or benefit. Intangible elements are very important. They often provide an extra-positive "oomph" in justifying a modification. Intangible benefits might not lend themselves well to specific dollar savings, but they might align themselves well with a business plan that supports corporate goals. Because of this, intangible benefits might influence a decision to make a modification, even if it is not cost-effective.

For example, a software development company that develops network applications would want to maintain a good corporate image and employee job satisfaction by keeping their network state-of-the-art, even if the modifications result in benefits that do not counter the implementation costs. Otherwise, clients might not consider the company as credible network application developers if they did not have an up-to-date network themselves.

Feasibility Study Document

It is important to fully document the costs and benefits of making the network modification. Be sure to cite as accurately as possible the dollar cost and savings for each cost/benefit element. State any intangible benefits that the modification will realize. The feasibility study should also end with some type of recommendation about whether to proceed with the modification.

In most cases, such as modifying the network to support new user needs or incorporating shifts in technologies, the feasibility study must clearly identify tangible cost-saving benefits. Managers normally need to see definite cost savings before making a decision to spend large sums of money on changing an existing network.

The feasibility study document should:

- Identify real assumptions.
- Describe realistic and achievable benefits.

- Describe complete and realistic costs.
- Accurately compare benefits and costs.
- Provide a justifiable recommendation on whether to change the network.

Figure 2.11 shows a typical outline of a feasibility study document.

Obtaining a Decision to Modify the Network

After identifying influencing factors that warrant changing the network, the next objective is to obtain a decision from upper management to fund the modification. This might not be an easy task, especially if the feasibility study relies mainly on intangible benefits. The best way to get an affirmative decision to modify the network is to review the feasibility study with upper management and sell the idea.

The review should cover all tangible and intangible costs and benefits. It is very important to show how the benefits of making the modification fall in line with the corporate business plan. For example, show how the modification will allow the organization to better meet company goals of increasing revenue and entering new business areas. Explain how the modification will create new business opportunities and allow the company to keep up with

Feasibility study
for modification X

I. Introduction
   A. Executive overview
   B. Proposed modification

II. Modification benefits
   A. Tangible
   B. Intangible

III. Modification Costs
   A. Tangible
   B. Intangible

IV. Conclusions
   A. Recommendations

Figure 2.11 Typical outline of a feasibility study document

competitors. Also, do not forget to show what will happen if the company does not make the modification.

If the modification is large or covers multiple sites, suggest a pilot program in which only one site or portion of the company will receive the modification first. After fixing all the bugs you can extend the modification to the remaining users. The pilot approach reduces the risk of causing corporate-wide havoc. If considering the pilot approach, be sure to pilot the modification in a part of the company that has supportive users.

If the decision to proceed with a network modification is positive, then the organization should proceed with making the modification. This entails proceeding with the network reengineering methodology described in Chapter 1; that is:

1. Plan the network modification.

2. Redetermine requirements.

3. Redesign the network.

4. Prepare for operational support.

5. Install the components of the modification.

6. Transfer the modification to operational mode.

The remaining chapters discuss how to perform each of these steps.

3

Planning a Network Modification

Once an organization decides to change a network, a project team should carefully plan the network modification. The implementation of a modification requires the use of project management principles and knowledge of issues related to the specific type of modification being undertaken. This chapter covers basic project-management concepts and the principles necessary to properly plan each type of modification. These aspects of project planning apply to all types and sizes of network modifications.

Project Management Concepts

As defined by the Project Management Institute, "Project management is the art of directing and coordinating human and material resources throughout the life of a project." Project management is the oversight needed to make sure actions are planned and executed in a structured manner. More specifically, good project management ensures that the project team will achieve objectives in defining project scope, cost, time, quality, and end-user satisfaction. The scope of a project defines all activities, end products, and resources. Costs consist of estimating, budgeting and control. Initially, the project team must estimate and plan the cost of a project, then track and regulate expenditures of money. The time objective deals with when the team will accomplish certain tasks. Project management also ensures proper planning, estimation, scheduling, and control of time.

Project management consists largely of planning and monitoring the execution of the project. Planning, which establishes a predetermined course of action to achieve a particular objective, involves identifying goals, creating work plans, budgeting, and committing resources. Monitoring the execution of the project ensures that project events will conform to the plan. This conformance involves:

- **Measuring** which determines the amount of progress toward objectives.
- **Evaluating** which identifies the cause and possible corrections to performance deviations.
- **Correcting** which involves taking a control action to correct an unfavorable trend.

Project Management Benefits

Project management is an essential part of any network modification, because it establishes and maintains a structure for the effort, providing support for the planning and execution of the network modification. Without project management, an organization might aimlessly modify the network and end up with results that do not meet the expectations of the organization.

Good project management can ensure effective planning and implementation of a network modification, by offering benefits such as:

- Improved communication among project team members, upper management, and the customer organization
- Increased understanding of the modification
- Accurate projections of resource requirements
- Identification of problem areas
- Clarification of project goals
- Control of project scope
- Quantification of project risk

These benefits help an organization complete a quality modification on time and within budget.

Planning Objectives

The project planning process defines what needs to be done, when and how it is going to be accomplished, who is going to do it, and how much it is going to cost. In other words, planning includes defining the work, scheduling activities, allocating resources, and budgeting.

With most projects, planning objectives map into the following project elements:

- **What** Statement of work
- **How** Work breakdown structure

- **Who**   Resource requirements
- **When**   Schedule and milestones
- **How much**   Budget

Later sections of this chapter will describe these project elements.

Risk Management

A successful project is one that satisfies all objectives and is completed on time and within budget. The project team must carefully manage risks in order to ensure project success. In general, risk is an element within a project that might cause undesirable outcomes, possibly causing the project to fail.

To avoid serious negative consequences, the team can effectively manage risks by identifying risk factors and establishing methods to reduce them. A risk factor is anything that could affect the outcome of the project. It is crucial to initiate risk-management practices at the very beginning of the project, because problems tend to be more expensive and take longer to fix at later stages.

Risk factor identification

Many people do not like to identify risks, because knowing risks is not pleasant. However, managing a project with unknown hazards is very dangerous, because when trouble finally surfaces it can cause much more damage than if it had been associated with a risk and managed earlier. Usually, a very small number of factors cause the most risk.

The key to risk management is to identify risk factors and implement methods to reduce them. It is important to communicate the risks to upper management, and in appropriate cases, the customer, so that informed decisions can be made. It is the responsibility of everyone on the project to monitor risk on a continuous basis.

The project team should examine the following risk factors, plus any others specific to the project:

- **Organizational risk factors**
  ~Level of management commitment
  ~Funding constraints
  ~Level of user involvement and support
  ~Firmness of benefits

- **Technical factors**
  ~Range of solution alternatives available
  ~Complexity of the interfaces to existing systems
  ~Familiarity and prior experience with the type of modification being accomplished

- **Project factors**
  - ~Clarity of project objectives
  - ~Working relationships among the project team
  - ~Size of the project team
  - ~Team geographical dispersion
  - ~Project duration
  - ~Tightness of delivery date constraints
  - ~Prior experience of the project manager

- **Resource factors**
  - ~Prior experience of team members
  - ~Team learning curve
  - ~Use of contractors
  - ~Possible loss of team members due to other projects

Risk analysis

The project team should classify the degree of risk for the occurrence of each identified risk factor. One approach to classifying risk is to label risk factors as low, medium, or high. The degree of risk indicates the level of probability that the factor will cause the project to fail.

The team could assign risks to each factor as follows:

- **Low risk**   The factor will probably not cause the project to fail (0–30% chance of failure).

- **Medium risk**   The factor might cause the project to fail (30–60% chance of failure).

- **High risk**   The factor is likely to cause the project to fail (60–100% chance of failure).

Having multiple risk factors classified as medium or high could indicate a very unstable project. High risk factors often include lack of upper management support and lack of user involvement. Senior management commitment is often the most important factor affecting the successful completion of a network modification project, because management involvement ensures that funds will be available throughout the project lifecycle. Without this commitment it is very difficult to obtain true management *buy-in*, a lack of which usually results in partially completed projects. User involvement is also critical for the completion of most network modification products. To guarantee that the end result of the project fully meets the needs of the entire organization, the potential end users need to be part of determining requirements and system acceptance criteria.

Risk management techniques

The project team should strive to reduce risk by following these steps:

1. Review the existing network and project work plans to identify risks.
2. Assess the impact and severity of each risk.
3. Pinpoint the causes of the risks.
4. Commit additional resources (including time and funding) and establish additional checkpoints and controls to manage these risks.
5. Refine the work plans to reflect the overall risk-reduction strategy.
6. Reassess overall risk.

The project team should keep repeating the above process until the overall risk is acceptable. If attempts by the team are unsuccessful in reducing risks, then the project team should communicate the risk factors to higher management for recommendations.

Often, the project team must deal with unrealistic schedules. If not handled adequately, this rushes the team and does not allow enough time to complete a quality modification. In this situation, the team should first determine the flexibility of the schedule. In other words, find out whether the schedule is really set in concrete, and if so, why. If changing the schedule to allow more time for the modification does not cause higher risk for other projects, then the schedule should be stretched out. It might also help to remind people that it is better to have the project completed late than to have a defective system that will cause bigger problems over a long period of time. Of course, if rescheduling does cause serious problems the team should redefine the requirements and reduce the scope of the project. In this case, the team could recommend a phased delivery of system functionality.

Quality Control

Quality is the extent to which an end product satisfies the needs of its users. In relation to network reengineering, the degree of quality is how well the network modification satisfies user needs in a cost-effective and efficient manner. To achieve quality control, the team must implement a solution based on accurately defined requirements. In addition, a quality modification must incorporate well-planned quality control practices.

The project team should accomplish these steps to increase the quality of the modification:

1. Obtain management commitment to quality control.
2. Define quality objectives.
3. Identify procedures to detect quality problems.

Many organizations agree that quality control is an important aspect of all projects, but very few companies actually use methodologies that implement it. Therefore, the team might need to obtain management commitment to the establishment of quality control mechanisms before pressing on with the project. To accomplish this, the team might need to educate management on the benefits of quality control. Benefits include the delivery of a product that fully satisfies user and organizational needs, ensured compliance with standards and procedures, and the detection of errors during the early stages of the project. All of these reduce the cost of the project.

To obtain an information system modification that meets its intended purpose, the project team must clearly state quality objectives. These objectives provide a level of excellence the modification team should strive to meet. To develop quality objectives, the project team should create a quality plan that instills a chosen level of quality in each project deliverable. Project deliverables relate to project planning, project execution, and end products.

For example, an organization should produce these deliverables to provide effective network reengineering:

- **Planning deliverables**
  ~Strategic information system plan
  ~Modification plan (including budgets, schedules, and resource allocations)
  ~Quality plan
  ~Feasibility study
  ~Installation plan
  ~Test plan
  ~Operational support plan

- **Execution deliverables**
  ~Requirements document
  ~Design specification
  ~Schematic
  ~Cabling diagram
  ~Test results and corrective actions
  ~In-process reviews/inspections
  ~Management reports
  ~System releases

- **End product deliverables**
  ~Final system release
  ~User manual
  ~Training program
  ~Continuous monitoring of user satisfaction

Later chapters will describe each of these plans and documents. For each deliverable, the quality plan should describe the deliverable itself, its acceptance criteria, and measurement methodology. The deliverable description should clearly describe each deliverable's purpose, main attributes, and how it relates to other deliverables. Deliverable criteria identify what attributes the deliverable should have in order to have acceptable quality. The measurement methodology shows how to determine whether the deliverable meets the criteria.

Public Affairs

It is beneficial to plan on dealing with public affairs early on in the project. For most network modifications, the users will experience some noticeable loss in productivity during and shortly after the installation phase. This is mainly caused by disturbing users while installing hardware and software within or close by the users' offices. In addition, most people resist change, even if the change will eventually make them more productive. This might cause them to initially reject new applications or services a modification brings forth. Thus, the project team should have a strategy in effect to counter these problems.

One method of dealing with the public-affairs aspect of the project is to keep the potential end users abreast of any upcoming changes to the network. Be sure to give plenty of advance warning before making the actual change. An effective method to keep users informed is for the system management organization to publish a concise monthly newsletter identifying strategic plans, upcoming modifications, and results of past modifications. The newsletter should also solicit various means to enable users to provide comments to the modification teams. This is a good way to make the users feel they are a part of the modification. Plus, their comments can help validate requirements and identify operational problems.

Management Reports

Management reports summarize the technical, schedule, and cost progress of the modification. Project leaders should periodically send management reports to upper management, to keep them abreast of the status of the network development. It is normally best to alert management to any conditions that might have an impact on the project as early as possible, to allow enough time for upper management to assist in developing workarounds to counter the problems.

A typical management report should focus on the:

- Current and accumulative costs
- Current schedule status
- Past and present utilization of resources
- Issues having negative impacts on the project schedule, budget, and quality of the deliverables and end products

- Identification of successful and unsuccessful deliverables
- Changes made to the modification plan

The management report should not only identify status; it should also explain how the project team will counter all deficiencies. For example, the management report could state that the modification project is on schedule but $10,000 over its budget. In this case, the report should also describe how the team expects to resolve the problem, whether it is to reduce the functionality of the system (through, perhaps, fewer hardware and software procurement expenses) or to ask for more money.

Modification Planning

To ensure a successful network modification, it is extremely important to plan each step of the project. The team should develop a modification plan addressing all aspects of the project. At this point, the team should refer to the modification plan as *initial*, because it might change throughout the project as solutions and budgets become more defined.

As described in Chapter 1, the reengineering team should modify the network according to the process shown in Figure 3.1. The project team should plan each of these modification steps. Some steps might not be necessary or might be needed only in varying degrees, depending on the type and scope of the modification. For instance, a network move would mainly focus on installation of the existing network at the new location, with much less emphasis on requirements analysis and design. However, the incorporation of new technologies would focus on all steps. Figure 1.6 of Chapter 1 identifies the degree of importance for each modification step, based on types of modifications. This can help the team determine which steps of the modification project to focus on when planning.

Project Initialization

The first step in modifying a network is to initialize a project and start planning the modification. This marks the very beginning of the project. Without proper project initialization and planning, the network modification stands very little chance of being successful.

Here are some project planning steps an organization should accomplish:

1. Create a statement of work (SOW).
2. Develop a work breakdown structure (WBS).
3. Determine and allocate resources.
4. Create schedules.
5. Determine a budget.
6. Review background information, if applicable.

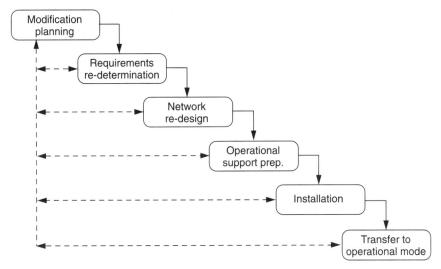

Figure 3.1 Network modification process

Some of the project initialization activities could have been completed before the project was officially started, depending on the scenario. As an example, if the project is part of a proposal developed in response to an organization's request for proposals, then these elements would have been part of the proposal. The team could then get started immediately with reviewing requirements. On the other hand, if the project is to modify an organization's internal network, then all of the above elements would have to be accomplished.

Creating a statement of work

The statement of work (SOW) describes what needs to be done to accomplish the network modification. The SOW should clearly define project goals by stating expected end results. These goals are the vision of the project and gives all project team members something common to strive for.

The SOW does not need to cover all aspects of the project, because other project elements, such as the work breakdown structure and schedule, will provide much more detail. For example, the SOW might merely state the need for the incorporation of desktop video conferencing for a specific group of users, to be accomplished by a certain date. The work breakdown structure and schedule will further define milestones and activities necessary to complete the project.

Figure 3.2 identifies an outline of a SOW.

The SOW should explain which influencing factor or factors the modification will counter, as well as a description of the tasks necessary to develop and implement the modification. At this point in the project, though,

---

Statement of work

I. Introduction
    A. Executive overview

II. Project description
    A. Work description
    B. Work basis
    C. General schedule
       and cost

Figure 3.2 Outline of a statement of work (SOW)

---

the factor(s) influencing the organization to change the network might be well understood, but not much might be known about how to modify the network. Later on during the design phase, the team will determine more details about the modification. For example, the SOW might explain that the goal of the project is to migrate the current system from a centralized mainframe system to a distributed client-server architecture. Or, the SOW might identify the major milestones to modify the network to accommodate a new application, such as desktop conferencing. But the technical details of how to accomplish these goals might not be known yet.

The SOW should include the scope of the project; that is, the magnitude of the modification. As an example, the SOW should identify how much of the existing network should incorporate the modification. Will the modification cover all sites or just specific locations?

Developing a work breakdown structure

The work breakdown structure (WBS) is a task-oriented tree showing what the team needs to accomplish to complete the project. The WBS lists all tasks the team will need to perform, and the products they must deliver. The project team should base other planning elements, such as resource allocations and schedules, on the WBS. The WBS provides a road map for planning, managing and controlling items such as work definitions, resource allocations, cost estimates, expenditures, changes, and cost and technical performance.

The WBS should identify major tasks, subtasks, and even lower-level tasks if necessary. Major tasks usually tie directly to the major milestones of the project, which, for a network modification, could include requirements determination, design, installation, testing, and determining new levels of support. For each major task the WBS should identify a group of subtasks that provide more detail. For example, subtasks for the major task "installation" could include the following: install cabling, configure client workstations, and install servers. It might also be beneficial for the WBS to include a set of tasks for each subtask as well. Thus, for the subtask "install cabling" the WBS might list another series of steps. The general rule of thumb for creating the WBS is to continue dividing the project into work units small enough so the team can reasonably estimate the resources needed to complete both the individual and the overall task(s). This makes it possible to more accurately determine the overall costs associated with the project.

As part of the WBS, the project team should produce a WBS dictionary that documents the scope of each task and product. This becomes a valuable tool, because all team members will have a common understanding of the project tasks and products.

The following is a sample WBS for a typical network modification:

1. **Project initialization**

1.1 Create work breakdown structure.

1.2 Determine and allocate resources.

1.3 Identify milestones.

1.4 Create schedules.

1.5 Create a budget.

1.6 Establish a project team.

1.7 Review background information.

2. **Requirements analysis**

2.1 Determine which requirements need revision.

2.2 Determine validity of existing requirements.

2.3 If necessary, redetermine requirements.

2.4 Identify constraints.

2.5 Develop a requirements prototype.

2.6 Validate new requirements.

2.7 Document requirements.

2.8 Initiate test planning.

2.9 Baseline the requirements.

3. **Network design**

3.1 Develop a design prototype.

3.2 Determine design specifications.

3.3 Identify network components.

3.4 Review the design.

3.5 Produce documentation.

3.6 Baseline the design.

3.7 Procure components.

4. **Operational support planning**

4.1 Identify support mechanisms requiring change.

4.2 Determine new levels of operational support.

4.3 Produce a support plan.

4.4 Develop training courses.

4.5 Develop user manuals.

4.6 Baseline the operational support mechanisms.

5. **Network installation**

5.1 Prepare for the installation.

5.2 Install components.

5.3 Perform testing.

5.4 Update network documentation.

5.5 Baseline the installed system.

5.6 Prepare for the transfer to production mode.

6. **Transfer to operational mode**

6.1 Review network documentation.

6.2 Ensure that the network is ready for operational mode.

6.3 Produce a support turnover agreement.

Determining resource requirements

Resource requirements identify people and equipment the project will need to accomplish the project's goals. Figure 3.3 shows a sample outline for a resource requirements document. The resource requirements document should cover the entire project duration and should list names of people and

Resource requirements

I. Introduction
    A. Executive overview

II. Labor requirements
    A. Employees
    B. Consultants

III. Material requirements
    A. Work space
    B. Storage space
    C. Office equipment

Figure 3.3 Outline of a resource requirements document

their expected level of utilization on the project. The document should specify whether these people are employees of the organization, contractors or consultants. This information is very useful when staffing the project, and managers can use the utilization forecasts to plan future workloads for their employees.

Resource requirements should also identify necessary items needed to complete the project, such as PCs, software, and reference books. It is usually too late to acquire these items at the time they are actually needed. The resource requirements document should state the location of these items, as well as the serial numbers of any hardware.

Be sure to confirm the availability of any resources planned for a particular project. Joe might be available this week to work the project, but three months from now he might not be available, unless some commitment is obtained from Joe and his superior. In addition, that PC sitting in an unused office might be available today, but someone might take it before you need it for your project. Therefore, it is best to make known *who* and *what* you plan to use on the project.

The project team

A successful network modification requires a project team that can efficiently satisfy all the steps of a network modification. This means the capability to plan and control all aspects of the project. Thus, it is important to establish a complete set of human resources, a project team, which has appropriate levels of expertise to handle the modification.

For small projects, the project team commonly consists of one person who performs all tasks associated with the network modification. For larger projects, additional people should be involved in performing the modification. The makeup of the project team should encompass all skills necessary to develop and implement the network and provide insight into network support. Figure 3.4 identifies necessary team members of a network modification project.

The succeeding paragraphs explain the roles of each team member.

Project manager

The project manager is one who manages and directs the entire network modification. This person coordinates the people and resources to ensure that all objectives of the project are met. Periodically, throughout the project, the project manager should schedule Technical Interchange Meetings (TIMs) to address issues needing attention by project team members and customer representatives. The project manager should coordinate all activities with applicable organizations, such as the customer site, configuration management, and network operations. In general, the project manager should at least be familiar with networking concepts. The project manager can rely on the education and experience of the rest of the team to accomplish the objectives of the project.

Customer representative

The customer representative portrays the interests of the users who will be receiving the network modification. In general, this person is the focal point for

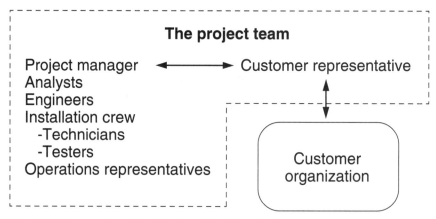

Figure 3.4 Team members of a network modification project

aiming the project team in the right direction when dealing with the organization, especially the users. The customer representative should be very familiar with the user population and should be able to speak honestly for the users.

In most cases, the customer representative should participate in determining network requirements. As a minimum, the representative should validate requirements that the team discovers. For example, the customer representative might identify who the team should see to assist the members in gathering data to support the redetermination of network requirements. Also, the customer representative can help the project team plan initial site visits and can help develop the installation schedule. To best fill these needs, the customer representative should have a good feel for the organizational structure and missions of the organization.

System analysts

System analysts determine the requirements for the network; therefore, they will be gathering information from a variety of sources. This means the analyst should be able to work well with other people, especially the potential users of the system. The analyst should have good interviewing skills and should be able to translate true needs into realistic requirements.

Engineers

Engineers provide the technical know-how to meet the objectives of the project. The engineers might assist in determining requirements, but primarily they design solutions that will counter the influencing factor(s). This entails identifying technologies and products that will satisfy network requirements. In addition, engineers can assist in managing or implementing the installation of the network modification, and can help plan new levels of operational support. Engineers should have a solid background in current network technologies and products.

Installation crew

The installation crew consists of installers and testers who implement the network modification. It is best to have the installation crew work under the direction of the engineers for efficient problem resolution, because the crew normally does not participate in other modification activities. The installers should have a good background in installing network hardware, software, and wiring. Testers will need to make sure that the network being installed or modified meets the users expectations, the system requirements, and quality standards. The testers should understand quality control techniques, should be diplomatic, and, if possible, should be independent of the installers.

Operations representative

It is important to have an operations representative on the modification team, to coordinate the modification with existing network support organizations. This ensures that the network modification will be integrated effectively into the existing network infrastructure and support mechanisms. Thus, the operations representative should have a broad understanding of the existing network, and some knowledge of current network support mechanisms.

The entire project team should initialize the project by having a kickoff meeting to review project goals, milestones, and schedules. This starts the team operating as a whole group rather than having people stray off course from the primary goals. Both large and small network modification projects can be frustrating, intimidating, and demeaning. Therefore, it is extremely beneficial to keep all team members motivated during the network modification project.

One of the top team motivators is personal achievement. People tend to perform much better when they know they will be achieving something valuable during and at the conclusion of the project. Projects with unclear milestones, especially conclusions, will frustrate team members. Thus, with networking projects it is best to clearly identify the beginning, midpoint, and end of the project, plus all the positive benefits the team members will receive.

Recognition is also high on the list of motivators. Be sure to identify people who have gone that extra mile towards achieving project objectives. This is where awards, such as plaques and certificates, are effective. It is usually best to present the awards at larger company functions, but do not wait too long.

The chance to practice true craftsmanship is also something that will motivate people to continue doing good work. In other words, if the team feels they have been allowed to produce a quality product they will continue to do so. To enable good craftsmanship, be sure to have available quality tools and a good working environment.

Professional growth is something very important to most people, especially networking professionals. People are also interested in learning new skills that might pay off in the future. It is important to communicate to team members the value of the skills they will learn by working on the network modification.

Of course money is also a motivator. But believe it or not, the motivators discussed above tend to be more effective in getting people to do their best. However, if team members are underpaid they will probably not perform well. Thus, if possible, keep the team members' salaries or fees at reasonable levels.

Creating a project schedule

The project schedule identifies when the project team will accomplish specific tasks and milestones. Schedules show when project actions will occur, establishing an organized flow to the project. The simplest type of scheduling tool is a GANTT chart, which shows the start, finish, and duration of each task. Figure 3.5 shows an example of GANTT chart schedule. Other more sophisticated tools show precedence relationships among tasks; that is, which ones depend on each other.

The schedule should differentiate between working time and elapsed time. Working time refers to the time that people will be working on the project. Typically, working time is eight hours per day and does not apply to weekends, holidays, and vacations. On the other hand, elapsed time is the actual amount of time that transpires, which is normally twenty-four hours per day and seven days a week. Resources that operate continuously, such as computers and other nonhuman resources, might be scheduled according to elapsed time. The point here is to be sure to schedule resources only during the time that they will be available.

Determining a budget

The budget specifies how much it will cost to meet the objectives of the project. Initially, the team will have to base the budget on estimates of the labor and other costs. As the project continues, the team might need to adjust the budget to reflect more precise information to accommodate changes and unexpected expenses or cost reductions.

Reviewing background information

Before getting into the details of the project, the team should review background information, such as management plans and existing system archi-

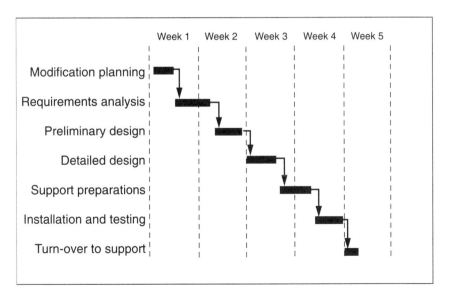

Figure 3.5 Sample network schedule

tecture. The network modification will get off to a smoother start if the team studies background information first.

The team should consider the following actions for reviewing background information:

- Review the organization's information management plans. Consider preferences, goals, and strategic plans the organization has for their information system. This will help lead the team to solutions that fall in line with the organization's expectations.

- Determine the general makeup of the existing system by reviewing the existing information system architecture. This will enable a well-integrated network modification.

- Identify all documentation and points of contact the team will need throughout the entire project.

- Perform a site visit to verify building layouts and existing system cabling.

Requirements Analysis Planning

Network requirements define what the network is supposed to do; therefore, requirements analysis is a critical part of the network modification. If the requirements are not accurate, then the network modification can easily become a failure because the network will not meet the expectations of its users.

For planning the requirements analysis portion of the project, the team should consider the following question: Does the modification project demand a full redetermination of user requirements, or does the project merely necessitate a review of existing requirements?

The answer to this question depends on whether there is an accurate existing set of user requirements. Of course, if no user requirements are specified it is wise to fully determine the user requirements before continuing with the project. Also if the organization has experienced significant growth or a change in mission since the latest requirements determination, it is best to redetermine the requirements. If the existing requirements are well-documented and no sizable organizational changes have occurred, then the team could just review the existing requirements. For more details on analyzing network requirements, refer to Chapter 4.

Network Design Planning

Network design describes how the network will meet requirements, by defining the technologies and products necessary to satisfy the network requirements and to counter factors that might have influenced the network change. The design requires the use of engineering principles, which includes finding a least-cost solution that satisfies requirements but also falls within constraints.

The project team should form a design team and should plan on splitting the network design phase into two parts, the preliminary design and the detailed design. The goal of the preliminary design is to identify and compare a solution set consisting of technologies and standards that will satisfy the requirements. The design team should plan to have a preliminary design review meeting, at which the team can select the best solution from the set of solutions. The purpose of the detailed design is to fine-tune the chosen solution by selecting products and producing (or just updating) design documentation. The detailed design consists, among other things, of materials lists, schematics, cabling drawings, and installation plans. The design team should plan to have a detailed design review meeting to ensure that all team members agree the design is complete. At the conclusion of the detailed design, the team should procure all components needed for the modification. For more details on designing the network, refer to Chapters 5, 6, and 7.

Operational Support Preparations Planning

The network modification might change requirements for operational support of the network. It is not advisable to wait until after the installation team installs the new components to start thinking about how to support the reconfigured network. After modifications are completed, people might start using the network immediately. If the appropriate degree of support is not available, the network might fail and there would not be a mechanism in place to fix the problem. Therefore, the team should start planning new levels of operational support as early as possible. A complete and accurate operational support plan should be ready for implementation before installation takes place. The plan should specify what support is needed and who is going to provide it. For more details on preparing for operational support, refer to Chapter 8.

Network Installation Planning

The network installation consists of installing components and testing the network modifications. The network installation will often interrupt employee productivity, especially when the modification involves a change in technology, the correction of an operational problem, or a network move. Thus, careful planning is necessary to avoid problems during the installation stage.

At the conclusion of the installation and testing of the modification, the team should transfer project management responsibility to supporting organizations. This officially ends the project by transferring the network modification to a production mode. This entails the transfer of all network modification documentation, such as schematics, cabling diagrams, and support plans to organizations that will provide the necessary operational support for the network modification. For more details on how to install the network, refer to Chapter 9.

Production Mode Transfer Planning

The transfer of the modification to production mode consists of handing the network or modification over to the users and the operational support staff. The project team should plan for an official transfer to avoid misunderstanding of when the modification has attained operational status. The transfer also clearly ends the project and places the responsibility of supporting the network on proper operational support mechanisms. For more details on transferring the network to operational mode, refer to Chapter 10.

Planning Specific to Factors Influencing Change

Each type of network modification resulting from a particular influencing factor requires a varying perspective in terms of planning. This section covers the planning peculiarities of each type of network modification. Later chapters include more information on how to accomplish each type of modification. As mentioned before, Figure 1.6 identifies the degree of importance of each modification step, based on each type of modification. This figure can help the project team determine which modification steps to focus on.

Planning for Changes in User Needs

A modification responding to changes in user needs, such as the need for access to a distant database, generally includes all general modification steps. However, the team should concentrate most of the effort on analyzing requirements, especially user requirements.

An organization might have discovered changes in user needs by performing a previous user requirements analysis. If so, the network modification team should base the redesign upon these requirements, as long as the existing requirements are accurate and complete. If the requirements are inadequate or nonexistent, then the team should plan a full requirements analysis. In this case, be sure to have someone on the modification team who is familiar with performing requirements analysis.

The team should plan to redesign and reconfigure the network based on the new user requirements. This could entail software development if off-the-shelf interfaces and applications that meet new user needs are not available. Be sure to plan new levels of operational support and project management responsibility for the reconfigured network.

Planning for Special Services

The planning for special services, such as mobility or desktop conferencing, is very similar to planning for changes in user needs. It is very important to review accurate requirements to gain a full understanding of the needs for special services. Special applications, though, often require significant redesign of the network. Thus, the team should plan to spend most of its time in the design stage of the modification process. In addition, the special service could significantly alter the required operational support; therefore, be sure to adequately plan new levels of operational support.

Planning a Technology Migration

If faced with implementing a technology migration, a network manager should develop a solid migration plan that identifies every step necessary to migrate from the older technology to the newer one. This is necessary because the process of migrating to a different technology can seriously affect the operation of the system. In addition, the results of a technology migration are not easily visible to users and most management. Thus, it is highly recommended that you carefully plan every step. The migration plan should include a vision of the eventual system, accurate tangible costs and benefits of migrating, and a preliminary schedule and installation plan phasing in the newer technology. The team should concentrate extensively on planning the migration. This will significantly reduce problems, such as system outages and unclear expectations.

Planning for Organizational Resizing

If the modification project is to accommodate the resizing of an organization, the system modification project will differ depending on whether the resizing involves the addition or deletion of users. In the case of deleting users, the current network, if initially designed correctly, will probably continue to support the remaining users. In fact, the network will most likely perform better. Therefore, the team might not need to perform any modification steps. Some system components, such as computers and networking components, might even become available for other uses.

The modification team should perform all modification steps if the organization wants to add users to the network, especially if the increase of users is substantial. One word of caution, though, is to monitor the gradual addition of users. It might seem like one or two additional users will not affect the performance of the network. But, the network might be close to saturation, and that one additional user might have requirements that result in periodically crashing the network. In addition, adding one or two users periodically will eventually add up to a substantial number. Sooner or later, an organization will need to perform some redesigning and reconfiguration of the network to meet its increased demands. Thus, the modification team should at least plan to analyze user requirements of the new users and should make necessary changes to the design, system configuration, and operational support infrastructure.

Planning a System Move

When making organizational moves, the team should concentrate on planning the removal and reinstallation of the system. This involves moving networking components and users' computers to the new location. As a result, the team must make detailed plans to move the system without making users ineffective and angry.

Because network and application software is already installed on the servers and client workstations before the move, it will not require reinstallation at the new site. Most software can just be transported within the hard platform it resides on. However, it takes a relatively great amount of time to recable and reinstall network hardware at the new site.

A very important objective in moving a system is to ensure that all users at the new site will have proper connectivity, primarily because the new facility will probably have quite a different layout and type of construction. Therefore, the team should plan some redesigning of the network configuration. Typically, the redesign will concentrate on network wiring and distribution. The team can better plan the network move by asking the following questions:

- Is there existing wiring in the new location, and is it adequate?
- Where will we locate the servers and wiring hubs?
- Is there adequate ventilation and cooling for all network equipment?
- Is the power adequate to support the network?
- Will any renovations be taking place?
- Are rooms identified to contain the network equipment?

Before moving to a new location, an organization will normally prepare the new building by performing some degree of renovation. This renovation could include recarpeting, painting, reconstructing walls and ceilings, and installing office partitions. Therefore, the project team should be coordinating the system move with teams responsible for moving furniture and renovating the facility. It is much easier to install network cabling and equipment during or after renovations but before the furniture goes in place. Plan the installation of network cabling and taps to take place at the most effective time. Avoid installing cabling in a wall or ceiling that someone eventually will change as part of the renovation. It is also easier to install network taps without having obstacles such as desks and bookcases in the way.

Planning for Countering Operational Problems

Countering operational problems has two distinct phases. The first is to identify the problem (not just the symptoms) and the other is to fix it. The maintenance function of the operational support organization should determine the sources of the operational problems by first performing testing. Often the maintenance group will be able to fix the problem readily. However, these operational problems sometimes require a network redesign. In such a case, the modification team should plan to concentrate on design, installation, and testing modification steps.

Planning to Expand the Network's Coverage

If planning to enlarge the network to expand coverage across the organization, the modification team should carefully review the existing user requirements and network architecture. One problem with this type of modification is that significant time might have elapsed since the existing network was put in place, causing the requirements and possibly the existing network to be out-of-date. Thus, plan to redetermine user requirements if they are not accurate, and carefully review the existing network architecture to prevent premature obsolescence.

Another problem with this type of network modification is that it is prone to the creation of network pockets within the organization that do not interoperate. Therefore, the team should plan to implement a modification that interfaces with the existing network and allows the new users to interoperate with the rest of the organization.

Planning to Create an Initial Network

If planning an initial information system for the entire organization, this is a good opportunity to "do it right the first time." Thus, the organization should plan the system by developing strategic plans, schedules, resources, and budgets. The modification team or, in this case, the "initial implementation team," should fully exercise all modification steps. The team should carefully analyze user requirements, create a design that meets these requirements, install and test the system components, train the users, and establish an operational support infrastructure.

The Modification Plan Document

The modification plan should contain details on how to modify the existing information system to respond to influencing factors, such as changes in user needs, technological changes, organizational moves or resizing, operational problems, and limited network coverage. Project managers use the plan to effectively manage information system modifications. Figure 3.6 shows an outline of a modification plan.

The modification plan document should:

- Define the modification objectives and scope.
- Identify a clear set of milestones.
- Contain a complete work breakdown structure.
- Completely identify available resources.
- Spell out a realistic schedule.
- Contain an accurate budget containing realistic costs.
- Define all major risks.
- Describe mechanisms that will reduce risks.
- Describe how the project will produce quality end products.
- Describe the roles and responsibilities of a complete project team.
- Identify plans for analyzing requirements, redesigning the network, reconfiguring the network, implementing new levels of operational support, and transferring project management responsibility.

After arming the project with a sound modification plan, the team is ready to begin analyzing requirements.

Modification plan

I. Introduction
   A. Executive overview

II. Modification description

III. Attachments
   A. Feasibility
   B. Statement of work
   C. Schedule
   D. Budget

Figure 3.6 Outline of a modification plan

Analysis and Design

4

Requirements Analysis

After planning the network modification, requirements analysis is the next step in the project. An initial network creation will always demand a complete requirements analysis; however, other types of modifications might only need a review and perhaps an update of existing requirements. Properly completing a requirements analysis simplifies the design and maximizes the implementation of a modification that effectively satisfies user and organizational needs. This chapter explains the concepts and types of network requirements, general requirements analysis procedures, and how to determine requirements for each factor that might have influenced the network change. These topics explain what is necessary to prepare requirements in a form that eases the design of the network.

Concepts of Network Requirements

As shown in Figure 4.1, requirements analysis determines the *what* in the development of a system and describes attributes the system must contain. It is the job of the system analyst to determine requirements. The design phase of the network modification defines the remaining elements not specified by requirements. Collectively, the requirements and design specifications support the overall goals of the modification project.

The implementation of the network, which includes the design and installation phases, depends heavily on requirements. Not specifying solid requirements often results in a network that does not adequately meet the needs of the organization and users. There is a tendency, however, to rush the project through the requirements analysis and design and hurry on to

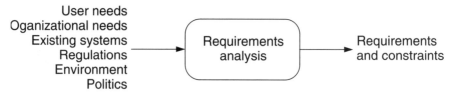

User needs
Oganizational needs
Existing systems
Regulations
Environment
Politics

Requirements
analysis

Requirements
and constraints

Figure 4.1 Concepts of requirements analysis

the procurement and installation of network components. This often occurs because upper management and/or the users are anxious to see results in the form of hardware and software. But, this approach might miss or not clearly define requirements, resulting in poor network operating character-istics. In many cases, users might not be able to effectively utilize all the ser-vices they need, or the network might be full of bugs that take many months to fix. Also, these bugs are much more expensive to fix after the network becomes operational. Therefore, be sure to define requirements before pro-ceeding to the remaining phases of the modification.

The project team should strive to define worthy requirements. This is a big step in the application of quality control, because defining full-bodied requirements significantly reduces expensive reworks later on during the project. As a product of requirements analysis, the project team should be sure requirements are unambiguous, verifiable, and describe the *what*, not the *how*.

Requirements should be clearly and completely stated to avoid clarifica-tion questions later. For example, the requirements might identify the need for electronic mail, but state nothing else about necessary functional fea-tures. Ambiguous requirements cause the designer, later on during the pro-ject, to seek the finer details of the requirements. As a result, the designer might attempt to contact the analysts who initially identified the require-ments. This could take a considerable amount of time, causing the project schedule to slip. To save time, the designer might guess at the values of the remaining requirements details. The problem with this is that the designer might choose characteristics of the requirement that are not the best in terms of satisfying the users' needs. Either case is most likely a no-win situ-ation. So, be sure to specify unambiguous requirements from the beginning.

Another element of a good requirement is that it be verifiable; that is, it will be eventually possible to test whether the requirement is satisfied. For in-stance, a requirement might state that the network must utilize user names and passwords to provide access control. How can you test this requirement? To perform adequate testing you need to test the range of valid and invalid inputs. But this requirement does not identify the valid inputs, such as char-acter string length. Therefore it would not be possible to fully test the re-quirement. To be verifiable, the requirement in this example should also indicate the maximum length of user names, as well as the maximum and minimum length and required use of characters for the password. The requirements should emphasize what the network is supposed to do instead of how it will work. Therefore, requirements should avoid specifying technologies and actual products, unless there are corporate policies or regulations stating otherwise. This maximizes design flexibility because it allows more freedom in choosing the most cost-effective solution.

At a minimum, requirements should describe overall system attributes and network functionality. System attributes define anything the network must interface with and how the overall network must operate. For example, requirements might specify that the network must interface with a specific type of mainframe computer, and the network must be operational twenty-four hours per day with a minimum downtime of two hours over the next year. Network functionality describes what applications and services the network must perform. As described before, these applications and services include electronic mail, resource sharing, file transfer, shared databases, desktop conferencing, and document management.

It is important to not over- or under-specify requirements. Too many requirements can limit the choice of solutions, because designers will not have the flexibility to offer the most cost-effective solutions. Not enough requirements can leave designers with a vague understanding of needs, which prompts the development of solutions which are not satisfactory. Figure 4.2 illustrates these concepts. A key in developing requirements is to concentrate on specifying those that clearly increase the effectiveness of the organization and its employees.

Concrete requirements are normally referred to as *constraints*. Constraints are usually requirements dealing with money, regulations, and the environment. However, any requirement could be a constraint if that requirement is absolutely necessary and not feasible to change. Money is commonly a constraint, because an organization either has it or it does not.

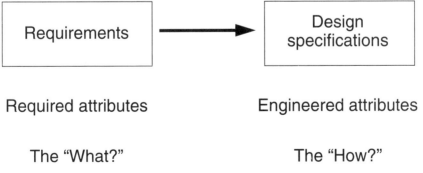

Figure 4.2 Comparison of requirements and design specifications

For example, if an organization absolutely cannot spend more than $100,000 on the network modification, then money is a constraint. Regulations are normally constraints because they often carry mandates directing a particular form of conformance. As an example, local laws might require the use of plenum grade cable. The environment, such as building size and construction, establishes constraints as well because the facility might be too expensive to change.

Network Requirements Basis

Many elements can provide the basis for requirements, resulting in some requirements that are flexible to some degree, but others that are very rigid. For example, as part of the requirements specification, an organization might require users to send graphic files to a distant location. But the organization might have only a set amount of money to spend on the modification to support this requirement. If the designers find it is impossible to supply a solution for this requirement based on the funding limitation, then the organization would need to alter one of the requirements. In this case, the organization could change the requirement of where graphic files are sent to a requirement more manageable within the funding limitation.

The project team can derive requirements from many sources, which the following paragraphs describe:

Plans and documentation

When determining requirements, the project team should utilize any existing documentation that provides an accurate basis for network requirements. As an example, the concept of operations defines system-level functionality, operational environment, and implementation priorities for an organization's information system. In effect, the concept of operations identifies a partial set of requirements. Thus, project team members should use the concept of operations, if it exists, as a basis for network requirements.

The organization might also have an overall strategic information system plan, which provides long-term vision and general procedures necessary to manage the efficient evolution of the corporate information system. This plan identifies a clear set of implementation milestones that support projected business objectives, identify long-term and short-term technical goals, and often specify recommended technologies and standards. The project team should make certain that requirements for the modification are consistent with the strategic plan.

In addition, the organization might have other plans, such as business plans and employee projections, which the team can use to derive requirements. Business plans describe the future markets and strategies the company wishes to pursue, which is useful in determining the types of applications and services the users might require. Of course, employee projections give insight into the size of the workforce, which the team can use to estimate the dimension of the future network.

User and organizational needs

An effective network modification must satisfy the needs of the users and the organization. To accomplish this, the team must include user needs as part of the requirements. User needs contribute to the network requirements, because they identify necessary applications, interfaces, communications, and features. The overall organization might also have needs, such as a desire to increase communications among its employees or cut operational costs.

Existing systems

Existing systems, such as the current networks, applications, and mainframes, might create requirements for the network modification to be compliant with certain protocols and standards. If the network modification does not include these types of requirements, then the eventual modification might not interoperate with existing systems. For example, the network modification might need to allow its users to communicate with users of a network located at a different site. A requirement might then specify the need for the networks at the two sites to be compatible.

Regulations

Regulations and policies normally map directly into requirements. For example, a safety regulation might state, "All cabling used within the facility must be of plenum grade." Or, an information management policy might declare, "All electronic mail applications must interface with X.400 standard." Both of these statements would become requirements for any network modification dealing with cabling or electronic mail applications.

Environment

The environment also plays a role in identification of requirements. For instance, if the facility has space for a communications room measuring ten feet long and fifteen feet wide, then a requirement should specify these dimensions as a size constraint for the communications room. The size and layout of the facility containing the users also identifies requirements specifying the separation between users. For example, users might reside in buildings separated by a two-lane street. The requirements should then describe this situation as part of the requirement for communications between the two buildings.

Politics

Some large organizations have highly political information management groups. That is, managers primarily make decisions based on reasons that give them more power and career advancement. Thus "politics" often finds its way into the formation of requirements, because some managers can benefit by including their technical "solution" as part of the requirements. For example, a manager might have political reasons to utilize a particular vendor's network operating system. This motivates the manager to fund a solution utilizing that network operating system. As a result, political forces will cause requirements to specify much of the technical solution, whether it is effective or not. This usually constrains the designers in choosing cost-effective solutions because they are left with very little choice over the selection of technologies and products.

Types of Network Requirements

Through both the requirements analysis and design, the project team will define all elements contributing to the network modification. As mentioned before, the requirements define necessary elements describing what the network is supposed to do, and the design specifications define the remaining elements and identify how the network will satisfy requirements. Figure 4.3 identifies the kind of requirements that system analysts will need to define. The rest of this section describes each type.

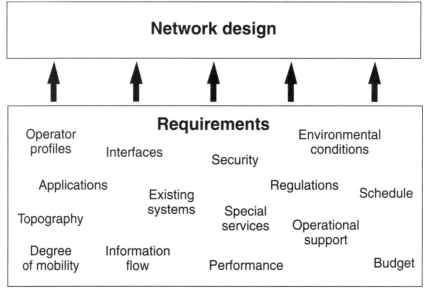

Figure 4.3 Classes of requirements

Operator Profiles

Operator profiles identify and describe attributes of each person who will be utilizing the network. It is crucial that the requirements fully explain the profiles of the users and operational support staff. The operator profiles are human factors the designers must take into consideration when finding solutions for other requirements and design specifications. Operator profiles play a large part in the selection of any network element that provides a human interface, such as applications, special services, and network operating systems.

What should the operator profile include? The answer to this depends on many things. If the network modification focuses on the addition of new applications or special services, then the profile should specify as much about the users as possible. For example, the user profile requirements should recognize the person's name, whether the person is strictly a user or serves some network operations role, the person's level of networking experience and knowledge of applications, and the person's job title and description.

For modifications dealing with changes that are transparent to users, the team might need to specify only the profiles of operational support staff. As an example, consider the situation in which an organization decides it is cost-effective to transition from the use of T1 communications lines to frame relay service. This type of change would probably not affect the users in any way. But people supporting the network will need to maintain a different type of long-haul communications. Therefore, it would be best to describe operational support staff profiles, not users profiles in the requirements. These requirements would enable the designers to make the right choices when deciding on which level of support to lease from the frame relay provider, or possibly to recommend appropriate training for the support staff.

Existing Systems

Requirements should identify and fully describe any existing systems that could affect the design of the network modification. This could include the system the modification directly affects or any peripheral system. Normally, the interfacing requirements will describe any necessary interfaces to these systems. In general, existing systems requirements include the network being modified and other peripheral systems, as shown in Figure 4.4.

The design team will need to fully understand the existing systems, especially the one upon which the modification is supposed to take place. A description of the existing systems will aid in determining how to integrate the modification into the existing system, or how to interface the network under development with external systems. Therefore, requirements should fully describe attributes of existing systems, such as:

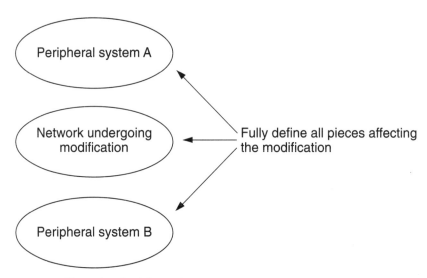

Figure 4.4 Illustration of existing systems

- Operational functionality and hardware, such as CPU type, memory size, and configurations
- Software, such as type applications and network drivers
- Protocols and standards
- Operational support methods

The team can probably find the above information through the network manager who presides over the system of interest.

Interface Requirements

As shown in Figure 4.5, the network will require interfaces for people and other systems to interact effectively with what the network offers. The interfaces are the network's input/output ports. The network might require several types of human and system interfaces. Interface requirements specify what type of interfaces are needed to meet the needs of the users and the operational support staff and to facilitate proper interconnectivity with other systems.

Human interfaces

Users will need some sort of interface to allow them to utilize network applications and services. As discussed in Chapter 2, examples of user interfaces are GUI and command-line interface. In addition, operational support personnel must have some method of interfacing with the network to facilitate network administration, monitoring, and maintenance. This could take the form of a network management station or a system administration console that is part of the network operating system. Thus, system analysts should base human interface requirements on applications and services the people must be able to access. Also, be sure the selection of interfaces matches well with the operator profiles.

System interfaces

Interface requirements should recognize the need of the network to interface with other systems, both internal and external to the organization. These systems could be anything not considered part of the immediate network, such as a network residing in another place in the organization, a wide area network, a mainframe computer, or a database located at a distant site. As part of this specification, analysts should clearly identify the protocols and standards other systems require for interoperability.

Topography Requirements

The topography of a network defines the network's physical surface spots. In other words, it specifies the type and location of nodes with respect to one another. Figure 4.6 shows the elements of topography. Nodes are end-devices having network addresses, such as PCs, printers, mainframes, and routers. Topography is different from topology. Physical topology goes another step beyond topography by identifying the interconnectivty between nodes in terms of links. Topology is normally considered a design specification, which Chapter 5 will address.

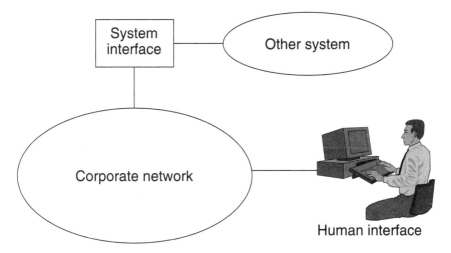

Figure 4.5 Illustration of network interfaces

Building floor plan

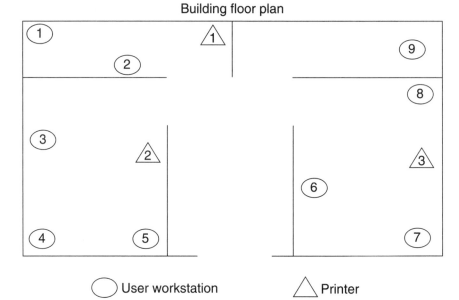

○ User workstation   △ Printer

Figure 4.6 Illustration of network topography

Topography requirements should address the type and location of users, operational support personnel, computers, and printers. Designers will use these locations to determine the type of medium and medium-access techniques to employ. Requirements might not fully identify the number and location of all end devices. For instance, routers and bridges might not be specified until during the design phase of the modification. Topography requirements should also identify space available for communications equipment and servers, and the general layout of the organization's facility. This will aid the designers in choosing a place to locate the network components, and in deciding where to run the cables.

Application and Special Service Requirements

The users of the network might need a variety of applications that requirements should specify. Office applications consist of financial tracking software, word processors, spreadsheets, and databases. Typical network services include resource sharing, file transfer, and electronic mail. Specialized services comprise desktop conferencing, telecommuting, document management, and electronic data interchange.

The network requirements should, as a minimum, specify the types of applications and services the users need, required application features, and the expected utilization plan of each type of application. The types of applications and required features aids the team in choosing actual products. Knowing the expected utilization levels of each application allows the designers to develop a network topology to support likely traffic patterns generated by users accessing the applications.

The requirements might describe necessary application attributes but might or might not name the software vendor. Whether or not to include actual product vendor names in the requirements depends on the amount of current investment and satisfaction with existing applications. If the organization does not have much investment in application software or is dissatisfied with current applications, then the team should not identify the actual product vendors in the requirements. Instead, the team should select the application products during the design phase of the project. This reduces the constraints on the designers and allows more flexibility finding in cost-effective solutions. However, an organization having a great deal of investment in software from specific vendors might consider stating requirements that specify the use of particular vendors.

Mobility Requirements

The mobility requirement describes the movement specific users require while interfacing with the network. People needing to constantly move in order to perform their job usually require some degree of mobile access to the network. Ordinarily, mobility demands that both the users and their respective user interfaces can move.

Mobility requirements should distinguish whether the degree of movement is continuous or periodic. Continuous movement requirements occur when the user or network component must have the ability to utilize network resources while freely moving at any time. Examples of users requiring access to network resources while continuously moving include emergency vehicles, military personnel on a battlefield, delivery services, and healthcare professionals. Periodic mobility, which is often referred to as portability, implies the utilization of network resources from temporary locations, but not necessarily while the user is in transit between locations. Portability implies a temporary connection to the network from a stationary point. The interface associated with a portable connection, though, should be easy to move, set up, and dismantle to facilitate efficient temporary operating locations. Examples of users requiring access to network resources through portable interfaces include point-of-sale cashiers, conference organizers, and employees working from temporary office facilities.

When specifying mobility requirements, the analysts should address the following items:

- Identification of users and components needing mobility
- Degree of movement each user or component requires

- Geographical coverage the user or component requires, such as:
  ~Local, within the immediate building
  ~Semi-local, within the immediate city or campus
  ~Non-local, or anywhere on Earth

The above requirements attributes will aid designers in the choice of effective wireless connectivity.

Information Flow Requirements

Figure 4.7 illustrates the concept of information flow. The use of network applications requires the flow of information among various points on the network. If a user retrieves a file from storage located on the network, the file must be able to flow from the storage location to the user's workstation. If a user would like to send an e-mail message to a co-worker located in another part of the building, the e-mail message would need to flow between the co-workers. The mail message might flow directly from the sender to the receiver, or the mail message might travel through a mail server.

Designers need to know details of information flow to properly determine the connectivity between every pair of end devices. Information types, such as text, video, voice, and imagery, generally demand different types of connectivity. For example, the need to transfer video signals is best satisfied by using lots of bandwidth on a synchronous network, while data can be sent over lower-bandwidth, asynchronous lines. Therefore, requirements should

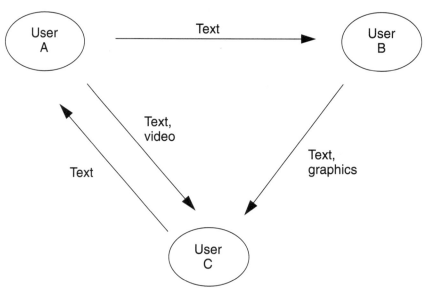

Figure 4.7 Concept of information flow

specify all information flows within the network. As a minimum, information flow requirements should specify the paths of information flow between end devices, types of information sent between end devices, how often the information requires transmission between end devices, and maximum allowable error rates.

Performance Requirements

Performance identifies how well a network provides its applications and services. If a network does not perform well, users easily become disgruntled because they cannot accomplish their functions as quickly as they want. Thus, it is extremely important to address performance in the requirements specifications. Then designers will be able to create a solution that satisfies performance expectations. Performance includes measurable attributes such as reliability, availability, and delay.

Reliability

Reliability is a function of how long the network will continue to provide its services without disruption. In other words, it is a feel for how long it will work without breaking. Reliability needs are normally stated as the number of occurrences and length of downtime that the users can tolerate. A typical business, such as a grocery store or consulting firm, might be able to accept a network that could be nonoperational three times a year for a duration of thirty minutes each occurrence. However, organizations doing more critical work, such as hospitals and law enforcement agencies, might require much higher degrees of reliability.

Availability

Availability describes when the network must be operational. For example, the degree of availability could identify that the network will be usable twenty-four hours a day, or twelve hours a day from 6:00 AM until 6:00 PM. Even though normal business hours are from 8:00 AM to 5:00 PM, the company must anticipate people coming in early, staying late, and working on weekends. Thus, most businesses operate their networks twenty-four hours per day. However, these businesses might require a higher degree of reliability during the day.

Delay

Delay is how long users are willing to wait for the network to deliver its services after a request is made. Figure 4.8 illustrates the concept of network delay. Predominantly, the delay tolerance is specified as the maximum amount of time users can tolerate waiting for applications to boot, files to transfer, etc. Network delay is a parameter which, if excessive, can reduce the effectiveness of the communication process. Causes of delay depend on factors such as spacing between nodes and whether the data traffic is light or heavy. As distance between nodes increases, the propagation delay (time the data takes to traverse the line) increases to a point at which it becomes the significant contributor to overall delay. Under light traffic conditions and assuming insignificant propagation delays, delay is primarily caused by the time each node needs to store and forward the packet. However, under heavy loads, queuing delay (the amount of time a packet waits at a node to be processed) is most significant.

Delay is normally stated as the maximum number of seconds it should take to initiate an application or send a file. There is no magic formula to determine the amount of delay users will tolerate. In fact, different users will give you different answers. Users who have had a great deal of experience using network applications will normally demand shorter delays than the novice users. The reason for this is that the new network users do not know of anything better. However, most users require that they will be able to complete a file transfer in less time than sending it manually through the postal system or in person.

Security Requirements

Computer security ensures the use of network resources without negative consequences, such as compromise of sensitive information and loss of equipment and files. The amount of security needed depends on the severity of the consequences the organization will face if it damages or compromises information. Some organizations (such as the military) require

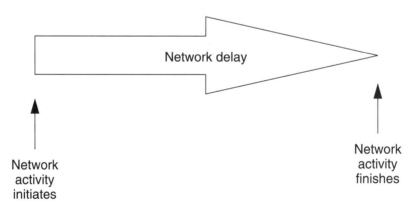

Figure 4.8 Concept of network delay

maximum security. But other organizations, such as a manufacturing facility or an employment agency, might not require security to be as high.

The proper identification of security requirements is critical in the protection of company secrets. Therefore, the analysts should address these items when assessing security requirements:

- The organization's security regulations
- The sensitivity level of all information processed on the network
- The access rights of all users
- The probability of disasters such as equipment failure, power failure, viruses, and fire

Environmental Requirements

Requirements should state conditions about the environment that could affect the operation of the network. This helps designers construct solutions that will maintain expected levels of reliability. To alert the design team of possible negative environmental effects on the network, analysts should include the following environmental operating conditions: temperature and humidity profiles of communications and server rooms, heating and cooling system ratings, and presence and intensity of electromagnetic waves from other systems and devices. Designers can use this information to determine whether it is necessary to make changes to the heating and cooling systems, or to think twice about placing radio communications gear within the facility.

Without environmental requirements, the resulting network modification might not work properly. For example, the environmental requirements could specify, "The network modification must operate within close proximity of a particular ground radar system." Designers would then choose solutions that would avoid interference with the radar system.

Operational Support Requirements

The requirements should highlight any need to base the network modification on the existing operational support infrastructure. For example, the current network monitoring stations could utilize the Simple Network Management Protocol (SNMP) to gather network statistics. If this were the case, the project team could state that all critical network devices must be able to support SNMP.

Budget Requirements

An organization might have only a certain amount of money to spend on the network modification. This funding limit should be listed as a requirement (which is usually considered a constraint) so that designers can discover a solution that does not cost more than the limited amount. Conversely, if requirements do not specify cost limits then the team could spend unnecessary amounts of time designing solutions that cost more than the organization can afford. Requirements should also state the funding plan for the project; that is, a schedule of how much money will be available at specific times. This allows designers to find solutions the organization can incorporate in a stepwise manner.

Schedule Requirements

The requirements specification should include any definite schedule demands, because the schedule might affect the design approach. For example, a lengthy schedule might allow the design team to test the functionality of products before purchasing them, which would favor a better decision on which products to include in the design specification. A shorter schedule, because of time constraints, might encourage an organization to implement the network modification by contracting with a company which has a great deal of experience with implementing that particular modification.

Within an organization, many conditions could be imposing schedule requirements on the modification, such as:

- Availability of project funds

- Availability of project team members

- Urgency to reap the benefits of the modification

- Interdependency between the network modification and other projects

The availability of project funds can drive schedule requirements. A company might currently have enough money to modify its network, but due to budget constraints it might not have access to the money after a certain date. This occurs frequently with government organizations. Such time constraints on money often mandate a certain deadline for the project team to complete the modification. Another case in which funding can affect the project schedule occurs when a company must wait until the beginning of the next budgeting cycle to receive funds to proceed with the modification. This might require a more lengthy project schedule.

Other projects and activities could also mandate a particular schedule for the network modification. For example, a company might have to move to another facility by a certain date, say August 1. This date would become a schedule requirement the modification team would need to consider when planning the installation, testing, and turnover to operational support.

Regulatory Requirements

There are many official federal, state, city and organizational regulations that companies must uphold. Some, such as safety and environmental regulations, impose definite requirements on network modifications. Often the law enforces these types of regulations strictly, making them constraints. In addition, the company itself might have policies and procedures, such as strategic plans and cabling standards, which the requirements should identify.

Network Requirements Analysis Process

As discussed before, the project team must properly analyze requirements, especially user requirements, to provide a solid and accurate basis for the design. The inclusion of the users in requirements analysis is a must, and it cannot be overstated. The project team, namely the analysts, should plan the requirements analysis process before getting started. Proper planning is needed to avoid wasting the time of the organization while the team is collecting information.

The team should utilize the following requirements analysis process:

1. Identify requirements needing revision.
2. If necessary, redefine or initiate new requirements.
3. Identify constraints.
4. Validate new requirements.

The following paragraphs describe each of these steps.

Identifying Requirements Needing Revision

In most cases, the team will need to revise only the existing requirements. For instance, the organization might need to integrate the existing network with one from a newly acquired company. In this case, the team might need to revise requirements to reflect needs of the users from the new organization. For initial network implementations, or in cases in which no requirements were originally expressed, the team should develop a complete set of requirements.

The team should review existing requirements and determine which requirements might need revision. The requirements review process should consist of reviewing current requirements documentation. The team should then identify which requirements might be invalid based on the influencing factor prompting the modification. The team can then focus on redefining these invalid requirements.

Defining Network Requirements

After identifying which existing requirements need revision, the team should define these requirements and any new requirements necessary to support the modification objectives. The project team can determine network requirements by gathering information and then assessing requirements.

Gathering information

Gathering the right information can ensure the best possible choice of requirements. Too often a project team will gather information without regard to what they will use it for. The team should base the choice of requirements on user needs, existing systems, regulations, and the environment. Thus, the team should concentrate on finding information dealing with those areas.

Analysts can use several methods to accumulate information, such as performing interviews, reviewing existing documents, conducting Joint Application Development (JAD) meetings, and surveying the facility. The remaining paragraphs of this section describe each of these methods.

Performing interviews. The team should utilize personal interviews to determine the organization's structure, departmental missions, work flow, operator profiles, and existing network infrastructures. This type of information will assist in determining user needs. Before conducting interviews, explain the purpose and methods of the information-gathering activity to management. The concurrence of management adds a degree of perceived importance to the interview; therefore, the interviewees might make more effort to respond fully to questions.

The interview questions should address applicable requirements the team is striving to define. Be sure to draft the questions in advance and distribute them to the interviewees several days before the meeting takes place. This allows the participants to at least think about the information the analyst is looking for. If possible, the project team should schedule the interviews with a complete cross section of user types, which will facilitate a complete set of opinions and needs. During the interview use two interviewers, one to ask questions and the other to take notes. This will ensure the capturing of all comments. A recording device, such as an audio tape recorder, might also prove beneficial.

Reviewing existing documents. Another source of information is existing system documentation. By reviewing system documentation, the team can identify existing systems that might affect the design of the network modification. The team should inventory existing hardware and software, and should identify existing documentation supporting the system. The team will usually need to require the network modification to interface with the existing systems.

As mentioned earlier, regulations and company policies are often a basis for requirements. Thus, the analyst should review all applicable regulations and policies when collecting information for requirements. In fact, the project team should consider regulations as constraints. For example, most facilities have regulations stating the need to meet certain safety codes. This mandate will require designers to utilize types of cabling that are fire-retardant. In addition, some organizations might have frequency-management policies restricting the operation of radio devices, such as radio-LAN components. This might cause the designer to rule out the use of some radio-based network components if the frequencies conflict.

Conducting JAD meetings. Conducting a series of JAD meetings is an excellent way to collect information for requirements. JAD, which many organizations utilize to develop software, gets the customers, eventual system users, and designers all working together to determine requirements for the network. This ensures that users will play a definite role in the creation of requirements, which results in a more accurate definition of what the system is supposed to do.

Basically, a JAD meeting consists of a facilitator and, as participants, the customer representative, a representative sample of users, and the project team. The facilitator manages the JAD meetings and should remain neutral and impartial. Therefore, if any problems occur during the meeting, the facilitator should attempt to resolve them without taking sides with anyone. The JAD participants should start the meetings off with a series of questions that probe the needs of the users and the organization, and then continue until requirements details are known. All participants should engage in the meetings; therefore, it is a good idea to have someone who can record or document the outcomes of the JAD sessions.

Performing a facility evaluation. The project team should consider performing a facility evaluation, which assesses the environment in which the network will reside. The purpose of the facility evaluation is to determine the facility's capability of supporting the network. In some cases the environment might constrain the choice of design solutions; however, in some cases designers might recommend changing the environment to facilitate the network modification. For example, the length and width of a building requires cabling to span a certain range. It probably would not be feasible to change the building's dimensions to lessen cable span lengths. Thus, the building size is a constraint. But, if the building does not have adequate power to operate the potential modification, then designers could feasibly recommend changes to the electrical system to boost the availability of power.

As part of the facility evaluation, the team should visually inspect the building, evaluate electrical capabilities, identify server room locations, and recommend cable layouts. The facility evaluation should identify any issues associated with installing network cabling, such as the presence of firewalls and other obstacles. Before embarking on a facility evaluation, the team should obtain the most up-to-date building drawings. If possible, a building custodian should escort the team through the facility. The custodian usually knows every nook and cranny of the building, and he should also have keys for access to all parts of the building.

Here are some items to accomplish during a facility evaluation:

- Verify the building drawings. Organizations commonly remodel facilities by moving walls and office partitions. Therefore, as part of the facility evaluation, it is important to verify the accuracy of building layout drawings by visually comparing the drawings to actual facility construction. This avoids designing the network modification based on false architectural information.

- Investigate ability to run cables throughout the facility. The team should check above the ceilings to determine whether there is enough room for running cabling, and should also locate and assess all vertical cabling conduits.

- Check ability to install cable outlets. The team should check the spacing and construction between walls to assess their ability to place network outlets.

- Check for the presence of asbestos. It is dangerous to install cabling within an area containing asbestos, and it is very expensive to remove the asbestos to allow safe installation.

- Evaluate the electrical system. The electrical evaluation provides information on whether the building's electrical system will support the network modification. The team should determine if there is adequate building power for the modification, and whether the building has experienced power outages. If there are problems with the electrical system, the team should recommend appropriate corrective action.

- Investigate server and communications room locations. If applicable, determine the location for the system servers. The room(s) should have adequate power, air conditioning, and space for all server components. If the chosen room(s) requires enhancement, specify what is needed.

- Identify the location of users. The team should mark the location of network users, printers, and other devices requiring a network tap. The team can annotate these locations on a copy of the building drawings. This location information might be included as topography requirements, explained earlier in this chapter.

- Assess requirements. The project team can assess requirements by reviewing all gathered information, and can then redefine or initiate new requirements. When reviewing the gathered information, focus on what is necessary and not just desired. Overspecifying wants instead of real needs will highly constrain the choice of effective solutions.

As part of the requirements assessment, the project team should prioritize each requirement and should indicate when each requirement should be met. The design team can then focus on finding solutions for the higher-priority requirements first. For example, users might need to have access to a particular database to satisfy short-term objectives, but they might not need e-mail immediately. Therefore, the project team should prioritize the implementation of the requirements accordingly.

Identifying Constraints

As part of the requirements analysis, the team should identify all constraints placed on the modification. Designers will utilize the constraints as boundaries for determining solutions. The team can define these constraints by identifying those requirements the team and even the organization cannot change.

Validating New Requirements

As mentioned earlier, requirements are extremely important because inaccurate requirements will drive the design to ineffective solutions. Thus, the project team should validate the requirements. Requirements validation attempts to answer the question, "Are we building the right product?"

One of the most effective methods to validate network requirements is to build a prototype representing some or all of the network requirements. A prototype creates a simulated visual representation of the user interface. Prototyping reduces the risk of an unsuccessful completion of a project, because it encourages greater user involvement in the development of requirements.

With a prototype, users can validate requirements by actually performing most or all of the functions being established by the modification project. A sample set of users can operate the prototype under observation, providing a check on whether the stated requirements are optimum. This gives an opportunity to restate requirements so they best match the needs of the users.

Requirements Analysis Documentation

Because the requirements set the stage for the remainder of the project, the team should carefully document the requirements. Designers will use the documentation as a basis for determining solutions, and testers will use the requirements to verify the network implementation. Therefore, the team should prepare a requirements specification, clearly stating all requirements and constraints.

Drawbacks of Not Documenting Requirements

If the project team does not properly record the requirements, the modification can easily derail. As the project continues under these conditions, the requirements of the modification become more unclear because of memory lapse and the handover of project information from person to person. Also, people who were involved in determining the requirements could leave the company or be reassigned to different positions before the modification is complete.

A design and implementation of the modification, based on foggy requirements, will certainly lead to an ineffective end product for the users. Undocumented requirements also make it very easy for an organization to change requirements in an uncoordinated manner during later stages of the project. This wastes time and causes ill feelings with most designers.

The Requirements Document

The requirements document is very important, because all the following modification activities are based on it. The team should prepare a requirements document clearly defining all network requirements. These requirements should reflect the concurrence of the entire project team, including the potential users.

To produce the requirements document, the project team should refer to various items, such as interview and JAD meeting notes, regulations, facility evaluations, analysis results, and prototypes. The team should always completely define each requirement and should show the method used to verify and validate the requirement. Also, be sure to list the requirements in terms of their priorities. Figure 4.9 identifies an outline of a requirements document.

Reviewing and Approving Requirements

Before proceeding with the design phase, the project team should review the completeness of the requirements by holding a requirements review meeting. The goal of the requirements review meeting should be to review and approve the content of the requirements specification. All project team members, including the customer representative, should attend the meeting and should come to an agreement on the requirements. The team should send a copy of the requirements specification to team members a few days before the meeting, to provide adequate review and preparation time.

```
┌─────────────────────────────────────────┐
│                                          │
│      Requirements document               │
│     ─────────────────────                │
│   I.   Introduction                      │
│        A. Executive overview             │
│                                          │
│   II.  Requirements                      │
│        A. Operator profiles              │
│        B. Topography                     │
│        C. Application                     │
│        D. Mobility needs                 │
│        E. Information flows              │
│        F. Performance                    │
│        G. Security                       │
│        H. Operational support            │
│                                          │
│   III. Constraints                       │
│        A. Cost and schedule              │
│        B. Regulatory                     │
│                                          │
│   IV.  Requirements basis                │
│        A. Prototype results              │
│        B. Interview results              │
│                                          │
└─────────────────────────────────────────┘
```

Figure 4.9 Outline of a requirements document

Requirements Review

Each project team member, especially customer representatives, should read the requirements document and assess its quality. This is very important to accomplish before baselining the requirements and then moving on to the design phase of the project.

The team should expect affirmative responses to the following questions:

- Do the requirements include all user and organizational needs?
- Are the requirements clearly stated?
- Are the requirements verifiable?
- Do the requirements state only what is really required?

If any answers to the above questions are "No," then the project team could consider baselining the acceptable requirements and proceeding with the design. This might be necessary if there are critical requirements that must meet a certain schedule. However, to avoid future risks, incomplete or vague requirements should be perfected before baselining them.

Requirements Acceptance and Approval

The customer representative of the network modification should agree on the requirements by signing an acceptance and approval letter included as part of the requirements document. The letter documents the customer organization's acceptance of the requirements. The acceptance should also indicate that both the organization and modification team agree to consider the set of requirements as a firm baseline from which to design the network.

The requirements baseline should not hinder the customer from changing requirements at a later stage in the project. However, to avoid requirements creep, procedures must be in place for reviewing the impact of recommended changes on the project budget and schedule. Chapter 8 covers a change control procedure as part of the configuration management process.

With accurate and approved requirements in hand, the project team is ready to move into the design phase of the project.

Network Design

Organizations commonly "design" the network by haphazardly selecting and purchasing components. This often leads to a network full of operational problems, such as excessive delay, non-interoperability, and missing functionality. A structured and well-planned design yields superior results. This chapter explains a top-down design methodology that steps the design team from the selection of an initial solution to the detailed configuration of the network.

Network Design Process

As shown in Figure 5.1, the next step after determining requirements is to specify how the network will satisfy these requirements. This process is network design. The overall goal of network design is to identify and describe how the network will satisfy requirements at the least cost. Based on requirements, the design identifies technologies, standards, components, and configurations that comprise the network.

As identified in Chapter 3 and shown in Figure 5.1, the project team should design the network in two stages—preliminary design and detailed design. The preliminary design identifies a set of multiple solutions, from which the design team selects the best one in terms of cost and the ability to satisfy requirements. Preliminary design allows the project team to ease into a solution to requirements by selecting and evaluating potential technologies and standards capable of satisfying requirements. This helps the project team avoid wasting a great deal of time and money on solutions that might not be the most effective. Designers might ask "How much of the de-

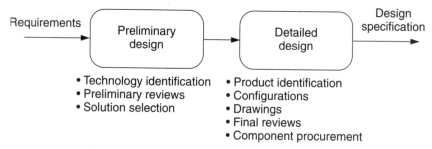

Figure 5.1   Concept of network design

sign do you complete during the preliminary design?" Figure 5.2 helps answer this question. Within the preliminary design phase, the team should determine enough detail to cost and then decide on a solution.

As part of the preliminary design phase, reviews will catch defects in the design before these defects become problems. It is much easier and less expensive to correct these defects as early as possible during the design. Thus, preliminary design can help the project team maintain better control of the modification, producing a higher quality network.

The detailed design phase is a continuation of the preliminary design, completing the overall network layout. The project team should begin the detailed design after everyone, including the customer organization, commits to a particular solution. The detailed design produces the remaining elements needed to facilitate the implementation, such as network configurations and final documentation. For example, the preliminary design might identify the type of network operating system, and the detailed design would explain disk space allocations, printer setups, directory structures, and similar decisions. At the conclusion of a final design review, the team should procure applicable network components.

Many designers will utilize past experience and publications to determine the design. Previous experience and lessons learned in satisfying particular requirements have tremendous benefits. Experience in a particular technology or product lessens the time necessary to find a solution, because the design team will not need to do as much guesswork and prototyping. Designers can find guidance from publications, because many include test reports on network technologies, and books cover implementation techniques.

The project team should design the network using a structured process, providing the basis for a smooth, orderly and efficient design. Not doing so can lead to the development of a network that does not effectively meet requirements and for which it is difficult to attain a comfortable degree of operational support. An unstructured and unplanned network design will certainly lead to operational problems and unhappy users.

The project team should design the network by completing the following major steps:

1. Determine preliminary design specifications.
2. Develop a prototype, if necessary.
3. Document preliminary design specifications.
4. Perform a preliminary design review.
5. Determine network configurations.
6. Document final design specifications.
7. Perform a final design review.
8. Procure components.

The following sections describe each of the steps above.

Determination of Preliminary Design Specifications

Specifications, which describe how the network will satisfy requirements, are at the heart of the overall design. For example, a design specification might state that the network should use Category 5 twisted pair cabling as the medium, and ethernet as the medium access method to facilitate the requirements dealing with the flow of information between network devices. Chapters 6 and 7 will explain the many different types of design specifications.

The process of determining design specifications is as follows:

1. Recognize which specifications to change.
2. Select technologies and standards.
3. Identify components and products.

The succeeding sections will describe each step of determining specifications.

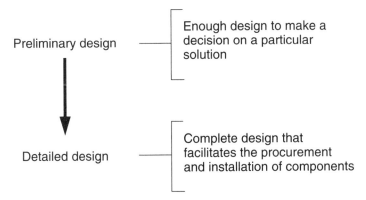

Figure 5.2 Comparison of preliminary and detailed design

Recognizing Specifications to Change

Before defining specifications, the designers must first recognize which ones to change. Designers can identify a rough cut of elements requiring change by first analyzing the factor(s) influencing change. The factors influencing the network modification can help designers choose which specifications need attention. This process provides a list of specifications to define during the remaining steps of the design phase.

Figure 5.3 illustrates a set of design specification types that comprise most networks. Therefore, designers will need to focus on these specifications when identifying which ones to change. The high-level specifications tend to directly satisfy requirements, whereas low-level specifications usually support other design specifications in addition to requirements.

In some cases, conditions might affect all network specifications. For example, a non-existent network would result in most design specifications needing fulfilled because the designers would need to specify every element of the network. In contrast, the designers might only need to find a solution for the signal distribution if the influencing factor for change was to move an existing network from one facility to another. Therefore, not all factors influencing a network modification require every network element to change.

The following paragraphs explain how each factor influencing network change can affect which design specifications to alter.

Changes in user needs

Changes in user needs directly affect the selection of network applications and hardware platforms, because most user needs are satisfied by applica-

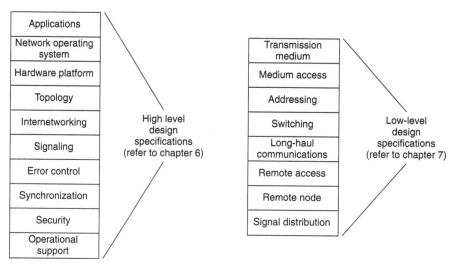

Figure 5.3 Specifications to consider when designing a network modification

tions residing on various platforms. However, changes in user needs can indirectly affect any of the specifications. For instance, users might require the ability to send electronic mail to another company's mail system. In this case, designers would probably need to identify changes in specifications such as applications, communications, internetworking, and security. As another example, users might need to utilize an application that does not run on an existing workstation. Then designers would identify a change in the hardware platform specification.

Here are some additional examples of how requirements changes can affect the identification of which specifications to alter:

- Significant changes in user profile requirements might prompt a change in the selection of applications.

- A new requirement to support the interface to a different system might create the need to change internetworking specifications, such as the addition of a gateway.

- The need for a new application or service might indicate the change of data rate and medium to support more bandwidth.

- A new requirement for mobility or portability could necessitate a change in medium to a wireless form.

- A change in information flow requirements might create a need to alter the internetworking (segmentation) specification.

- The requirement for shorter response times might give reason to tune the network operating system and client workstations.

- A new requirement for tighter network security could lead to changing security specifications, such as file backup or encryption.

Special services

Special services, such as desktop conferencing, telecommuting, and document management, often require an increase in network performance. To adapt the network to support special services, designers will at least need to recommend changes to the network's applications. For example, if the requirements call for the incorporation of desktop conferencing, then the designers will need to specify which desktop conferencing method and products would best satisfy requirements. Designers should also recommend changing any specification that supports an improvement in the network, to maintain performance requirements of the special service. For instance, the incorporation of desktop video might require designers to increase the performance of the network to support the data rate and synchronization requirements of video across the network.

Technological changes

Technology changes, such as the migration from mainframe to client-server or replacement of T1 circuits with frame relay service, can affect most types of specifications. Modifications of these types will primarily affect those specifications the technology change deals with. As an example, changing from T1 to frame relay requires changing specifications related to T1 and frame relay, such as medium and medium access. But this particular change will have little if any affect on the network operating system and applications.

Organizational resizing

Organizational resizing usually changes the number of network elements, such as application and network operating system licenses, and network connections. In some cases, though, an organization might grow to a size that warrants changes to the network operating system, communications, and internetworking functionality. For example, the network might grow to a larger size, requiring the interconnection of different workgroups or dissimilar networks.

Organizational moves

Barring any other change, an organizational move will only warrant changes to the signal distribution. Because the new facility will probably have a different structure, it might require a network having media of different layout. It is common, though, for organizations to include other network modifications in the move to another facility. Companies move locations when they require a larger or smaller facility to house their employees. This basis for a move normally warrants an expansion or contraction in the size of the network.

Operational problems

Operational problems vary and can motivate the designer to change a few or all of the specifications. For example, if users experience a great deal of delay when using applications from a particular server, the designer should recommend changing the network elements affecting performance, such as the network operating system, hardware platforms, medium, and signal distribution. If the operational problem is that the network is difficult to administer, the designer could recommend changes to the network operating system. If users are unable to connect to a distant host computer, then the designers should consider changes to specifications such as communications and addressing. Some networks might be based on obsolete technologies and products, making them very difficult to maintain and modify. In this case, the designers could consider scrapping most of the existing network definition and starting over.

Limited network coverage

An organization might have initiated the implementation of a network a year or so ago, which is not complete. Assuming the network requirements are still valid, changes to the network based on limited network coverage usually involve increasing the span of the network. As with organizational resizing, this can change the number of network components, such as servers and client workstations. Designers might also need to redefine other specifications, such as topology, signal distribution, internetworking, medium, security and addressing. This all happens because the expanded network could encompass additional workgroups, requiring segmentation from the overall network or residing in different facilities.

Non-existent network

Of course if the organization has no existing network, then designers will have to define all design specifications. Starting from scratch is often easier than modifying an existing network, because no specifications are present to constrain the choice of solutions. This provides an opportunity for doing it right the first time.

Funding reduction

If a company is striving to reduce expenses, designers could redefine the design specifications to make users more productive and lessen overall operational support costs of the network. As explained before, the company will save money in labor expenses if users are more productive. For this case, any of the specifications might be affected.

Selecting technologies and standards

With an idea of the specifications requiring changes, the design team should proceed with selecting technologies and standards that comprise one or more solutions. In general, technologies describe systematic methods and science involved in accomplishing specific objectives. Network technologies describe the protocols and physics necessary to transport information from one point to another. Standards are well-defined and acceptable descriptions of technologies. The selection of some standards might encompass more than one network specification. For example, choosing the IEEE 802.3 standard defines both medium access and error control. The point here is that the designer might not be able to separate some of these specifications from standards. Chapters 6 and 7 describe and give suggestions on the many technologies and standards that apply to networks.

Top-down specification approach

The goal of defining design specifications is to identify technologies and standards that, taken collectively, will provide the most effective solution(s) for stated requirements. As a result, the design team should utilize a top-down approach, as illustrated in Figure 5.4, to determine the order of assigning values to design specifications. The top-down approach first defines the high-level specifications that directly satisfy network requirements. This ensures the proper beginning of an overall solution that best satisfies the requirements. The next step is to finish the design by addressing the lower-level specifications. In some cases, though, designers might not be able to complete the definition of some higher-level specifications without first describing some of the lower-level ones.

For instance, the designers should first define applications because they directly satisfy the users' requirements. Next, the designers should choose the best platform for these applications, which would consist of the network operating system and hardware/software platforms for user workstations and servers. Designers would then continue with specifying network elements that support the network operating system and platforms, such as medium access, medium, and bridges.

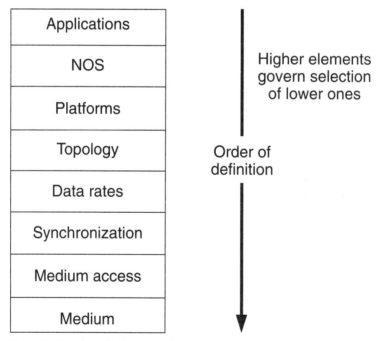

Figure 5.4 Top-down design approach

Requirements satisfaction matrix

The requirements satisfaction matrix, as shown in Figure 5.5, can aid designers during the selection of technologies and standards. The matrix identifies which requirements certain technologies (and standards) satisfy. It consists of one axis identifying the network requirements and the other axis specifying the design specification types. The elements of the matrix contain the values that satisfy the requirements. The matrix also provides a record of each solution, making it easier to review to ensure that the design team completely fulfills all requirements.

The process of selecting design specifications not only produces a solution, but also helps validate requirements. It cannot be said enough that catching inadequate requirements early on in the project is much less expensive and time consuming than correcting the resulting problems during later stages. If designers have too many choices of specification values, then requirements might be inadequately defined or even absent. As an example, ethernet and token ring employ different types of synchronization, and information flow requirements govern the necessary type of synchronization. Most data transfers can get by with asynchronous (e.g., ethernet), but video transfers typically require more synchronization (as provided by token ring). Thus, to select the proper medium access method in this case, the designer should question whether requirements are adequate. This could flag a missing requirement, and the project team would then refine the requirements before proceeding.

The need for standards

It is important to maximize the use of standards to ensure widespread acceptance of the solution and compliance among network components. The use of standards also decreases the learning curve required to understand specific technologies, because the standards forming group will have already invested the time to smooth out any wrinkles in the implementation of the applicable technology.

There are two classes of standards: official and nonofficial. Official standards are ones approved, and usually developed by, official standards organizations. Government or industry consortiums normally sponsor these groups. Nonofficial standards, often called *de facto standards*, are common practices that have not been produced or accepted by an official standards organization. These standards are the result of widespread usage. Often, nonofficial standards having high proliferation eventually pass through standards organizations and become official standards. Standards organizations work to ensure compatible transmissions between communications equipment at both the international and domestic levels. Figure 5.6 shows the relationships among various standards organizations.

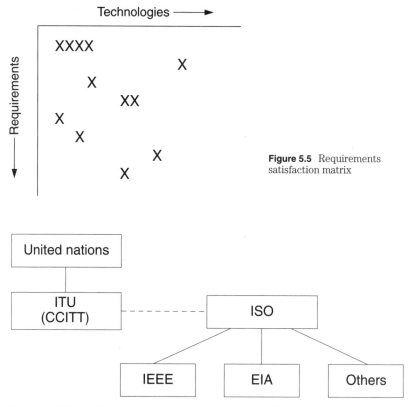

Figure 5.5 Requirements satisfaction matrix

Figure 5.6 Relationships among various standards organizations

Domestic U.S. standards organizations

Domestic U.S. standards organizations are active in standardizing American innovations. However, these domestic groups often invite international participation to produce standards that the entire world will eventually accept.

Electronics Industry Association

The Electronics Industry Association (EIA) is a trade organization which represents a vast number of United States electronics firms. This association has representatives in hundreds of commercial and governmental organizations. Since being founded in 1924, EIA has produced hundreds of standards and publications. Many manufacturers use recommendations by EIA, such as the RS 232 physical interface standard.

Institute of Electrical and Electronic Engineers

The Institute of Electrical and Electronic Engineers (IEEE), formed in 1884, actively participates in the development of standards for data transmission systems. The overall goal of IEEE is to promote electrotechnology by sponsoring numerous conferences, publications, and standards. Many societies fall under the umbrella of IEEE, including the Computer and Communications Societies. IEEE has made significant progress in the establishment of standards for local area networks, namely the IEEE 802 series of standards.

National Institute of Standards and Technology

The National Institute of Standards and Technology (NIST) is a government agency established by Congress "to assist industry in the development of technology needed to improve product quality, to modernize manufacturing processes, to ensure product reliability, and to facilitate rapid commercialization of products based on new scientific discoveries." NIST is part of the U.S. Department of Commerce's Technology Administration. The primary mission of NIST is to promote U.S. economic growth by working with industry to develop and apply technology, measurements, and standards.

American National Standards Institute

The American National Standards Institute (ANSI), founded in 1918, is the primary standards-forming body in the United States. ANSI is a nonprofit organization which coordinates U.S. voluntary standards and accredits organizations that develop standards, such as EIA and IEEE. ANSI consists of approximately 1,300 national and international companies, 30 government agencies, 20 institutional members, and 250 professional, technical, trade, labor and consumer organizations.

International standards organizations

International standards organizations are responsible for creating new standards and integrating standards from many countries. These associations represent the many federal governments, private businesses, and user communities around the world, thus providing the highest degree of compatibility for a world of diverse technologies.

International Telecommunications Union

The International Telecommunications Union (ITU) is an agency of the United Nations, and its function is to provide the coordination for the development of international standards. ITU consists of two main groups. One deals with international radio broadcasting, while the other is concerned with telephone and data communication systems. The latter is the International Telegraph and Telephone Consultative Committee, CCITT (which is actually an acronym for the French words: Comite Consultatif Internationale de Telegraphique et Telephonique).

The CCITT, established in 1865, is dedicated to establishing effective and compatible telecommunications among members of the United Nations. CCITT develops the widely used V-series and X-series standards and protocols. Two examples are V.24 (also known as EIA RS232), which identifies the physical (electrical and mechanical) connection between data terminal equipment (DTE) and data circuit-terminating equipment (DCE), and X.25, which specifies the necessary protocols for connecting a computer to a packet-switching network.

The membership of CCITT is broken into several classes. Class A members are the national telecommunication administrations of the member countries, such as the Federal Communications Commission (FCC) of the United States and the Post, Telegraph, and Telephone (PTT) administration in Europe. Class B members are recognized private administrations (e.g., AT&T), Class C members are scientific and industrial organizations, and Class D members are other international organizations. Finally, Class E members are organizations whose primary mission is in another field but which have interest in CCITT's work. When standards are up for approval, only Class A members may vote.

International Organization for Standardization

International Organization for Standardization (ISO) is a worldwide non-treaty federation of national standards bodies. ISO was founded in 1947 and is active in the development of international standards, such as the Open System Interconnection (OSI) network architecture. Constituents of ISO include national standards organizations of member countries. For example, ANSI is the United States' representative to ISO, and ISO is a Class D member of CCITT. Therefore, domestic manufacturers and user committees can voice their opinions in the development of international standards.

Technology and standards evaluation

The design team should strive to identify and evaluate all candidate technologies and standards. The evaluation process screens technologies and standards by utilizing a series of tests, which act as filters. The objective of the evaluation process is to identify technologies and standards that will satisfy requirements with a high degree of confidence.

The design team should evaluate technologies and standards by performing the following tasks:

1. Identify candidate technologies and standards that fulfill overall functional and performance attributes of the requirements.
2. Determine if the candidate technologies conform to cost constraints.

3. Determine whether the candidate technologies meet acceptable levels of maturity.

The next several paragraphs describe each of these tasks.

Designers should first identify technologies and standards that appear to match the functionality of the applicable design specification. For instance, if the particular designers or working group is focused on finding solutions for the medium access specification, they should identify all medium access protocols and standards. In this case, they could identify candidates such as IEEE 802.3 (ethernet), IEEE 802.5 (token ring), FDDI, and Fast Ethernet.

The next step would be to analyze the cost of implementing each candidate technology. For example, the designers could identify the average cost of implementing the medium access method, as well as other specifications. Designers could then sum all individual costs and compare them to the cost constraints identified at the beginning of the project. If the overall cost is too high, the team should then utilize lower cost technologies if possible.

An important step in evaluating each standard and technology is to determine its level of maturity. The maturity of a technology is based on its degree of standardization and proliferation. In terms of maturity alone, more mature technologies are superior to technologies having a lower level of maturity. A technology might appear to be superior in terms of functionality, performance and cost, but it might be based on an emerging technology that has not been fully standardized, resulting in low maturity. (The team should avoid choosing solutions based on technologies having low levels of maturity, because low maturity normally results in higher risk maintenance and lower longevity.)

As with performance and cost, maturity is something the team can measure. The following provides a level of maturity measurement for technologies:

- Low maturity
  ~No standard and low product proliferation
  ~De facto standard and low product proliferation
  ~Emerging official standard and low product proliferation
  ~Stable official standard, but reaching obsolescence; low or high product proliferation, with vendors and end users switching to other technologies.

- Moderate maturity
  ~No standard and high product proliferation
  ~Emerging official standard and high product proliferation

- High maturity
  ~Stable official standard and high product proliferation
  ~De facto standard and high product proliferation

Ideally, the design team should select technologies based on the highest level of maturity. Typically, high maturity is based on very stable (but not obsolescent) standards and high degrees of product proliferation. This will lead to solutions that will last for longer periods of time and be easier to maintain.

Research working groups

The design team might benefit from forming research working groups that will perform the identification and evaluation process. The design team should start by identifying all possibilities. Then, through a rigorous evaluation process, they should pare the list down to a set of alternatives they have confidence in. Figure 5.7 illustrates an organizational structure for research working groups. Typically, existing design team members will comprise the research working groups. However, the design team might consider hiring consultants having specific expertise in applicable areas.

A well-organized set of working groups decreases the amount of design time. It is often best to establish multiple working groups, with each one focusing on specific design specification. For instance, one group could focus on user applications, another group might research network operating systems, and a third group might be responsible for evaluating technologies dealing with medium access and cabling techniques.

The overall objective of the research working groups is to investigate technologies and standards by identifying, comparing, analyzing, and recommending a number of technologies that support given design specification types. The working groups should consider all technologies and standards, both cur-

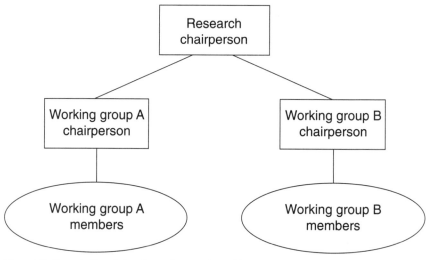

Figure 5.7 Organizational structure of research working groups

rent and emerging, which might satisfy requirements. Together as a forum, working groups should present, discuss, and screen applicable technologies and standards that have the potential for satisfying network requirements. When performing the research, working groups should utilize all possible sources of information, such as conference proceedings, test reports, networking magazines, product announcements, and past experiences.

The forum, or collection of working groups, should consist of a chairperson who manages the forum by establishing and leading forum meetings. Each of the working groups should consist of a leader and participants familiar with the applicable design specifications. Each working group can research their respective technologies independently from other working groups; however, the entire forum should meet periodically to ensure a well-integrated research effort. This is necessary because some specifications are dependent on each other.

In general, the working groups should operate as follows:

1. Participants should suggest potential technologies and standards by preparing short, one-paragraph summaries explaining each technology's function and main benefits.

2. The working group should meet to discuss all suggested technologies.

3. If the entire group feels the technology is viable, then the participants should develop a point paper or white paper that fully explains the technology's function, performance, costs, benefits, and risks.

4. As shown in Figure 5.8, the working group should develop and maintain a matrix that compares various technologies and standards. This will help consolidate the characteristics of each solution, making it easier to choose the best one.

Component and product identification

Based on the network requirements and the chosen technologies and standards, the design team should identify the type of components and products necessary to support the modification. The design team should attempt to utilize off-the-shelf products whenever possible, to satisfy the need for components. This is usually the least-cost method. If the team cannot find a product that supports the design specification, then the team will need to either develop the component or change the requirement or design specification to a value that makes use of existing products.

The design team should review test reports published by vendor-independent sources to ensure proper selection of the product. Of course, price should be a factor in determining which products to choose; however, be sure to take into account the fact that some products might cost more because they have more features. Also, consider the maturity level of the product before

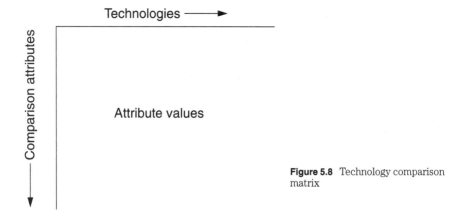

Figure 5.8 Technology comparison matrix

making a choice. As an example, avoid selecting emerging products and new major releases, unless the product can be proven through prototyping or contact with legitimate references. The team should also obtain product user satisfaction information before making a decision on which products to utilize.

Here are some additional guidelines for selecting products:

- Obtain bids from several sources before making a decision.
- Select vendors having a reputation for reliable products and support.
- Guarantee that the product meets all requirements.
- Use products that are flexible.
- Limit the number of vendors to two for each type of product.

The number one measure of a product vendor is customer satisfaction. Designers can obtain this type of information by contacting samples of the vendor's customer base. Some vendors will provide references of people who have utilized their products. Be sure the vendor has the ability to support the product after purchase. There should be easy access to technical support staff who can assist during installation and operation of the product. A sizable market share usually indicates user satisfaction of the product. In addition, a small company size should not, by itself, deter the selection of products from that company. Many effective products are produced by small companies which can operate efficiently with very little overhead. For more information about vendors who produce various types of network products, refer to the Appendix B, List of network component vendors.

Prototyping

A prototype is a flexible hardware or software model that represents the network. The process of prototyping can shorten the modification project by ensuring the proper selection of design alternatives. Figure 5.9 illustrates these concepts.

In some cases, especially if solutions are obvious, it might not be necessary to prototype. For instance, the addition of users or minor upgrades to applications usually does not necessitate prototyping. In general, it is beneficial to prototype if requirements and potential solutions are unclear, network downtime will cause serious consequences, the modification will affect a sizable number of users, or components supporting the solution are relatively expensive.

Types of Prototyping

There are two main types of prototyping: physical prototyping and simulation. Through physical prototyping, designers can build a physical (hardware and software) working model of a proposed network solution. The main attributes of physical prototyping are that it yields very accurate (real) results, is relatively inexpensive for a one-time design effort, takes time to reconfigure, and requires access to network components.

Simulation allows designers to fabricate a model of the modification to try out different solutions by easily reconfiguring the model and testing its resulting performance. A simulation model consists of a software program written in a simulation language. A designer can run the simulations and check results quickly, greatly compressing time by representing days of network activity in minutes of simulation run time. The main attributes of design simulation are that it reduces time needed to redesign a network (assuming the simulation model exists), does not require much geographical space, is relatively expensive for one-time design effort, and might not yield accurate results.

There are simulation tools on the market that can assist designers in developing a simulation model. Most simulation tools represent the network using a combination of processing elements, transfer devices, and storage devices. Processing elements identify entities that run programs (being simulated), such as central processors and relay nodes. Transfer devices model connections between various processing and storage devices. A stor-

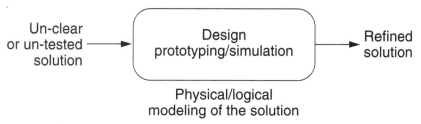

Figure 5.9 Physical prototyping and simulation

age device allows the simulated storage of data. Software modules can simulate actual programs that might reside within processing elements, and can also simulate the interaction between devices. These three major building blocks, in addition to software modules, can comprise the model of a proposed network.

As part of the simulation model, designers must estimate utilization levels of users. The results of a simulation highly depend on these predicted levels. Therefore, the accuracy of simulation depends on how close designers are in predicting utilization levels. The problem is that it can be difficult or impossible to accurately predict utilization. Thus, simulation can easily yield inaccurate results, especially performance.

Physical prototyping versus simulation

If the design team decides to utilize physical prototyping or simulation as a technique to determine design specifications, then the team must decide which method to use. The choice depends on several factors. The design team should review the attributes mentioned previously, and should then consider the following:

- Use a *physical prototype* if there must be a high degree of assurance that the design solution is optimum or it is unlikely requirements will change throughout the life of the network.

- Use *simulation* if it is very likely that requirements will change throughout the life of the network, the initial solution does not need to be highly accurate, designers need to find effective solutions quickly, or physical networking components are not readily available.

Sometimes it might be beneficial to use both a physical prototype and simulation. For example, an organization might maintain simulation models for the network. Designers could determine the initial solutions through use of simulation, then build a physical prototype to be sure the solution works as expected before transitioning the modification to the production phase. In this case, simulation quickly points the designers in the right direction by showing them where to start with the physical prototype. Designers can then tweak the physical prototype to demonstrate that the solution works.

Process of Prototyping

The approach to prototyping is typically a trial-and-error experimental process. Designers can start with their best choices of technologies and products, then see if the configuration provides the functionality, interoperability and performance necessary to support requirements. If the prototyped solution does not perform as expected, then designers can efficiently try other approaches by easily reconfiguring the prototype. Prototyping should continue until the design team clearly identifies and understands the most effective solution.

The team can use their best guesses and build a small prototype, allowing testers to evaluate performance. Selected users can operate the network in a nonproduction mode. The designers should continue modifying the prototype until it meets network requirements. Once the prototype meets requirements, then the team can document the elements of the prototype and use the results as a basis for the design. For example, an organization might have requirements stating the need for interoperability among dissimilar electronic mail products. The design team might not be aware of a reliable design that will provide full interoperability among the mail products. Therefore, the project team could consider identifying a design solution by first developing a prototype, modifying the prototype until it provides the best solution, then using the final prototype configuration to aid in developing the design specifications.

It might not be practical to prototype the entire solution, mainly because designers might already feel confident about certain parts of the design. Pretesting well-understood products and technologies would be a waste of time, unless these components are part of another solution that must be tested. The design team should concentrate on prototyping the least-understood parts of the solution. For example, the design team might feel sure the selected electronic mail system will support the delivery of binary attachments within the corporate network. But it might not be clearly understood how and if the selected internetworking solution will provide similar support to remote networks. In this case, the design team might wish to pretest the ability to send binary electronic mail attachments between local and remote network users.

When pretesting design solutions, ensure full compliance with network requirements. Through prototyping, designers will often discover that initial solutions do not work at all. For example, an attempt to login to a remote application might result in an error message stating "Cannot connect to distant host." In this situation, the designer would reconfigure components until a successful connection is made. After establishing a connection to the application, though, it is important to continue testing to ensure that the chosen design specification truly meets requirements by testing application functionality.

Designers should avoid prototyping too much of the network initially. It is best to break the network into individual parts and then to prototype each part separately. This allows the team to focus on the individual parts. After optimizing the selection of technologies and products for each part, designers can integrate the parts together. It is important to integrate the parts together one by one. This approach avoids having too many interdependencies that affect the determination of the overall solution. For instance, the design team might be unsure of which network operating system and electronic mail software best meets requirements. In this case, designers might accomplish the prototyping in two parts: network operating system and electronic mail software. The designers could prototype the first part by determining which network operating system best supports specified applications. The design team could then prototype the electronic mail part by experimenting with various electronic mail software in search of the package that best supports requirements. Designers could then integrate these two parts together to demonstrate that the network operating system and electronic mail software will effectively meet requirements together.

Prototyping Results

Designers should utilize the results of the prototyping effort to represent design specifications. Therefore, the team should adequately document the details of the prototype. The designers should document not only the technologies and products providing the best solution, but also which did not work well. This saves a great deal of effort the next time the organization wants to modify the network with similar requirements. Future designers can avoid using certain components if documentation shows poor performance for those components.

Documenting the Preliminary Design

After reaching conclusions on a set of solutions that satisfy requirements, the design team should document all design specifications for each solution to facilitate a preliminary design review. The team should produce a preliminary design document containing a description of the modification, an overall logical view of the design solution(s) identifying technologies and standards, a recommended solution and alternatives, and a materials list.

The modification description should explain the purpose and scope of the modification. In many cases, the team can do this by using a highly condensed version of the requirements. To identify the technologies and standards making up the solution, it is preferable to employ graphics to easily review the design. Be sure to clearly identify the recommended solution selected by the design team. The team should also describe the alternatives in case later reviews reject the recommended solution. Also, it is always good to document the less-desirable solutions because they might be optimum for future modifications. The materials list identifies all components, such as hardware, software and peripheral items, needed to implement the design. For each component, the materials list should identify nomenclature, model number, part number, manufacturer, source, price, and quantity. The design team will later use the materials list to purchase components.

At the beginning of the project, the project team will have developed an estimated budget based on requirements and design predictions. The preliminary design document should include enough detail for the project team to update costs and reflect a more accurate budget. This updated budget is still preliminary. The design team will not be able to produce a final budget until after the detailed design phase, when the remaining details are known. In addition, the project team should update schedule and resource allocations based on the preliminary design, if necessary.

Reviewing the Preliminary Design

After identifying and documenting design specifications, the project team should review the preliminary design to assess its technical qualities and coordinate any management or customer concerns. The benefit of this review is that it ensures that there are no roadblocks or dead ends before the team presses on with design details and component procurements. Therefore, the team should facilitate both a technical and customer review.

Technical Review

The technical review makes certain that the integration of all specifications contributes effectively to the satisfaction of requirements. The main concern here is to spot missing and inadequate specifications, as well as to mediate conflicts dealing with the choice of technologies and standards. It is paramount that the entire team concur with the design solution(s), and that all existing operational support organizations have knowledge of the eventual network. For the technical review, the design team should have enough documentation to enable the team and other outside participants to understand what the design entails. Each of the reviewing participants should have access to the design materials for an adequate period of time; then they should meet to discuss the technical quality of the design.

It is important to complete a thorough review at this point, because defects are much less expensive to correct early in the design. The technical design review participants should:

1. Review all design documentation.
2. Identify defects in the design.
3. Describe potential technical problems.
4. Recommend prototyping or simulating of unclear design specifications.

The team should implement lessons learned from other projects to spot potential problems in the ability of the specifications to meet requirements. As described earlier in this chapter, designers can also use prototyping and simulation to assist in verifying design specifications.

With technical projects, the design team could easily bury themselves in the details, making it difficult to see defects and problems within the design. Therefore, it is beneficial to have some external assistance to help review the design. This assistance could be in the form of other designers currently working other projects, or an independent consultant who has experience with the applicable technologies and products.

Customer Review

The project manager should make sure that all customer representatives and appropriate management people review the preliminary design to review funding, schedules, and future support. Based on a revised cost and schedule due to the creation of design specifications, this review verifies that there is still customer and upper-management commitment and support for continuing with the project. The team should explain the reasoning behind the chosen solution and alternatives. However, most customers will not understand highly technical networking concepts, so keep the technical jargon to a minimum. The customer review is also a good place to discuss any changes needed to the requirements to make it possible for the solution to work. Be sure to have the customer's approval for changes in requirements before proceeding on with the detailed design.

Determining Network Configurations

At the conclusion of the preliminary design review, the team must proceed with defining remaining design details. As mentioned earlier in this chapter, this begins the detailed design phase. At this point, the design includes the identification of technologies, standards, and most products. The next step is to determine configurations of these network elements, which describe component settings and interconnections between the components. Designers can identify network configurations by producing a cabling diagram, schematic, communications cabinet drawing, and software/hardware configuration plan. The following paragraphs define each of these documents.

Cabling diagram

This identifies where the team should install the hubs, repeaters, bridges, routers, network cables, connectors, and wall plates. It is convenient to utilize building facility drawings as a basis for the cabling drawing; however, the facility drawings do not always reflect recent remodeling efforts. Therefore, the project team should verify the accuracy of facility drawings by visually comparing the drawings to actual facility construction.

Network schematic

This illustrates how the components will be electrically connected. The team should utilize standard conventions and symbols when producing the schematic. Installers will use the schematic as a basis to install the modification, and support staff will use the schematic to maintain the network.

Communication cabinet drawings

These illustrate the placement of network components that require mounting within communications cabinets. These drawings should illustrate a floor plan of the communications room and should show where the team should install cabinets. The drawings should also show the precise location of equipment within the communication cabinets.

Software/hardware configuration plan

This describes the configuration of active components, such as directories, printer queues, hardware platforms, and network interface cards. For example, a hardware platform configuration plan would identify assignments of interrupts and base addresses, specify the amount of RAM and hard drive space, and identify the type of operating system.

Documenting the Final Design

The final design document fully defines all design specifications for the chosen solution, and includes references to other design documentation. Be sure to include a description and basis for each specification. The description should identify necessary technologies, standards, and products necessary for satisfying specific requirements. The basis should explain why each specification is needed and should give assurance that its chosen elements will support the overall solution. Figure 5.10 illustrates the format of a final design document.

Performing a Final Design Review

Before procuring most components or installing the network modification, the project team needs to conduct a detailed design review for the customer organization. All project team members, customer representatives, and appropriate management people should review the final detailed design. As with the preliminary design review, the project team should make certain that the customer representative is aware of all costs and schedules, that all engineers concur with the design, and that all operational support organizations know about and understand the eventual network modification. In ad-

---

Final design document

I. Introduction
   A. Executive overview
   B. Requirements overview

II. Design solution
   A. Alternatives
   B. Recommended solution
   C. Verification methods

III. Design issues

IV. Attachments
   A. Cabling diagrams
   B. Schematics
   C. Configuration

Figure 5.10 Final design document

dition, the review should guarantee that all documentation is complete and that plans are ready for procuring and installing the components. It is important to be certain the detailed design is acceptable, because the organization will base the procurement of components on it. If the design is not correct, the organization might waste a great deal of money.

After the final design review, the design team should incorporate appropriate changes to the design and should update all design documentation, budgets, and schedules. The project team should then treat the design as a baseline for the purchase, installation, and support of network components. As with requirements, though, the team could alter the design later in the project if they follow proper change control procedures, as described in Chapter 8.

Procuring Components

After performing a satisfactory detailed design review, the project team can procure the necessary components. The goal of component procurement is to purchase the lowest-priced products while meeting all design and support requirements. This involves locating network component distributors or resellers. The project team must find where and how to purchase each component on the design's materials list.

When to Procure Components

The project team should avoid purchasing products until after the final design review, to avoid the acquisition of inappropriate products. For instance, the project team might purchase network interface cards based on a preliminary design specification that identifies the type of medium access method, such as ethernet. But after the design team completes the definition of network interface card attributes during the detailed design phase, the purchased card might not satisfy all the remaining attributes, such as SNMP network management support. The card originally purchased might not support SNMP because the purchasers would not have known it would be a requirement. Thus, the team would have to deal with not having the necessary SNMP support or else buy another card. Either way, problems exist.

However, sometimes the project team must purchase components before completing the design. This occurs because some components might require long order lead time, or the organization might have to spend money by a certain date. If the team must order components early, then the organization must understand that these components might limit the satisfaction of requirements and could increase the cost of the project.

Warranties and Maintenance Agreements

When procuring components, the team needs to understand warranties and maintenance agreements included with the product. Most vendors include excellent warranties in the price of the product, and many vendors offer maintenance agreements at an additional charge. Knowledge of warranties and maintenance agreements for each product will enable the team to properly plan the maintenance support and operational budget for the network modification.

Here are some questions to ask about warranties and maintenance agreements:

- How long is the product covered?
- What are the limitations of the coverage?
- How should the product be returned if it becomes defective?
- Will the vendor provide on- or off-site maintenance?

Be sure to look for answers that best fit your requirements, organizational policies, and budget.

Delivery and Warehousing

Before actually ordering the components, the project team must identify where the components will be stored after delivery. This might be trivial for small network modifications, but in the case of large modifications it becomes critical. Imagine ordering 250 ethernet boards, 50 PCs, 8 hubs, and other miscellaneous items. Where would you store the components after they arrive?

Specifically, the project team should identify:

- The location to which the components should be delivered.
- Where the components should be stored while waiting to be installed.
- How the components will be moved from the delivery point to the storage area.
- How the components will be moved from the storage area to the point of installation.

6

High-Level Design Specifications

The previous chapter on network design described a top-down approach for determining design specifications. This included the need to first define high-level, then lower-level specifications. As stated before, the reason for assigning values to high-level specifications first is that they typically satisfy requirements directly. This chapter describes and offers tips on selecting high-level design specifications. The specification types are presented in an order that designers should address for most modifications; however, a different sequence might be more appropriate for other network changes.

Applications

An application is a software program that accomplishes a useful task. Applications provide the functionality necessary to directly satisfy network requirements, particularly user requirements. There are many types of applications, ranging from simple utilities to full-blown office automation and specialized functions. The following briefly describes various categories of applications:

- **Office Software** Generally consists of word processing, database, spreadsheet, graphics, and electronic mail programs.

- **Scientific applications** Analyzes real-world events by simulating them with mathematics.

- **Vertical market applications** Provides customized data entry, query, and report functions for various industries, such as insurance and banking.

- **Project management software** Provides the ability to efficiently track a project and analyze the impact of changes.

- **CAD (Computer Aided Design) software** Uses vector graphics to create complex drawings.

- **Desktop publishing software** Makes it possible to effectively merge text and graphics and maintain precise control of the layout of each page of a document.

- **Contact managers** Make it easy to keep track of clients and sales activities.

- **Infoware** Provides online encyclopedias, magazines, and other references.

- **Mathematical programs** Allows the creation and execution of complex mathematical equations.

- **Multimedia software** Combines graphics, sound, and video for use in education and specialized applications.

In most cases, the choice of applications is the first specification to consider, mainly because they are closest to directly satisfying requirements. In addition, the identification of applications first generally offers the most flexibility in choosing lower-level specifications, such as cabling and network operating systems. Most other specifications will support the chosen applications; therefore it is very important to ensure that the applications adequately satisfy requirements. To ensure proper selection of applications, designers should consider using trial offers from vendors or having the vendor or applicable representative demonstrate their products. The results of these activities can help support the right choices.

In some situations, the requirements will partially specify the applications. For instance, requirements might state the need for electronic mail. Designers would then further specify items, such as a particular vendor and product. In some situations, though, the requirements might fully define the applications. This often happens when an organization has a strong desire for one type of application over others.

As guidelines in selecting appropriate applications, designers should primarily focus on the following requirements types:

Operator profiles

Choose applications that satisfy the functions users require. Also, select applications that best match the users' degree of computer literacy and knowledge of similar applications. In addition, strive for application functionality that increases the users' productivity. Designers and analysts can satisfy these criteria by having a test group comprising a cross section of potential users utilize and provide feedback on the applications.

Existing systems

Make sure applications interoperate with existing applications on local and remote systems. Users should be able to access applications from existing systems.

Information flows

Select applications that support the type and flow of information needed by the users. As an example, if users can strongly benefit from sending scanned images, then identify applications that will support appropriate image formats.

Security

The applications must meet all security needs for passwords, file checking, and rights assignments.

Regulatory

The choice of applications must abide by all company policies for utilizing certain vendors. Some organizations might have established relationships with particular vendors and have significant investments in certain application types. It might be beneficial then to continue specifying vendor-specific applications to reduce training and support costs.

Network Operating System

The network operating system (NOS) provides a platform for applications and services to operate on. Thus, it is important to choose a network operating system that adequately satisfies network requirements and supports the chosen applications. A NOS normally offers communications, printing, and file services for applications residing on the network. Figure 6.1 illustrates NOS functionality.

A NOS provides the mechanisms that make resource sharing possible. Print services via a print server application are included within most network operating systems. A print server comprises software residing on a hardware platform and performs the functions necessary to share printers among multiple users on the network. Print servers connect directly to the network and augment network operating system printing functions.

Printers can be attached to the network server, dedicated print server,

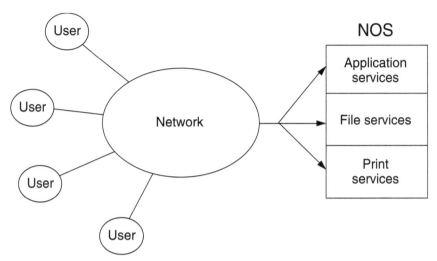

Figure 6.1 Functionality of a network operating system

user workstation, or directly to the network. Printers attached to a server or the network are commonly managed by the print server software located on the server. Printers attached to user workstations are managed by terminate-and-stay-resident (TSR) software that runs in the workstation.

Most NOSs allow network clients to have access to the disk drives located on the file server or other workstations. This is where users can store data files and applications. Through the network operating system, each user's workstation can have a set of drive letters mapped to drives located on the file server. This mapping provides transparent access to extended file storage.

Because a NOS supports the remote storage of files, an organization can store user applications on a file server. This provides centralized access to applications. If a user would like to run an application located on a file server, the user can change to the drive mapped to the directory on the file server on which the application resides, then run the application. The file server will send the application to the user's workstation, where the application will run.

Most NOSs are either peer-to-peer or server-oriented. In a peer-to-peer network, the NOS is distributed throughout the network. With server-oriented networks, a specific network device (the server) performs most of the network operations. Designers should consider whether to use a peer-to-peer or server-based network operating system. The choice commonly depends on the size and complexity of the network. For larger and more complex networks the server-oriented approach would be the best choice, because server-based networks have more functionality and are easier to manage. Peer-to-peer networks have limitations, such as lower performance, limited control over resource availability, and difficult management if the network grows to a larger size. However, a peer-to-peer approach might be best if it is difficult to justify a dedicated network server where there are few users, or where there is limited funding.

Designers should also indicate methods to maximize server performance. The network operating system typically resides on a microcomputer or minicomputer hardware platform, which includes a network connection via a network interface card.

Designers can maximize server performance by:

- Increasing server cache and RAM memory.
- Using a faster network interface card and more efficient drivers.
- Using a faster hardware platform.
- Using a faster hard drive interface.

To facilitate storage of system applications and user files, the design team will need to allocate an appropriate amount of storage space. Designers should calculate the amount of disk space needed by including space for applications, user files, and network operating systems. Also, be sure to pad the disk space calculation in anticipation of future growth.

When considering the network operating system, designers should primarily focus on these types of requirements and design specifications:

Existing systems

Ensure that interoperability will be possible with existing network operating systems. Designers should be certain that there are interfaces available to maintain both a cohesive name directory between platforms and proper cross-platform access to all applications and storage space. Network File System is a distributed file system allowing a set of dissimilar computers to access each other's files in a transparent manner.

Performance

Be sure the NOS will satisfy delay and availability requirements. The most efficient way to accomplish this is by prototyping.

Security

Choose a NOS that satisfied the need for passwords, file locking, rights assignment, and disk mirroring. Designers should also consider multilevel security mechanisms if it is necessary to have users with security clearances lower than the highest classification level of data on the network.

Regulatory

The choice of network operating system must incorporate all company mandates. Often, companies will standardize on one particular NOS to reduce training needs and ease support costs.

Applications

Be sure the chosen network operating system will support all specified applications. Most vendors indicate whether their respective applications operate on particular NOSs.

Hardware Platforms

The hardware platform consists of a central processor(s), memory, applicable interfaces, and an operating system. Hardware platforms support both servers and users. For example, a server hardware platform would contain the network operating system engine, and a user hardware platform would support the interface or client piece of the network operating system. Typical hardware platforms include the 386, 486, and pentium PCs, and UNIX workstations.

Many vendors classify their platforms according to the rate at which the machine can process instructions. This unit of measurement is MIPS (Million Instructions Per Second). High-speed personal computers, such as pentiums, are usually capable of operating at 100 MIPS or greater. A 386 PC usually runs between 3 to 5 MIPS. However, real-world MIPS rates are not uniform, because some vendors utilize the best-case value of the platform while others utilize average rates. Also, some platforms require more instructions to do the same thing that a different platform would do with fewer instructions. As a result, designers should not consider MIPS as the single factor when sizing up the performance of a hardware platform. Be sure to consider other attributes as well, such as bus and memory speed, memory management techniques, and the operating system itself.

To select an appropriate platform, the design team should focus on the following requirements types and design specifications:

Interfaces

Choose a hardware platform that facilitates the bus interface, such as ISA (Industry Standard Architecture), EISA (Extended ISA), and PCMCIA (Personal Computer Memory Card International Association), which best supports requirements, applications, and network operating system.

Mobility

If users require mobility, consider the use of portables, such as palmtops, laptops, and pen-based computers. Make certain on-board interfaces, such as PCMCIA slots, will support needed modems and ethernet boards.

Performance

Ensure that the platform will satisfy delay and reliability requirements. In most cases, application and NOS vendors can identify platforms that will provide adequate levels of performance. But, be sure to test each potential platform by actually loading chosen applications and NOS products on the platform and measuring their performance.

Security

Abide by any requirements for suppression of electromagnetic emissions. This is common when using computers for processing classified information. The suppression decreases the chance of unauthorized reception of information.

Environmental

Make sure the platform meets limitations for size, weight, and power. For typical networks, size is the most crucial environmental factor. The hardware platforms take up space that is often a prime resource in most organizations, especially in older facilities that were not designed to house computer equipment. In addition to size, weight and power are also of great concern in mobile environments, such as ships and aircraft.

Regulatory

Consider company policies identifying the recommended platform types.

Applications

Ensure that the platform is suitable for all applications.

Network operating system

For servers, utilize a very fast platform and install the maximum amount of RAM. Choose server platforms certified to support the chosen network operating system and applications. Ensure that the platform has enough card slots to support the network interface card(s) and other devices.

Topology

At a physical level, a network can be thought of as a collection of nodes and links. The nodes are any network-addressable devices, and the links facilitate the transmission of data between these nodes. The topology describes the network's geographical layout of nodes and links. In other words, the topology illustrates general attributes of the connectivity between nodes. Other design specifications, such as signal distribution, will provide more detail on the connections between nodes.

Network Connectivity

Connectivity exists between a pair of nodes if the destination node can correctly receive data from the source node at a specified minimum data rate. If the reception of data results in a number of bit errors that exceeds the maximum error rate for that link, then connectivity does not exist between the nodes. Communication systems and various types of media provide connectivity between nodes. For example, a pair of modems and a telephone line would provide connectivity between two remote locations.

Link connectivity

The link connectivity between two nodes is the minimum number of links between the two nodes that must be removed to disconnect them. As an example, consider the network topology in Figure 6.2. To determine the link connectivity between nodes A and E, simply find the minimum number of links that you must remove to physically separate nodes A and E. In this example, the answer is obviously three. This tells us that this network can lose

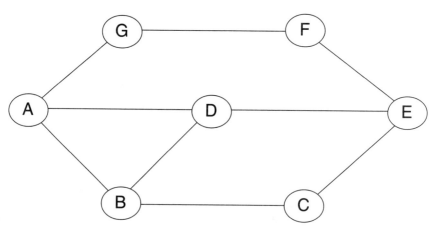

Figure 6.2 Sample network connectivity

any two links yet A and E will still be able to communicate. Thus, link connectivity is directly proportional to network performance. Networks having high degrees of link connectivity will be more reliable.

Node connectivity

Node connectivity represents the minimum number of nodes whose removal will disconnect two nodes of interest. As an example of node connectivity, again consider the network in Figure 6.2. What is the node connectivity between nodes B and D? Applying the above definition, the answer is two. Therefore, removing any single node will still allow a physical path between nodes B and D.

Nodal connectivity is more important than link connectivity, because the loss of a node could mean the loss of several links. If a node fails, all links connected to it will become inactive because they are no longer tied to a viable node. Network planners often employ strategies to increase the reliability of communications, such as dual-homing. This is where a user is tied to two source nodes. If the primary source node fails, the secondary node can still provide the connection into the network. This increases the node and link connectivity, thus lending a more reliable connection with other users. Backup channels are also used for high reliability circuits to provide an extra connection between users in a direct mode of communication.

Fully Connected Topology

One particular topology, which is very simple in form, is to physically connect every node directly to every other node in the network. This is called a fully connected network and it is illustrated in Figure 6.3. This type of network offers many advantages. Assuming all links are operational, there is no need to route data over more than one hop. Therefore, messages are delivered extremely fast. In addition, this topology offers high survivability, because each node is connected into the network at many points.

The low delays and high survivability of the fully connected topology are certainly appealing; however, the high degree of connectivity is very expensive, especially for networks with many nodes. In fact, the number of links necessary to fully connect a number of nodes together is $N(N-1)/2$, where N is the number of nodes in the network. As an example, consider a network having five nodes. This would mean ten links are necessary to fully connect the network. Not too bad yet, but now consider a network with 1,000 nodes! Get the point? The number of links grows exponentially as the number of nodes increases. Thus, a large fully connected network is too expensive because of the substantial number of links between nodes and interfaces needed at each node.

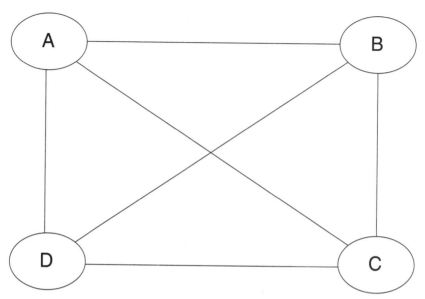

Figure 6.3 Fully connected topology

Partially Connected Topologies

Various partially connected topologies have arisen to eliminate the need for the costly fully connected topology. This trade-off in cost requires network nodes to share links with other node pairs. Thus, network nodes must use link-access protocols to regulate the use of the links. Common partially connected topologies have either a bus, ring, star, or hierarchical architecture.

Bus topology

With the bus topology as shown in Figure 6.4, all nodes share a common transmission medium. When a node is sending data, all other nodes are capable of receiving the data. This is a broadcast mode of operation sometimes called *multipoint transmission*. Because data being sent arrives at all nodes, no switches or repeaters are necessary to route data through the network.

One key attribute of the bus topology is that only one user can transmit at a given time. This is because there is really only one physical connection between all nodes on the network. As a result, the protocols for the bus topology must avoid collisions (when two nodes send data at the same time). The control over which nodes can send data is usually a centralized or distributed form.

Centralized bus control enables orderly transmission by having a controller node on the bus to regulate the data traffic. The controller polls individual nodes periodically to see if nodes wish to send data. A node must wait for this poll before it can send data. The advantage of centralized access is that throughput and delay are stable under heavy loads; however, the controller is vulnerable. If the controller is lost the network ceases to operate.

Whereas the centralized method of control leaves all responsibility for network access with a single entity, distributed access control allows all nodes to share the task of accessing the bus. There are two common types of distributed control—token passing and carrier sense. A section on medium access later in this chapter will cover these types of bus protocols in much more detail.

Ring topology

In ring topology, a set of nodes are joined together in a closed loop. Figure 6.4 describes the ring topology. With this structure, data is transmitted bit-by-bit around the ring. Each user has the ability to monitor the bits passing through the repeater to recognize address information and copy associated messages. As with the bus topology, stations connected to a ring structure cannot start transmitting at any time without first establishing access to avoid having collisions. Most ring networks utilize a token to gain the ability

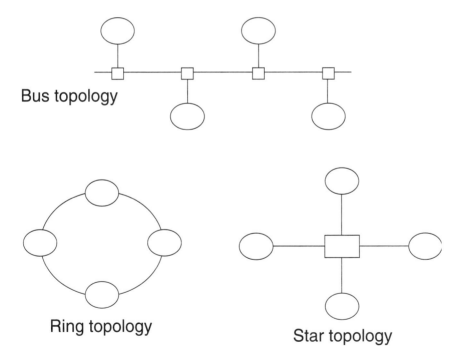

Figure 6.4 Partially connected topologies

to send data. The token circulates the ring, periodically passing by each station. If a station wishes to send data, it removes the token from the network and send its data. After it is finished sending data, the station inserts the token back onto the network. The token removal avoids collisions with the transmission of data from other stations. The main advantage of ring topologies is that they easily support synchronized transmissions, which makes them effective in supporting voice and video transmissions.

Star topology

In the star configuration, as shown in Figure 6.4, each station is connected to a common central switch or hub. Communication between a pair of users in this particular layout is normally done by circuit switching via a central controller. If a particular node wants to send data to another node, it must first obtain permission from the central controller. Assuming a line is available to the node of interest, the switch will provide the connection.

A star topology offers advantages of easier maintenance and fewer components. A network based on a star topology is easier to maintain because most of the active components are located in one location at the switch. The main disadvantage, though, is its vulnerability. If the central switch fails, all communications through that switch will cease.

Hierarchical topology

A hierarchical topology is shown in Figure 6.5. Within the hierarchical topology, nodes in the same geographical area are joined together, then these groups are tied to the remaining network. The idea is to install more links within high density areas and fewer links between these populations. This is the most effective and efficient method of connecting a large number of nodes residing within a vast geographical region, because links, especially long links, are expensive. Therefore, most WANs utilize a hierarchical topology.

Network Segmentation

Network segmentation is the concept of segregating data traffic. Most LAN protocols, such as ethernet, allow transmitted frames to go anywhere on the network, unless a bridge or router is put in place and configured to not forward the data. Segmentation improves the performance of the network because it avoids sending data to parts of the network at which they are not needed. This reduces unnecessary blocking of stations waiting to send data.

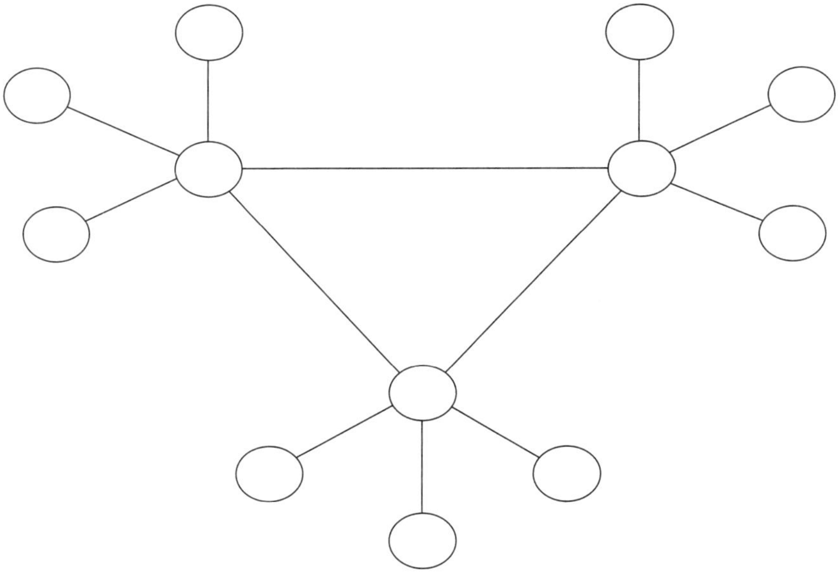

Figure 6.5 Hierarchical topology

Topology Design Considerations

Designers must choose a topology that effectively supports connections among users and network devices, as well as the flow of information. Therefore, the team should mainly base topology directly on requirements. The choice of topology will support the definition of signal distribution and internetworking specifications.

The design team should ascertain the topology as a ring, star, bus, hierarchical, or some hybrid form. In addition, the team should define a network topology consisting of a backbone and subnets. Traditionally, backbones provide a universal connection point for other networks (subnets) to connect. The backbone must be of high performance (an order of magnitude more than the subnets) to support internetwork traffic flows. Subnets consist of physical groups of network devices, typically within the same general geographical area. It is best to set up subnets that contain a group of users having common interests in (for example) utilizing applications, sharing files, or sending e-mail. The subnets can then share equipment, provide easy traffic segmentation, and be easier to administer.

Usually the topology should follow the administrative organization of the company. For example, the accounting department could be one subnet, the engineering department another subnet, and the administration department yet a different subnet. The backbone would then connect all these subnets together into a corporate network.

The overall goals of an optimum topology are to provide connections between every pair of nodes needing to communicate and to minimize topology "cost." Topology cost is based on the following elements:

- Delay in sending information through the network
- Reliability, availability, and maintainability of the network
- Security level offered by the network
- Economical cost of interfacing network devices to the network

An optimum topology can be found by minimizing delay and economics, and maximizing reliability, availability, maintainability, and security. Designers should base the topology on the following types of requirements and design specifications:

- **Topography** The topology must be capable of connecting all user and network device locations.
- **Mobility** If mobility is a requirement, be sure the topology can accommodate a changing topography.
- **Information Flows** The topology must provide necessary communications paths and must address the priority of information transmissions.
- **Performance** Be sure the topology satisfies delay and reliability needs. Multiple paths between locations might be necessary to support alternate routing, in case the primary path becomes inoperative.
- **Security** Abide by the need to protect data. The topology should contain sensitive information within secure protected areas.
- **Environmental** The topology must accommodate facility locations and floor plans.
- **Regulatory** Be sure the topology does not interfere with right-of-way restrictions stated by the company, city, state, or national government.

Internetworking

Internetworking defines the communications process necessary to connect two autonomous networks. An autonomous network has the capability of functioning on its own. For example, an ethernet segment is an autonomous network. Most networks will consist of many autonomous networks requiring internetworking functions that provide an interface between the networks. This is mainly needed to facilitate connectivity between end-devices located on different networks, and in some cases internetworking provides a means of interoperability.

Internetworking is necessary at various levels of the network architecture, which might include the physical, data link, network, and higher layers. Specific network components can provide internetworking at each of these layers. Figure 6.6 identifies each type of internetworking device and the level of internetworking it provides.

Repeaters

Repeaters provide internetworking functionality at the physical layer of a network's architecture. The physical layer is concerned with transmitting raw bits over a communications channel. Functions within the physical layer ensure that when a source sends a bit, the next network device down the line gets it. Physical layer standards deal primarily with electrical, mechanical, and procedural specifications for sending data bits.

As data propagates through a transmission medium, the signal will degrade because of noise interference and attenuation. If the signal degrades to the point where transmission noise is significant compared to the data signal, then errors are likely to occur. Thus, it is necessary to periodically restore the data signal to its original form. The repeater performs this restoration process by receiving the data signal and reshaping it back to its original form. Hence, repeaters will extend the length of the medium and avoid the possibility of transmission errors.

Bridges

Bridges provide internetworking functionality at the medium access (or data link) layer of a network's architecture. The medium access layer provides the functionality necessary to allow shared use of a common medium.

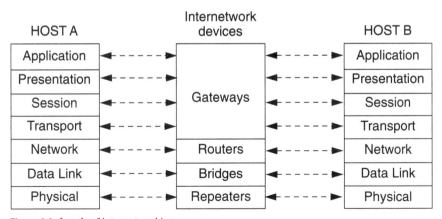

Figure 6.6 Levels of internetworking

Ethernet and token ring, which a later section in this chapter will explain, are examples of medium access techniques.

Bridges can interface similar or dissimilar LANs together, such as ethernet-to-ethernet or ethernet-to-token ring. Organizations use bridges to help form an enterprise network. In this fashion, the bridges segment data traffic by filtering each packet in terms of its medium access layer address. If a packet is destined within its immediate network, the bridge will not allow that packet to pass through. However, a bridge allows packets to pass if they are destined outside of the immediate network. Thus, bridges make sure packets do not wander into areas of the network where they are not needed. This increases system performance by making better use of network bandwidth.

As shown in Figure 6.7, there are two main types of bridges, local and remote. A local bridge connects two LANs within close proximity. Organizations use local bridges to segment traffic within a facility by having each department or work group connect to a corporate backbone via a local bridge. On the other hand, remote bridges connect networks separated by longer distances. A company will usually install remote bridges to provide network connectivity between buildings, cities, and even continents. This requires a pair of bridges, one at each site, and a circuit between them to provide a physical layer connection. Traditionally, organizations have used the analog telephone system and leased 56 Kbps and T1 digital circuits to provide the connection between remote bridges. Wireless remote bridges are very similar to traditional bridges, except that wireless bridges use a wire-free medium, such as spread spectrum radio or infrared laser light, to provide a physical layer link.

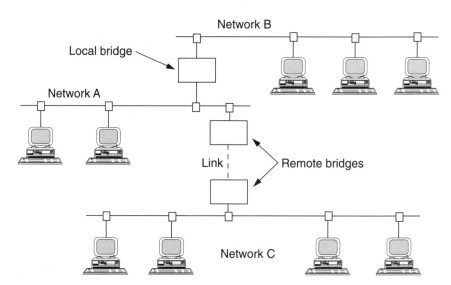

Figure 6.7 Local and remote bridging

Routers

Routers provide internetworking at the network layer of a network's architecture by allowing individual networks to become part of a WAN. As shown in Figure 6.8, routers provide an interconnection between LANs and WANs. Routers direct data packets through a wide area network by choosing from multiple forwarding paths stored in a routing table. Most routers are also capable of routing different types of protocols at the same time.

Gateways

Gateways provide interconnectivity and interoperability at the higher network layers. There are many instances in which an internetwork must provide interoperability among dissimilar protocols. But what is the most effective way to provide interoperability? Let us look at an example. Assume you are attending an international conference which includes participants from 30 different countries, all of whom speak different languages. Some participants speak only English, some speak only French, some speak only German, and so on. If you know how to speak only English, you could hire an interpreter or a set of interpreters who could translate between English and all other languages. This would allow you to communicate with the other participants.

However, it could be fairly expensive to hire a set of interpreters who knew the 29 other languages. Another method of solving this problem would be to agree that the conference would use a common language. Let us say the language chosen is French. Now each non-French person would need only one interpreter who could translate to the chosen language, French. This would be the most effective way to provide communications among all the participants.

Similar to the above example, the most effective way for internetworks to provide interoperability is to have all networks with different protocols convert to a common intermediate protocol. For example, electronic mail gateways can interconnect dissimilar electronic mail systems. If Company A employs Brand X mail software and Company B uses Brand Y mail software, then the companies can interconnect their mail systems through the use of gateways as shown in Figure 6.9. If someone from Company A sends mail to some individual in Company B, then the X.400 gateway would receive the mail message and convert it into the X.400 protocol. The mail gateway at Company B would eventually receive the mail message and convert it from X.400 into Brand Y software format before delivering it to the user.

Internetworking Protocols

Internetworking protocols support the end-to-end delivery of data packets over dissimilar networks. Some networks are able to handle large packets,

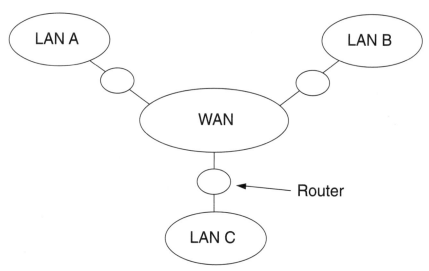

Figure 6.8 Internetworking LANs and WANs

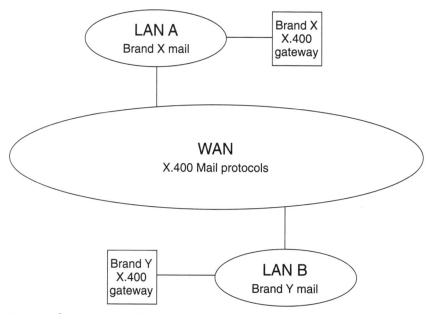

Figure 6.9 Interconnection of mail systems through use of gateways

while others can deal only with smaller packets. In addition, networks have varying support for delivery priorities and error control. Internetworking protocols must be capable of delivering packets over networks having these types of differences.

A popular internetworking protocol is Internet Protocol (IP). Normally, IP is utilized with Transmission Control Protocol (TCP). IP provides the functionality necessary for a data packet to traverse networks that are different in size and performance. TCP is a transport-layer protocol providing end-to-end connection establishment.

Internetworking Design Considerations

The selection of an internetworking device depends on the types of networks requiring interconnection. For example, it might be necessary to interconnect the new token ring network to an existing ethernet network. In this case, the designers should specify an ethernet-to-token ring bridge. Or, the new electronic mail application might have to interoperate with a different mail application located on another network. For this example, a mail gateway would be necessary.

Designers should base the internetworking specifications on the following types of requirements and design specifications:

Topography

Consider the locations of users, and utilize a bridge to separate workgroups. Often, users within close proximity, such as the same wing or floor, will primarily interoperate with each other and a local server. It is usually beneficial to segment these users into a workgroup to prevent their transmission signals from broadcasting to unwanted parts of the network.

Existing systems

If the need to interconnect dissimilar networks exists, establish a gateway to provide interoperability between dissimilar applications and protocols. This is often the case if the networks have different electronic mail software and directory services.

Information flows

Based on projected flow of information, place bridges to best segment the traffic.

Regulatory

Follow policies recommending the use of intermail transport protocols, such as SMTP or X.400, and internetworking protocols, such as TCP/IP.

Network access method

Select internetworking devices that satisfy the chosen network access methods, such as ethernet or token ring.

Medium

Employ repeaters, if necessary, to extend the length of the network medium. This is mainly applicable with older 10base5 (Thickwire) networks, because current 10baseT (twisted pair) networks utilize centralized hubs having built-in repeaters. It might be worthwhile, though, to use repeaters to extend optical fiber backbones.

Signaling

Signaling provides a representation of information through the use of electrical signals. There are two main types of signaling, analog and digital, both of which "carry" information through changes in amplitude, frequency, or phase. Designers need to describe the parameters of the network's signals that best matches requirements and higher-level design specifications. That is, should the signals be analog or digital? And what is their most effective frequencies or data rates?

Analog signals

An analog signal is one for which the amplitude varies continuously as time progresses. This is shown in Figure 6.10. Much of the natural environment

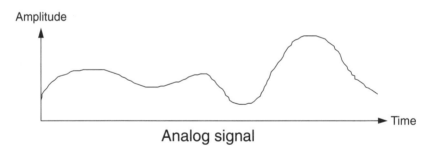

Analog signal

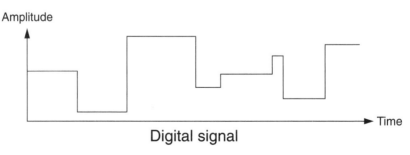

Digital signal

Figure 6.10 Analog and digital signaling

produces signals that are analog in form; examples of this are light and the human voice. In the early days of electronic communication, most systems processed signals in analog form; thus, they were termed *analog communication systems*. In the past, most inputs to the communication process were in analog form (such as voice); therefore, it was natural to design systems based on analog concepts. The introduction of the digital computer, which processes information in discrete form, led to system designs based on discrete-valued digital functions.

Digital Signals

In contrast to analog, digital signals vary in amplitude steps as time advances. Figure 6.10 illustrates the structure of a digital signal. In fact, at certain periods of time, the amplitude of a digital signal is theoretically discontinuous—there is no defined amplitude. In reality, digital signals have some specified value at all moments of time. Often digital signals are binary (two-state); therefore, it is common to refer to them as a string of binary digits (bits). Baseband signaling normally uses binary digital waveforms to represent information, while broadband signaling uses frequency modulated analog waveforms to represent information.

With computer networks it is most effective to process information as digital signals. One of the advantages of digital signals is easy regeneration. As a signal propagates through a medium, it might encounter noise that will change the appearance of the waveform. To clean-up (regenerate) a signal, a repeater detects if a pulse is present at a certain period of time. Detection circuitry can create a new pulse when it senses an incoming pulse even if it has a considerable amount of damage. Thus, regeneration is fairly easy. This is not the case for most analog signals because of the lower probability of predicting exactly what an analog signal looked like before noise affected it.

It is often necessary to encrypt and later decode a signal. This process is relatively easy with digital signals, because all that is necessary is to rearrange the bits using some type of keying process. When the data are received at the destination, a device can use the same key that is used for encryption and decrypt the data.

Another example of the advantage of digital signals over their analog counterparts is that of data and voice integration. It is possible to take analog voice signals and digitize them; that is, to perform analog-to-digital conversion and then integrate the digitized voice with other digital data (e.g., textual characters or telemetry). There is currently a strong push toward integrating voice, data, and video into a common network infrastructure, mainly because it eases management and supports new applications such as desktop conferencing.

Data Rates

The data rate identifies the speed of data transmission. The data rate of a digital signal gives some insight into how long it will take to transmit data from one point to another, and identifies the amount of bandwidth needed by the medium. Two primary types of data rates are baud rate and bit rate.

Baud rate

Baud rate, by definition, is the unit of signaling speed derived from the duration of the shortest code element of the digital signal. In other words, baud rate is the speed the digital signal pulses travel. To calculate baud rate, take the reciprocal of the width of the shortest pulse interval as shown below:

$$\text{Baud rate} = \frac{1}{T}$$

The unit of baud rate is Baud (Bd) if the width of the shortest pulse interval (T) is in seconds. For example, if 20 bits are transmitted in 20 milliseconds, then the width of each pulse is 0.02/20 = 0.001 seconds. The resulting baud rate is then 1/0.001 = 1,000 Bd.

Bit rate

Bit rate is equal to the total number of bits transmitted in relation to the time it takes to send them. Thus, bit rate represents the speed of a signal's data bits. Bit rate can be calculated through the following formula:

$$\text{Bit rate} = \frac{\text{Total number of bits}}{\text{Total time to send bits}}$$

The common unit of measure for bit rate is bits-per-second (bps). As an example, consider a signal with parameters as before for the baud rate example. You will find that bit rate is 20/0.02 = 1,000 bps.

Often people use the term baud and bit rate interchangeably because these measures often have the same numerical value (as they do in the case of binary signals). For multilevel digital signals, though, the bit rate will become greater than the baud rate. This is desirable because baud rate is really the parameter consuming bandwidth. At higher baud rates, more bandwidth is needed to support communications. Sending more bits per second while maintaining the same baud rate (as with multilevel signals) makes better use of the available bandwidth. It is possible to increase the bit rate by utilizing multilevel signaling. Calculating bit rate for a multilevel signal is possible by the use of the following formula:

$$\text{Bit rate} = (\text{Baud rate})\text{Log2}(M)$$

where M is the number of levels a pulse can assume. For example, if the baud rate is 1,200 Bd, and each pulse has 16 possible levels, what is the bit rate? Plugging in the numbers will give you

Bit rate = 1,200Log2(16) = 4,800 bps

Signaling Design Considerations

Based on what was included in the last section, designers should maximize the use of digital signals to take advantage of more effective signal regeneration, encryption, and integration of various information types. The design team will then need to focus on the selection of data rates necessary to support applications and communications needs. Be sure to define signal data rate specifications to satisfy the following types of requirements:

Information flows

The chosen data rates must be able to adequately deliver the types of information, such as data, imagery, video, or voice, that the network contains. For data and imagery signals, choose a data rate capable of sending the information within expected delay requirements. Good quality full motion (30 frames-per-second [fps]) video typically requires 200 Mbps signals without using compression. Lower rates will work if lossy compression is applied to the signal. As an example, only 30 Kbps is necessary for low quality (3 fps) video. For voice, 64 Kbps is good enough to sustain quality transmissions without compression. Table 6.1 identifies typical data rate and duty cycle requirements for various types of components and information types. This can further aid designers in determining data rate specifications.

TABLE 6.1 Typical Data Rate and Duty Cycle Requirements for Various Types of Components and Information Types

Type source	Peak data rate (Kbps)	Duty cycle (%)
Printers	19.2	50–80
File servers	100	10–30
Mail servers	100	30–50
Facsimile	9.6	5–20
Security alarms	0.1	100
Voice	64	50–90
Video	30,000	50–90

Performance

Make sure data rates are high enough to meet requirements to send information within a certain amount of time.

Error Control

Networks suffer from noise induced in the links between network elements. If the noise is high enough in amplitude, it can cause errors in digital transmission in the form of altered bits. This will lead to inaccuracy of the transmitted data, and the receiving network device might misinterpret the meaning of the information. As a result, it is very important to specify the error rate that signals can experience without being unacceptable at the receiving station. The error rate identifies the number of errors the network can tolerate. For example, an error rate of 0.00001 means the network must have fewer than 1 error for every 10,000 bits transmitted.

Types of Errors

The noise causing distortion within networks is usually Gaussian or impulse noise. Theoretically, the amplitude of Gaussian noise is uniform across the frequency spectrum, and it normally triggers random errors that are independent of each other. Impulse noise, the most disastrous, is characterized by long, quiet intervals of time followed by high amplitude bursts. This noise results from natural and man-made causes such as lightning and switching transients. Impulse noise is responsible for most errors in digital communication systems, and generally provokes errors to occur dependently in groups. This distortion is referred to as *burst errors*.

Error-control techniques can highly reduce the number of transmission errors to accommodate the required error rates. There are two main types of error control—automatic repeat-request and forward error correction.

Automatic Repeat-Request

With the automatic repeat-request (ARQ) technique, the receiver detects errors and uses a feedback path to the sender for requesting the retransmission of incorrect frames. Two main events must occur to correct errors with ARQ. First, a received frame must be checked at the receiver for possible errors; second, the sender must be notified to retransmit the frames received in error. The process of ARQ is illustrated in Figure 6.11. The ARQ technique operates at the data link layer of a network architecture.

There are two main approaches for retransmitting unsatisfactory blocks of data: *stop-and-wait* and *continuous* ARQ.

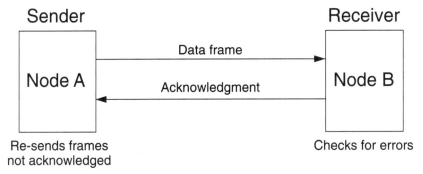

Figure 6.11 Automatic repeat-request (ARQ) process

Stop-and-wait ARQ

In the stop-and-wait method of transmission, the transmitter sends a block of data, then stops and waits for some type of acknowledgment from the receiver on whether a particular frame was acceptable. If the transmitter receives a negative acknowledgment, the previous frame will be sent again. The transmitter will send the next frame only after it receives a positive acknowledgment from the receiver.

One definite advantage of stop-and-wait ARQ is that it does not require much buffer space at the sending or receiving station. Only the outstanding transmitted frame needs to be stored at the sender (in case of retransmission). On the other hand, stop-and-wait ARQ becomes very inefficient as the propagation delay between source and destination becomes large. For example, data sent on satellite links normally experience a round trip delay of several hundred milliseconds; therefore, long block lengths are necessary to maintain a reasonably effective data rate. The trouble is that, with longer data blocks, the probability of an error occurring in a particular block is greater. Thus, retransmission will occur often, and the resulting throughput will be lower.

Continuous ARQ

One way of improving the throughput on longer links is to use the continuous ARQ method. With this type of ARQ, the transmitter sends data blocks continuously until the receiver detects an error. The transmitter is usually capable of sending a certain number of frames and keeps a log of which frames have been sent. Once the receiver detects a bad block it will send a signal back to the transmitter, requesting that the bad frame be sent over again. When the receiver gets the signal to retransmit a certain frame, several subsequent frames might have already been sent (due to propagation delays between the sender and receiver); therefore the transmitter must "go back" and retransmit the erred data frame.

The transmitter can retransmit frames in several ways with continuous ARQ. One method is for the source to retrieve the erred frame from the transmit buffer and send the bad frame and all frames following it. This is called the go-back-n technique, and it can be more effective than the stop-and-wait ARQ because the bandwidth of the channel is better utilized. One problem, though occurs when n (the number of frames the transmitter sent after the erred frame, plus one) becomes large, the method becomes inefficient. This is because, for the retransmission of just one *bad* frame, a large number of possibly "good" frames will also be re-sent, thus decreasing throughput.

The go-back-n technique is useful in applications in which receiver buffer space is limited, because all that is needed is a receiver window size of one (assuming frames are to be delivered in order). When the receive node rejects an erred frame (sends a negative acknowledgment), it does not need to buffer any subsequent frames for possible reordering while it is waiting for the retransmission, because all subsequent frames will also be sent.

An alternative to the continuous go-back-n technique is a method that selectively retransmits only the erred frame and resumes normal transmission at the point just before getting the notification of a bad block of data. This is the selective repeat approach. Selective repeat is obviously better than continuous go-back-n in terms of throughput, because only the erred data block is retransmitted. However, the receiver must be capable of storing a number of data frames if they are to be processed in order. The receiver needs to buffer data that have been received after an erred frame was requested for retransmission, because only the damaged frame will be sent again.

All ARQ types depend on the detection of errors and then the retransmission of the faulty messages. Overall, ARQ is best suited for the correction of burst errors because this type of distortion normally occurs in a small percentage of frames, thus not invoking many retransmissions. Because of the feedback inherent in ARQ protocols, half-duplex or full-duplex lines must be used because ARQ communication occurs in both directions. If only simplex links are available due to feasibility, then it is impossible to use the ARQ technique because the receiver would not be able to notify the transmitter of bad data blocks.

Forward Error Correction

With the forward error correction (FEC) technique, the receiver automatically corrects as many channel errors as it can without referring to the transmitter. Figure 6.12 illustrates this concept. This is possible because the transmitter sends not only enough redundant bits to detect errors but enough to enable correction as well. This makes FEC well suited for simplex communications lines.

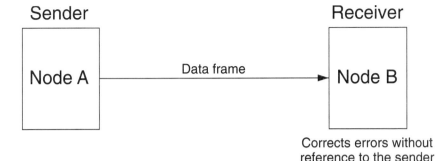

Figure 6.12 Forward error correction (FEC) process

FEC operates at the physical level of the network architecture. The FEC error control method uses two basic classes of error control codes to correct data at the receiver: hamming codes and convolutional codes. Hamming codes are capable of correcting single-bit errors, and convolutional codes can correct small-scale multiple errors.

FEC might be the best choice on long links, or where only simplex lines are available. However, ARQ is the most common method of error control. This is mainly because errors usually occur in clusters due to common impulse noise. This places a requirement to correct large numbers of errors, which FEC typically cannot accomplish.

More and more communications systems are utilizing a combination of both ARQ and FEC. In this case, the physical layer devices attempt to correct small numbers of errors to possibly avoid a retransmission. If FEC ends up correcting all the errors, the ARQ mechanism will not need to retransmit the data frame. If there are a large number of errors the sender will retransmit the frame.

Error Control Design Considerations

The design team should identify effective error-control techniques that will satisfy all requirements, especially the maximum allowable error rate. Most error control mechanisms are bundled with the network interface card or modem; therefore, the designer usually ends up choosing the error control type as part of the selection of the applicable medium interface. For example, Ethernet uses ARQ and some modems utilize FEC.

Designers should base error control specifications on the following types of requirements:

Information flows

If sending text files through the network, use error control that provides a high degree of integrity, such as ARQ.

Existing systems

Be sure the chosen error control technique adequately supports the transmission of signals across existing systems.

Performance

Base the error control mechanism on delay requirements and maximum allowable error rates.

Environmental conditions

The types of signal disturbances affect signals differently. If impulse noise might be present, burst errors are likely. ARQ would then be the best choice of error control because burst errors result in long streams of errors. For noise sources that cause random single-bit errors, such as thermal noise, FEC is effective.

Topography

For extremely long links when propagation delays are significant (satellite distances or beyond), utilize a sliding window ARQ method or FEC.

Synchronization

Synchronization refers to the timing between the transmission of information frames. Some information is sent via single frames, which is the case with most electronic mail. But, because of frame size limitations, networks must often transmit large files, video, and voice signals in multiple discrete frames. Thus, in some cases it is important to specify a degree of synchronization that allows for proper delivery of the information frames. For some information the timing between frames might not matter, but the transmission of continuous video and voice signals requires a high level of synchronization. The synchronization of information signals might require asynchronous, synchronous, or isochronous synchronization. Figure 6.13 illustrates these types of synchronization.

Asynchronous Transmission

With asynchronous synchronization there is no defined time relationship between transmissions of frames. Most network operations, such as server logins, electronic mail access, and file transfers, utilize asynchronous frame transmission. In this case it does not matter whether there is an irregular amount of time between frame transmissions. All carrier sense networks, such as ethernet and packet radio, provide asynchronous transmission of frames.

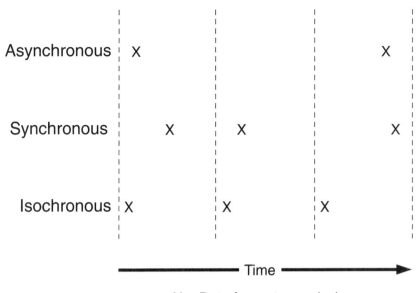

X = Data frame transmission

Figure 6.13 Illustration of asynchronous, synchronous, and isochronous signaling

Synchronous Transmission

A synchronous form of transmission guarantees that information frames can be sent within certain time periods. Information flows between automated equipment within manufacturing environments often require synchronous transmissions. Token passing medium access protocols, such as token ring and FDDI, allow the synchronous transmission of frames.

Isochronous Transmission

Isochronous transmission is very similar to synchronous, except that isochronous requires information to be sent at specific times. High-quality voice and video transmission requires isochronous transmission, because these signals require delivery at regular intervals to maintain integrity. Current LAN technologies do not support isochronous transmission; however, ANSI is considering an upgrade to FDDI (FDDI II) that will include isochronous synchronization.

Synchronization Design Considerations

The design team should select a form of synchronization that best supports the required type of information flow. For the design, the team should identify which type of synchronization, such as asynchronous, synchronous, or isochronous, is necessary for each part of the network. Most data can get by with asynchronous transmission, which ethernet provides, but voice and video both travel best over synchronous or isochronous circuits.

Security

Security mechanisms guarantee that the network resources are available and data is protected against theft and corruption. The three main methods to achieve security are access controls, data encryption, and backup methods. Access controls attempt to stop unauthorized people from entering a controlled area and accessing the network, applications and files. By definition, a controlled area is one in which users can freely distribute and utilize information without fear of unauthorized access. Most networks provide access controls to facilitate a controlled area through the use of locked doors, firewalls, system passwords, and restricted system access times. For data encryption, most networks encrypt sensitive information before sending it outside the controlled area. Backup methods include tape backup and disk mirroring of files residing within network storage devices, and the use of redundant power supplies. In case of power failure, uninterruptible power supplies (UPSs) can provide temporary power to servers and other critical network devices. In addition, backup generators can support long-term power requirements in case of power blackouts.

Firewalls

A firewall is a device that interfaces the network to the outside world and shields the network from unauthorized users. The firewall does this by blocking certain types of traffic. For example, some firewalls permit only electronic mail traffic to enter the network from elsewhere. This helps protect the network against attacks made to other network resources, such as sensitive files, databases, and applications. Firewalls also define a single "choke point" at which the organization can implement security and audit functions. Therefore, data gathered at the firewall is an effective tool in tracing unauthorized activities.

UPSs

As shown in Figure 6.14, UPSs are hardware devices that provide a short supply of power to servers and other critical devices if power discontinues. The limited power provided by the UPS allows the server to shut down gracefully, avoiding corruption of data files. UPSs directly support network security requirements and design specifications identifying the need to avoid loss of data. Most UPSs have unattended power shutdown and startup.

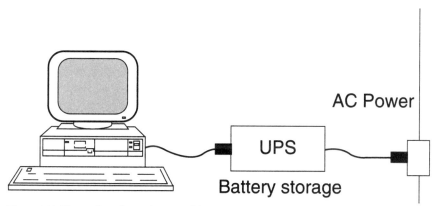

Figure 6.14 Illustration of an uninterruptible power supply (UPS)

That is, if the power fails, the UPS will automatically supply power to the server. If the power returns before the UPS battery drains, the UPS will automatically reestablish the primary power. As a result, the UPS can support continuous server operation during short power outages.

Security Design Considerations

Security requirements usually identify general access restrictions and needs for protecting files. The design team must then determine how to satisfy these requirements. Designers should primarily define security specifications to satisfy the following types of requirements and design specifications:

Operator profiles

The chosen information security system must accommodate any needs of the user population to have access to data having multiple levels of classification. In this case, a multilevel security system might be necessary.

Topography

Be sure to consider the location of users and network devices, and define a controlled area that encompasses the area of the network requiring protection. Designers should utilize firewalls to properly secure the controlled area.

Existing systems

Be sure to address information security requirements or limitations of existing systems. Always ensure that existing systems are capable of securing the information at the highest level of classification.

Mobility

If mobile users can travel outside the secured area, make certain there are provisions, such as encryption, to protect the transmission of sensitive information.

Information flows

Take into account anticipated paths of information flow when defining security specifications. Protect sensitive information that goes outside the controlled area. Also, minimize the possible entry points for viruses, and incorporate effective virus-detection software.

Performance

Be sure the chosen security methods maintain delay and availability requirements.

Security

The security design specifications should directly satisfy all requirements dealing with security.

Environmental conditions

Consider the "hardness" of the facility, meaning building construction and existing use of building entry/exit methods, when selecting an approach to handle security. Be sure to analyze the possibility of network disasters, such as power outages and flooding, and incorporate security mechanisms that will keep the network operational. Also, investigate the presence of environmental disturbances that could corrupt signal transmissions, and then implement counteractive measures such as error control and shielding.

Regulations

Abide by all applicable organizational security policies.

Medium

Examine the type of medium and its ability to contain information signals. Metallic media, such as twisted pair and coaxial cable, emit electromagnetic waves that an eavesdropper can receive from several feet away with special sensing equipment. For the transmission of sensitive information through metallic media, consider the use of encryption to avoid a breach of security. Optical fiber, on the other hand, is very difficult to tap because it does not radiate signals—the light carrier remains within the core of the fiber. Even if someone cuts the fiber to allow enough detectable light to escape, security equipment can detect the corresponding loss of carrier power and set off an alarm. This makes optical fiber the most secure type of medium. However, to be absolutely safe, designers should consider using encryption for highly classified transmissions even on optical fiber.

Operational Support

Planning for operational support is a significant phase of a network implementation. Most of this planning should take place after designing the network; however, it is very important to address applicable operational support specifications into the design as well. Operational support design specifications describe attributes the network must have in order to adequately facilitate support activities. For example, these design specifications should identify how to provide effective network monitoring, which is the ability to electronically view traffic flows, states of network devices, and data packets. Network monitoring systems depend on protocols that gather statistics necessary to provide the monitoring functions.

The reason designers should contemplate support issues during the design stage is to ensure the proper selection of network components. For example, network monitoring equipment might require the ability of each active component to interact with Simple Network Monitoring Protocol (SNMP). SNMP is part of the TCP/IP protocol suite and defines the transfer of information between Management Information Bases (MIBs). Most high-end network monitoring stations require the implementation of SNMP on each of the components the organization wishes to monitor. If the team does not specify these types of specifications during the design stage, purchasers might procure the wrong components.

Operational Support Design Considerations

Designers should primarily define operational support specifications to satisfy the following types of requirements and design specifications:

Existing systems

Be sure to consider the existing network management tools and protocols before selecting one as part of the modification. Designers should specify network management components that interface and interoperate with existing tools and protocols.

Performance

Make certain that the inclusion of network monitoring traffic on the network does not hamper expected delay and availability requirements. Passive (non-intrusive) network monitoring devices, such as protocol analyzers, do not affect network performance because they do not transmit data onto the network. They merely view and record data passing through the medium. However, active network management stations that gather statistics throughout the network utilize protocols (such as SNMP) which require some of the network's bandwidth, which might decrease the overall performance of the network. Designers should test the effects of active monitoring equipment before utilizing it on the operational network.

Regulations

Abide by policies mandating the use of specific network management protocols.

7

Low-Level Design Specifications

This chapter continues the presentation of design specifications, but emphasizes ones that deal with lower levels of the network architecture. Most of these low-level design specifications directly satisfy other higher-level design attributes, such as signaling and synchronization types.

Transmission Medium

The medium is a physical link that provides a basic building block to support the transmission of information signals. Most media are composed of either metal, glass, plastic, or air. Therefore, an active component must convert the particular information signal, usually an electrical digital waveform, into a form suitable for transmission over the medium.

There are many medium types. The following paragraphs will describe the ones most common to computer networks.

Twisted-pair wire uses metallic-type conductors to provide a path for current flow. The wire in this medium is twisted in pairs to minimize the electromagnetic interference between one pair and another. The greater the number of twists per foot, the greater the noise immunity.

Twisted-pair wiring is inexpensive to purchase and easy to install. Because of these attributes, twisted-pair wiring is currently the most common form of LAN medium. IEEE 802.3 (ethernet), 10baseT, IEEE 802.5 (token ring), and ANSI FDDI standards specify the use of unshielded twisted-pair (UTP) wiring. Figure 7.1 illustrates the use of twisted-pair wiring in an ethernet network. For ethernet, twisted-pair wiring is limited to 300 feet between repeaters.

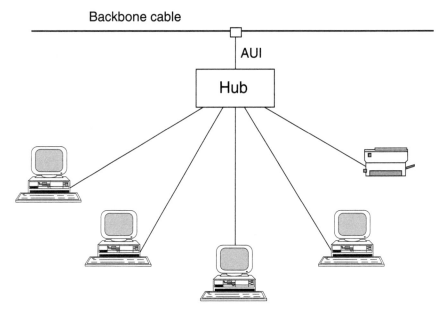

Figure 7.1 Use of twisted-pair wiring in an ethernet network transmission. Most telephone companies will lease 64 Kbps ISDN data channels.

The EIA 568 building wiring standard specifies the following five categories of unshielded twisted-pair wiring:

- Category 1: Old-style phone wire which is not suitable for most data transmission. This includes most telephone wire installed before 1983, in addition to most current residential telephone wiring.
- Category 2: Certified for data rates up to 4 Mbps, which facilitates IEEE 802.5 Token Ring networks (4 Mbps version).
- Category 3: Certified for data rates up to 10 Mbps, which facilitates IEEE 802.3 10baseT (ethernet) networks.
- Category 4: Certified for data rates up to 16 Mbps, which facilitates IEEE 802.5 Token Ring networks (16 Mbps version).
- Category 5: Certified for data rates up to 100 Mbps, which facilitates ANSI FDDI Token Ring networks.

Coaxial Cable

Coaxial cable has a solid metallic core, with a shielding as a return path for current flow. As with twisted pair, coaxial cable uses current flow to carry information from one point to another. The shielding within the coaxial cable reduces the amount of electrical noise interference within the core wire; therefore, coaxial cable can extend to much greater lengths than twisted-pair wiring.

Coaxial cable was very popular for use in LANs during the 1980s and is still an economical medium for small networks. The IEEE 802.3 (ethernet) standard specifies the use of coaxial cable in the 10base2 and 10base5 standards. Figure 7.2 illustrates the use of coaxial cable in ethernet networks.

The main disadvantage of coaxial cable is that it is bulky, making it difficult to install for large networks. In addition, most network standards utilize coaxial cable in a physical bus topology, which decreases the reliability of the network. If the cable breaks, a large part of the network becomes inoperative.

Optical Fiber

Optical fiber is a medium that uses changes in light intensity to carry information. As shown in Figure 7.3, an optical fiber system consists of a light source, an optical fiber, and a light detector. The light source changes electrical data signals into light, the optical fiber transports the light to the destination, and the light detector converts the light signal back into an electrical signal.

The light source simply turns the light on and off according to the data being sent. The light source converts logic 1s and 0s into on and off light. The typical span of optical fiber between repeaters is several miles; however, hun-

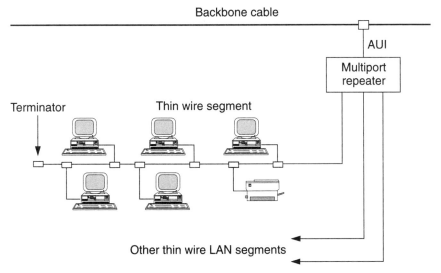

Figure 7.2 Use of coaxial cable in ethernet networks

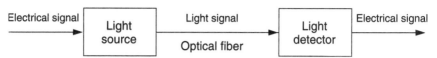

Figure 7.3 Optical fiber communication system

dreds of miles have been reached using specialized optical components. Optical fiber medium can also support data rates in the Mbps, Gbps, and Tbps ranges.

Optical fiber offers many advantages over other types of medium. These advantages include high data rate capability, excellent noise immunity, long distance transmission without signal regeneration, security, and light weight. The main disadvantages of utilizing optical fiber as a medium are expense and the brittle nature of the fiber itself.

A typical optical fiber consists of three parts: a core, cladding, and a buffer. The core is the optical transmission path and is surrounded by the cladding, which provides a reflective surface to keep light within the core and allow it to propagate light along the core to the distant end. The core and cladding are encased in the buffer, which adds strength and protection in the operating environment.

Light sources. Light sources include either a light-emitting diode (LED) or an injection laser diode (ILD). An LED emits incoherent light when current is passed through it. Advantages of LEDs include low cost and long lifetime, and they are capable of operating in the Mbps range. The ILD generates light that is highly monochromatic and very directional. Although ILDs are much more expensive than LEDs, they are capable of much faster operating speeds.

Optical fiber types. There are three main types of optical fiber: multimode step index, multimode graded index, and single mode. Figure 7.4 illustrates the attributes of these types of optical fiber.

The simplest fiber is the multimode step-index fiber, which has a relatively large core. This type of fiber has a sharp difference in the material content of the core and the cladding. The large core allows the many modes of a light pulse to travel through it. Because light reflects differently for different modes, some rays follow longer paths than others. The lowest-order mode, the axial ray, travels down the center of the fiber without reflecting and arrives at the end of the fiber first. The higher-order modes reflect at the core-cladding-interface many times and therefore take a longer route. Because of this, a narrow pulse of light spreads out as it travels through the fiber. The result is a smeared pulse at the destination, which hinders high-speed transmission.

A multimode graded-index fiber is constructed with its core as a series of concentric rings. Basically, the core's index of refraction changes according to how far light is from the cross-sectional center. The density of the glass fiber is highest in the core center. As light travels out from the core center, it will encounter less core density. This core density change forces the light wave to start refracting as it passes through each density layer, causing it to arc back toward the core's center. Because light travels faster in less density, light farther away from the fiber's axis (center) travels faster. Thus, modes of light tend to arrive at the end of the fiber at nearly the same time. This reduces the amount of pulse smearing at the destination, which enables higher-speed transmission.

The single-mode step-index fibers have a very small core diameter of two to ten micrometers. These fibers, ideally, propagate only one mode of light and are the most efficient at reducing dispersion. This type of fiber is very efficient and is suitable for very high-speed, long-distance applications.

Optical detectors

The optical detector serves the opposite function of the source and converts light signals back into electrical signals. There are two types of detectors that coincide with the wavelength of the LED and ILD light sources. These are the positive-intrinsic-negative (PIN) photodiode, and the avalanche photodiode (APD).

The PIN diode, which operates best with an LED as a light source, works on the principles of photoelectricity. The PIN diode is made of a semiconductor material which emits electrical current internally when illuminated sufficiently by short wavelengths of light. The APD acts as a light detector for the ILD light source. The APD provides some gain and is also sensitive to lower-power signals than the PIN. The advantage of the APD is that it is very fast, turning on and off much faster than the PIN. The APD operates at high voltages of 30 to 300 volts. The power supply required for this adds to the cost. The high voltage also leads to higher sensitivity to temperature variations.

Multi-mode step-index	Multi-mode graded-index	Multi-mode step-index
• Utilizes LED/PIN • High degree of pulse smearing • Not recommended	• Utilizes LED/PIN • Moderate degree of pulse smearing • Operates at Mbps	• Utilizes ILD/APD • Low degree of pulse smearing • Operates at Gbps

Figure 7.4 Optical fiber types

Carrier Currents

Electrical power wires within facilities effectively transport 60 Hz alternating current (AC) to wall outlets and supply power to lights, radios, and computers. These electrical wires are also capable of supporting the transmission of data as well. Figure 7.5 illustrates the concept of using AC circuits to interconnect network components. This form of media is often referred to as *carrier currents*.

The interface units typically convert RS-232 (20 Kbps) digital signals into an analog signal suitable for transmission over the electrical circuit. The data signals do not conflict with the AC power signals because the data signals are transmitted at a much higher frequency than 60 Hz. However, transformers within the electrical system highly attenuate (block) the higher frequency data signals, limiting data interconnections to individual power circuits.

Radio Waves

The use of radio waves through the atmosphere supports wireless communications, which can offer effective network node mobility, portability, and transmission through areas where it is difficult or impossible to install wires or optical fiber. Many long-haul communications systems, such as satellite,

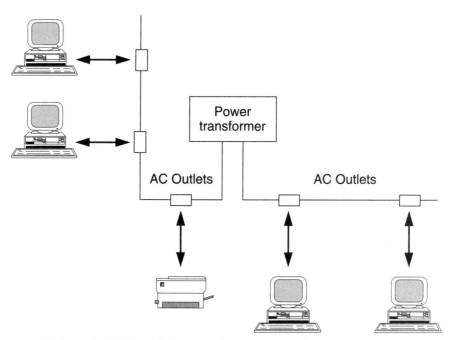

Figure 7.5 Concept of utilizing AC circuits to interconnect network components

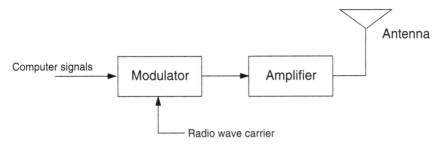

Figure 7.6 Radio wave system

LOS microwave, and packet radio, utilize radio waves as a transmission medium. There are also wireless LAN network interface cards and modems that utilize radio waves as the medium.

A radio wave system has an architecture as shown in Figure 7.6. The modulator mixes the source information signal with a radio wave carrier, and the result is coupled to an antenna. The modulated wave leaves the antenna and propagates through the atmosphere. The atmosphere causes the modulated wave to attenuate exponentially as the wave propagates farther away from the antenna. Therefore, the modulated wave must have enough power to reach the desired distance at an acceptable signal/noise level. The receiving station antenna couples the modulated wave into a demodulator, which derives the information signal from the radio wave carrier.

Antenna directivity

Figure 7.7 compares omnidirectional versus highly directional antennas. Broadcast radio wave systems, such as radio LANs and packet radio, use omnidirectional antennas that broadcast the radio signal in all different directions. Omnidirectional antennas provide relatively short ranges because the antenna spreads the signal power in all directions, minimizing the power in any specific direction. However, this is desired with most networks requiring mobility because it does not require realignment of antennas.

To maximize range, radio systems use antennas that produce a directive radio signal that adds gain to the signal transmission. These antennas focus the power into a narrow beamwidth aimed at the receiver. LOS microwave, satellite systems, and interbuilding wireless bridges utilize directive antennas to increase range between sources and destinations. The directive nature also increases the security of the signal, because is does not cover as much area as an omnidirectional system.

Modulation types

Modulation is a mixing of the information signal with a modulating waveform to transform the information signal into a form suitable for transmis-

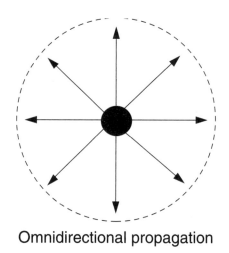

Omnidirectional propagation

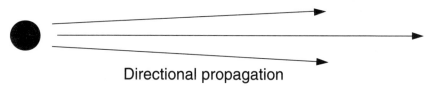

Directional propagation

Figure 7.7 Omnidirectional versus directive antennas

sion through a medium. Most radio wave networks use either spread spectrum or narrowband modulation.

Spread spectrum, developed originally by the military, spreads a signal's power over a wide band of frequencies. The main reason for spreading is that the signal then becomes much less susceptible to electrical noise and is less interfering with other radio-based systems. Most interfering noise is narrow in bandwidth; therefore, noise only interferes with a narrow part of the wideband spread spectrum signal. As a result, when the receiver despreads the signal, the resulting noise power is negligible. The reason spread spectrum systems don't cause much interference with other systems is that the spread signal is much lower in amplitude than conventional radio signals. Therefore, very little interference occurs.

Spread spectrum radio components use either direct sequence or frequency hopping for spreading the signal. Direct sequence modulates a radio carrier by a digital code with a bit rate much higher than the information signal bandwidth. Frequency hopping quickly hops the radio carrier from one frequency to another within a specific range.

Most radio LANs operate within the Industrial, Scientific, and Medicine (ISM) bands, which the Federal Communications Commission (FCC) authorized for wireless LANs in 1975. The ISM bands are located at 902 MHz, 2.400 GHz, and 5.7 GHz. Radio wave systems operating the ISM band must use spread spectrum modulation and must operate below one watt of output power. Commercial users who purchase ISM band products do not need to obtain or manage FCC licenses. This makes it easy to install and then relocate the bridge because you won't need to haggle with managing licenses. Because the ISM bands are open to the public, though, care must be taken to avoid radio interference with other devices operating in the ISM bands.

Radio wave issues

The use of radio waves offers many important advantages, such as support of long-haul communications and mobility. However, there are several issues to consider in implementing a radio wave medium. The two most important are security and interference.

In terms of security, the main difference between radio-based and wire-line networks is that a wireless network propagates the information signal power over a larger area. Because of this, an intruder can easily receive the radio signals at a significant and safe distance. However, an organization can easily prevent an intruder from decoding the data by using an encryption process.

Interference between two signals occurs when the two signals are present at the receiving station at the same time in frequency or phase (depending on how the receiver demodulates the signal). The FCC regulates the use of most frequency bands and modulation types to avoid the possibility of signal interference between systems. However, radio interference can still occur, especially with systems operating in license-free bands.

Radio signal interference might be inward or outward. Figure 7.8 illustrates this concept. When inward interference occurs, other system signals interfere with the radio transmission. This interference can cause errors to occur in the system, possibly causing retransmissions and unacceptable delay to the users. Significant inward interference might occur if another radio system is operating nearby with the same frequency and modulation type, such as two radio LANs operating in the license-free ISM bands within close proximity. Less significant inward interference could be caused by systems that generate harmonic frequencies within the ISM band.

Outward interference happens when the signals from the radio wave system interfere with other systems. As with inward interference, significant outward interference can occur if a wireless network is in close proximity to another system, where both systems utilize the same signal frequencies and modulation.

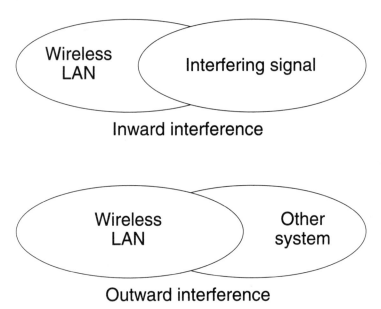

Inward interference

Outward interference

Figure 7.8 Inward and outward interference

Laser Light

Some wireless LANs and interbuilding products use laser light to carry information between computers. Laser systems have functional components very similar to optical fiber and radio systems. The laser modem mixes the information signal, which is typically digital, with a laser carrier. The result is a laser signal that changes intensity (on/off) according to the information signal.

Most laser modems produce light with a wavelength of 820 nm, just below the color of red. Under most lighting conditions, these laser beams are invisible to the naked eye. Laser light is naturally highly directive, producing a line-of-sight propagation pattern. Typical transmission distances with laser-based modems is 4,000 feet, which is relatively short because of limited laser power.

The advantage of an infrared connection, because of its very high frequency, is that it does not currently require special FCC or government licensing. In addition, it offers high data rate capability and very little interference with other emanating devices. Laser systems also provide a greater degree of privacy when compared to radio-based wireless techniques, because the laser light covers very little area while propagating to the destination. Thus, intruders would be forced to place themselves directly between the source and destination in order to receive the signal.

Diffused and direct laser are two main types of laser transmission. Figure 7.9 illustrates these two concepts. Diffused laser light is normally reflected off a wall or ceiling, and direct laser is directly focused in a line-of-sight fashion. Most laser LANs utilize diffused laser, and most interbuilding laser modems use the direct laser technique.

Infrared light is characteristic of very high bandwidth; however, the diffusing technique severely attenuates the signal and requires slow data transmissions (less than 1 Mbps) to avoid significant transmission errors. In addition, this technique limits wireless component spacing to around 40 feet, mainly because of geometry. The advantage, though, is relatively easy installation with inexpensive components.

The direct infrared approach intensifies the laser signal power in a manner similar to that of a directive radio wave antenna. This increases the range of low-power laser systems to a mile or so at data rates up in the Mbps.

Laser systems require more caution than radio wave systems. In the United States, the Center for Devices and Radiological Health (CDRH) of the U.S. Food and Drug Administration specifies four classes of lasers according to their ability to cause harm. These classes range from Class I, where there is no hazard whatsoever under any circumstances, to Class IV, where danger is always present. The CDRH rates most supermarket bar code scanners as Class I laser devices. An example of a Class IV device is a scalpel that surgeons use in laser surgery. The CDRH rates most laser net-

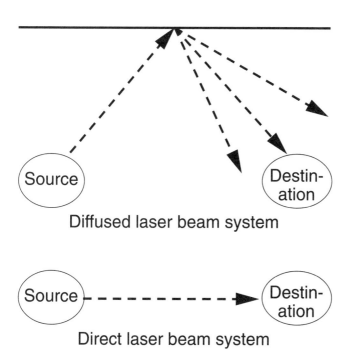

Figure 7.9 Diffused and direct laser systems

work devices as Class III, which have the potential of eye damage if someone looks directly at the beam. Thus, care should be taken when aligning the lasers during installation.

Medium Design Considerations

Designers should base the choice of medium on mobility requirements and data rate specifications. For the design, the team should determine which type of medium, such as twisted-pair, coaxial cable, or optical fiber, is necessary for every network segment. The team should also identify the standards that apply.

Most office LANs utilize twisted-pair wiring because it is the most flexible and least expensive. However, in general, focus on the following types of requirements and design specifications when selecting the type of medium:

Topography

Consider the distances between network elements and the number of users when choosing a medium type. For WANs, utilize the appropriate type of communications, as described in a later section. For interbuilding connections, examine the use of directive radio waves for typical applications and laser light for high bandwidth and high levels of privacy. The use of twisted-pair wire is most practical for LANs.

Mobility

For highly mobile LAN and WAN applications, utilize radio waves. Laser light might be best for portable situations.

Information flows

Ensure that the bandwidth of the chosen medium will support expected traffic patterns.

Security

Be sure to satisfy all needs to avoid the compromise of information during transmission on the medium. For corporate network backbones or highly secure data transfer, utilize optical fiber.

Environmental conditions

For areas having a high degree of electromagnetic interference, utilize optical fiber.

Regulations

Follow any company policies that call for the use of specific medium types.

Data rates

Be sure the medium will support data rate specifications.

Medium Access

Medium access techniques control the use of a common network medium, which is a data link layer function. Most medium access protocols work by allowing only one network device to send data on the medium at one time, avoiding collisions with other network devices. A network interface card normally implements the medium access technique. Two main types of medium access protocols are *carrier sense* and *token passing*.

Carrier Sense Access

Carrier sense access is based on a listen-before-talk protocol for regulating distributed access to a common medium. A common carrier sense protocol is Carrier Sense Multiple Access (CSMA), which provides distributed access to a bus-type network topology. With CSMA, each node has the capability of sensing transmissions from other nodes connected to the same network segment. For example, refer to Figure 7.10 which represents a network topology utilizing CSMA. If node A has data to send, then node A first checks (senses) if any other nodes are transmitting data. If the medium is clear (no transmission present), node A can transmit one frame of data. If node A senses transmissions from another node, then node A is blocked from transmitting and waits a random period of time before sensing the channel again. The sensing operation will continue until a node sends the frame or the node reaches a certain limit of retries.

With CSMA, collisions can occur even though the transmitting node senses the channel first before sending data. The factors contributing to these collisions is nonzero propagation time between nodes. Because of nonzero propagation time, the neighboring nodes are not blocked from transmitting until the transmission from a particular source node reaches all of its neighboring nodes. Once the transmitting signal has reached all neighbors, no collisions will occur because all nodes will be blocked. Hence, the vulnerability period (period of time when a collision might take place) because of nonzero propagation delay is the length of time the transmitting signal takes to propagate from the source node to the most distant neighboring node.

CSMA operates in an asynchronous form because a network device has no guarantee when it will be able to access the medium and send data. Therefore, packet transmissions with CSMA are not constant. This poses a problem for the transmission of real-time information, such as voice and video, because the network will not deliver pieces of information regularly enough.

The succeeding sections will describe common network carrier sense protocols.

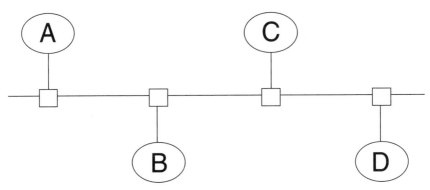

Figure 7.10 Bus topology utilizing a carrier sense protocol

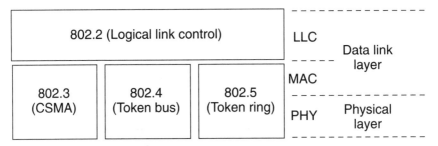

Figure 7.11 IEEE 802 standards hierarchy

IEEE 802.3

The IEEE 802.3 is a standard specifying the use of the CSMA protocol to provide access to a shared LAN medium, such as twisted-pair, coaxial cable, and optical fiber. This standard is normally called ethernet, and it is the predominant medium access standard in use today. Currently most organizations utilize the 10baseT version of ethernet, which specifies the use of twisted-pair wiring that supports baseband signals at 10 Mbps.

IEEE 802.3 fits into the overall IEEE standards hierarchy as shown in Figure 7.11. Notice IEEE split the data link layer into two layers, the logical link control (LLC) and medium access control (MAC) layer. The LLC, which is IEEE 802.2, provides link synchronization, whereas the MAC layer has functions related to sharing access to a common medium. Also, note that 802.3 specifies not only the medium access method but also the type of medium.

The 10 Mbps data rate of ethernet is misleading. A person cannot assume 10 Mbps will be available continuously between each network device. This is because network devices must access the network first before sending data, and under heavier network usage a device will probably have to wait before being able to send a data frame. Thus, this delay significantly decreases the effective aggregate data rate.

The IEEE 802.3 working group has formed the Higher Speed Ethernet Study Group to increase the performance of ethernet. The working group has established the following objectives for the new standard:

- 100 Mbps data rate

- Retention of the existing 802.3 frame format and error detection

- Twisted-pair wiring that conforms to EIA 568, building wiring standard

- Support of existing 10 Mbps data traffic

- Use of the ISO 8877 connector, which is similar to the existing the RJ-45 connector

Packet radio

Packet radio networks typically have a partially connected topology and employ a carrier sense access protocol. Therefore, the medium access method only pertains to the stations or nodes that share the same propagation space. For an illustration, refer to Figure 7.12. Nodes A, B, and C would compete for access to their common propagation space. Other node transmissions would not interfere with that space.

With packet radio systems, hidden nodes can pose a problem to CSMA protocols, mainly because of partial connectivity. As shown in Figure 7.13, a hidden node is established where two nodes (A and B) can both communicate with a third node (C) but cannot communicate with each other. Here, no direct connectivity exists between nodes A and B because of some

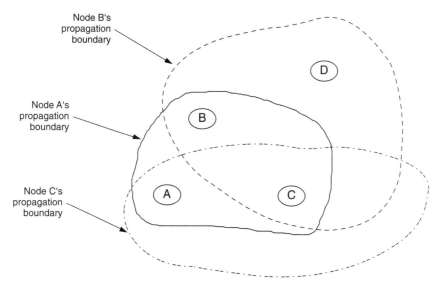

Figure 7.12 Topology of a packet radio network

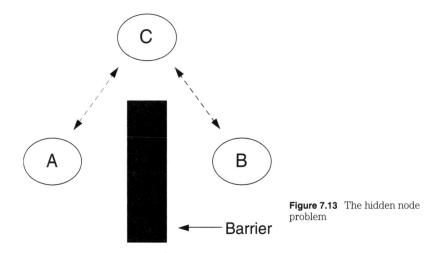

Figure 7.13 The hidden node problem

obstruction, although nodes A and B can both communicate directly with node C. This configuration causes problems with packet radio networks employing CSMA because of the following scenario.

Assume node B senses the media, finds it clear, and starts transmitting a packet. Node C will directly receive the transmission because nodes B and C have direct connectivity. But while node B is still transmitting, suppose node A senses the media, finds it clear, and starts transmitting a packet also. As a result, node C will start receiving garbage (i.e., a collision takes place at node C) because of the reception of two signals. Note that the transmission from node B never blocks node A; therefore, a packet radio network that has hidden nodes will suffer from a higher probability of collisions. In addition, the vulnerability period with the presence of hidden nodes is the time it takes to transmit a packet.

The Busy-Tone Multiple-Access (BTMA) technique can counter the problem of hidden nodes in a packet radio network. BTMA is similar to CSMA, except that BTMA employs a mechanism to alleviate the collisions hidden nodes cause. With BTMA, a node broadcasts a busy tone on a separate channel if it is currently receiving a packet. Each neighboring node will receive this tone, and the tone will inhibit the neighboring nodes from transmitting. Again, assume the hidden node problem where two nodes (A and B) can both communicate with a third node (C), but cannot communicate with each other. Assume node B starts transmitting with a packet destined for node C. When node C first detects the incoming signal, node C broadcasts a busy tone on a separate channel. Node A, being a neighbor of node C, will receive the tone, which will inhibit node A from transmitting a new packet. Therefore, the relatively long vulnerability period encountered in CSMA with hidden nodes is greatly reduced because the vulnerability period between hidden nodes with BTMA is two propagation hops. Thus, the addition of the busy tone to CSMA will significantly decrease the number of collisions when hidden nodes are present.

Radio LAN

Radio-based wireless LANs use the CSMA protocol to allow a group of computers to share the same radio frequency and space. For radio LANs, the medium access method must support a topology as shown in Figure 7.14. The operation of a radio LAN is very similar to ethernet. A radio LAN does not have to hop packets to the destination because the network generally has full-connectivity among nodes. In addition, radio LANs do not employ BTMA because the hidden node problem seldom exists.

Diffused laser LAN

With a diffused laser LAN, each computer uses an infrared transceiver aimed at a centralized place on the ceiling. As shown earlier (Figure 7.9), laser light reflects off the ceiling for each node to receive data from other nodes. Diffused laser LANs use the same carrier sensing principles that apply to ethernet and radio-based CSMA. The CSMA protocol ensures that only one station can transmit data at a time.

Token Passing

The token passing medium access method ensures that only one node can transmit within a given time through the use of a token. A token, which is a

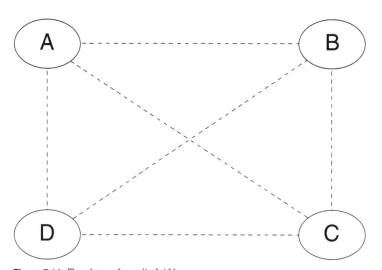

Figure 7.14 Topology of a radio LAN

small group of data bits, is circulated from station-to-station. A node can send data to another only if the sending node has acquired the token. Because there is one token, only one node can transmit during any interval of time.

Token passing protocols are more stable under heavy loads than carrier sense protocols. Therefore, designers utilizing a token passing protocol can specify the system in such a way to offer acceptable and predictable delays even at maximum load. This allows token passing networks to operate in a synchronous or isochronous mode, which will effectively support real-time information transmissions.

Most token-passing protocols are either token ring or token bus.

Token ring protocols

As shown in Figure 7.15, a token ring network consists of a physical ring topology in which stations are connected by point-to-point links. A token circulates the ring, periodically passing by each station. If a station wants to transmit a frame, the station "removes" the token from the ring by not re-peating the token. After a station captures the token, the station might transmit for a short amount of time then relinquish the token and send it to the next station downline. The order of token passing for a ring topology is fixed and is dependent on the order of connections.

Each token ring node constantly monitors data passing by its connection and continually looks for frames with its address in the destination field of each frame. If a node detects an incoming frame, the node copies the data into its memory and continually repeats the frame downstream with an ac-knowledgment (if received okay) attached to the end of the frame. After the frame circulates the ring and returns to the sending station, the sender removes (does not repeat) the frame. If the frame has not been acknowl-edged, the sending station will retransmit it.

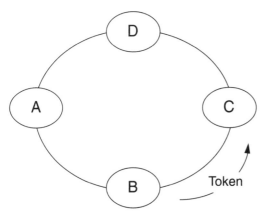

Figure 7.15 Illustration of a ring token network

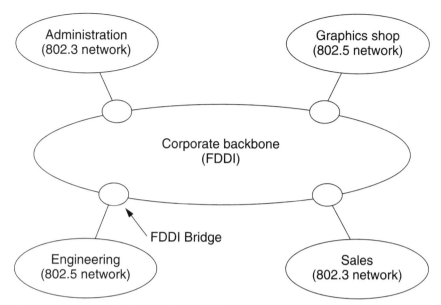

Figure 7.16 Corporate backbone utilizing FDDI

Common standards that specify token ring protocols are IEEE 802.5 (token ring) and ANSI FDDI.

IEEE 802.5. The IEEE 802.5 standard specifies a 4- and 16-Mbps token ring LAN. Each station might hold the token for a period of time decided upon during initialization of the network. While holding the token, the station can transmit frames until its token holding time has expired. IEEE 802.5 offers a priority scheme that supports different classes of traffic.

IEEE 802.5 is the second most popular LAN medium access technique. 802.5 supports heavier traffic under more stable conditions than 802.3 ethernet. In addition, 802.5 can handle synchronous-type information transfers.

ANSI FDDI. The Fiber Data Distributed Interface (FDDI) is an ANSI standard specifying a 100-Mbps dual token ring LAN. FDDI specifies the use of optical fiber medium and will support simultaneous transmission of both synchronous and prioritized asynchronous traffic. There is a version of FDDI called CDDI (Copper Data Distributed Interface) which specifies the transmission of FDDI signals over level 5 twisted-pair wiring. FDDI is effective in providing a corporate backbone as shown in Figure 7.16. Other networks can interface into the FDDI backbone through FDDI bridges.

FDDI supports both synchronous and asynchronous data transmission. Synchronous transmission ensures that each node can transmit within a definite time period. The synchronous mode is used for those applications whose bandwidth and response time limits are predictable in advance, permitting them to be preallocated by the FDDI Station Management Protocol. Asynchronous transmission is sporadic, and there is no guarantee when a node might transmit. The asynchronous mode is used for those applications whose bandwidth requirements are less predictable or whose response time requirements are less critical. Asynchronous bandwidth is instantaneously allocated from a pool of remaining ring bandwidth that is unallocated, unused, or both.

ANSI is currently active in the development of FDDI II, which is an upwardly compatible extension to FDDI. FDDI II will have two modes. The Basic Mode is identical to FDDI; therefore, it will accommodate both asynchronous and synchronous traffic. The Hybrid Mode will incorporate the functionality of basic mode plus circuit switching. The addition of circuit switching will allow the support of isochronous traffic. Isochronous transmission is similar to synchronous, but with isochronous a node is capable of sending data at specific times. This simplifies the transmission of real-time information because of decreased source buffering and signal processing.

In 1990, ANSI initiated the FDDI Follow-On LAN (FFOL) Project to develop the next generation of high-speed local area network protocols. Goals of these projects are to develop a network architecture that will match the payload of SONET (Synchronous Optical NETwork), support data rates up to one Gbps, and provide backup communication links for reliability. The resulting FFOL network will support FDDI traffic, but it will probably not incorporate FDDI architecture. Much of the work for FFOL is in early stages of development.

Token bus protocols

As shown in Figure 7.17, a token bus network consists of a physical bus topology. A token is sent in a logical ring from station to station in some predefined order, normally in sequential order based on each station's address. As with token ring, each node constantly monitors data passing by its connection and continually "looks" for frames with its address in the destination field of each frame. If a node detects a frame addressed to itself, that station copies the frame into its memory.

If a station wants to transmit a frame, the station must first receive the token. After a station captures the token, the station might transmit data for a period of time determined during network initialization. When a node is finished transmitting frames, it transmits the token to the next node on the bus.

An advantage of token bus protocols is that token passing order can be easily changed without making physical changes. For this reason, manufacturing plants can effectively utilize token bus protocols they make it easy to retool the manufacturing process. However, network reconfiguration with token bus is more complex with the token bus protocol. Periodically, a sta-

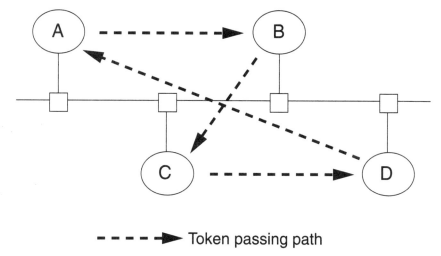

Token passing path

Figure 7.17 Illustration of token bus protocol

tion holding the token will solicit a bid for inactive stations to join the ring. Nodes are only allowed to join with an address that falls between that of the token holder and the current successor to the token holder. A node leaving the ring simply sends its predecessor a message identifying the address of its new successor.

IEEE 802.4. IEEE 802.4 is a token bus standard that operates at 10 Mbps. There are very few off-the-shelf products that implement the 802.4 standard. In fact, 802.4 is almost always embedded in other systems systems.

Network Interface Cards

The network interface card (NIC), consisting of primarily hardware and firmware, provides the interface between network elements and the medium. Network interface cards employ the medium access functions. Therefore, the NIC is a component that directly satisfies the preliminary medium access design specification. Figure 7.18 illustrates a NIC.

Most NICs are equipped with a 10baseT connection and an AUI (Attachment Unit Interface) connector. The 10baseT plug couples the card to twisted pair media, and the AUI is a standard interface that interfaces the NIC to other medium types via a transceiver.

Medium Access Design Considerations

The design team should select an appropriate medium access method based primarily on the type of information flow requirements and synchro-

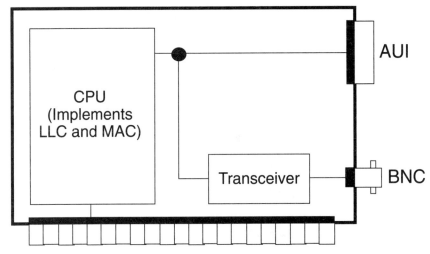

Figure 7.18   Illustration of a network interface card (NIC)

nization specifications. The team should also identify standards. Designers should focus on the following types of requirements and design specifications when selecting the type of medium access method.

Information flows

Utilize ethernet for pure data information types under normal loads. For high network utilization, consider the use of token passing protocols because they will offer more stability under this circumstance. For high-speed corporate backbones, consider the use of FDDI.

Regulations

Abide by company policies to use a specific medium access technique.

Network operating system

Network operating systems support various types of NIC drivers, such as IPX, ODI, IPXODI, NDIS, NETBIOS, and TCP/IP. Designers should make sure that there is a driver available that interfaces the network operating system to the NIC.

Synchronization

Utilize a medium access method that is most suitable for the specified type of synchronization. For example, ethernet will satisfy most asynchronous forms of synchronization, and token ring or token bus provide higher levels of synchronization.

Hardware platform

Be sure to choose a NIC that matches the hardware platform's bus interface, such as PCMCIA, ISA, EISA, NDIS, MCA, Windows NT, or UNIX. Also, utilize a high performance NIC in servers.

Operational support

The chosen NIC must support any chosen network management protocols, such as SNMP or CMIP.

Data rate

Ensure that the chosen medium access method will support data rate specifications. For high speed asynchronous transmission, consider using the 100-Mbps version of ethernet. For relatively high-speed synchronous information flow, utilize either IEEE 802.5 token ring or FDDI.

Addressing

All network devices must have addresses, distinguishing network elements from all other network elements. The network interface devices, such as network interface cards (NICs), are designed to respond to a particular physical address which the interface device continually monitors. If the network interface discovers its address within a data frame, it will hand the frame over to the proper application for processing.

Physical Versus Logical Addresses

All IEEE 802.3 ethernet NICs come with a unique, unchangeable physical address, programmed in during manufacturing of the NIC. The NIC will understand and respond only to data frames carrying the physical address. Often, applications must utilize internetworking protocols enabling the interconnection of different types of networks. For this case, each network connection is usually assigned a globally unique and logical address. The network will utilize the global address for routing the data packets across the internetwork until the packet arrives at the destination network. The global address, such as an Internet Protocol (IP) address, is normally different than the physical address the network interface is listening for. Therefore, a mechanism must map the logical addresses to the corresponding physical addresses. This is often handled by the Routing Information Protocol (RIP).

Internet Addressing

IP addressing is the most common method of ensuring that all network connections have a unique address. These addresses correspond to network connections, not necessarily the actual device. For example, a network device such as a server could have three NICs. This would require three IP addresses, because there are three network connections.

As shown in Figure 7.19, there are three classes of IP addresses: Class A, Class B, and Class C, based on a 32-bit address. Each IP address has a network and host portion. An organization normally is assigned a specific network address and has the freedom to assign the host portion as desired.

The Network Information Center (NIC) in Menlo Park, California, manages and assigns all IP addresses. Because of the dramatic increase in use of the Internet, unused 32-bit addresses are becoming rare. Therefore, the Internet Society is revising this structure to accommodate more addresses.

Address Design Considerations

The design team should specify addressing by developing an addressing plan that effectively describes the format and assignment of unique addresses to network devices. Most components on the network will require a unique address. The design team must carefully plan the use of addresses to make sure that no more than one network device has the same address. Duplicate addresses would cause lots of problems. In the case of IP addressing, the address plan should identify proper address masking to partition networks within the IP network address domain.

Designers should primarily choose an addressing plan to satisfy the following types of requirements and design specifications:

Topography

Designers should base address assignments on the location of network devices. To facilitate effective routing and easier disbursement of addresses, utilize a hierarchical address structure.

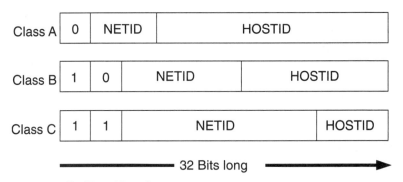

Figure 7.19 IP address hierarchy

Existing systems

Be sure to take into account any current addressing schemes for existing systems.

Mobility

Ensure that the address plan covers the anticipated movement of subnets.

Topology

Utilize the definition of subnets to form a hierarchical address structure.

Switching

Switching is a network function that enables transmission of data packets across a network having partial direct connectivity. Traditionally, switching techniques apply to WANs, decreasing the number of expensive long-haul links necessary to connect networks over a large geographical area. LANs normally do not require switching, but incorporating switching in a LAN can increase performance. Circuit switching and packet switching are the two primary types of switching.

Circuit Switching

With circuit switching, there must be a dedicated physical path between two nodes before these nodes can send data back and forth to each other. A series of links could compose the path, but these links are available only for communications between the specific pairs of nodes. Typically, circuit switching allows a steady, uninterrupted stream of data to flow between source and destination.

Packet Switching

The concepts of packet switching are as follows. The source divides its data into packets and sends the packets separately through the network to the destination. With packet switching, communication between the source and the destination does not require dedicated physical paths. Packets traveling between a pair of nodes share the links with other node pairs.

Virtual circuit and datagram are two types of packet switching.

Virtual circuit service

With virtual circuit service, there is a virtual circuit in place between the source and the destination. This is often called connection-oriented packet switching, because there must be an established connection between the source and the destination before the source can send data. The "circuit" in virtual circuit packet switching is not a physical circuit. Instead, a virtual circuit is composed of directions residing at each node (router) that tell data packets which way to go, depending on the destination address in the packet.

Datagram service

Datagram service, which is sometimes called "connectionless," is a form of packet switching whereby the source does not need to establish a connection with the destination before sending data packets. Instead, the source can immediately start sending data packets to the destination, and the packets travel independently to the destination. The routers will direct the packets based on its current routing table entries. Automated routing protocols update the routing tables as the network topology changes or congestion occurs in parts of the network. Therefore, a group of related packets could take different routes and could arrive at the destination out of order. The destination must reorder the packets after receiving them.

Many switching protocols utilize packet switching concepts. Some of the most common packet switching protocols and standards are X.25 and frame relay. A later paragraph on long-haul communications discusses these protocols.

Routing

Switching depends largely on the ability of intermediate nodes to route data and control packets across the network. The goal of routing is to provide the "least cost" route for data to reach a specified destination. Most networks that employ switching utilize protocols that automatically update routing tables at each node. These routing protocols should be able to adapt well to changes in the network's traffic load and topology.

Most routing protocols store routing information in tables that show which outgoing line should be chosen, based on the destination address located in the packet. Figure 7.20 is an example of a routing table for node A of the network shown. Routing tables can be static or dynamic. If the tables are static, the routing protocol is classified as nonadaptive; that is, the table entries do not change. Dynamic (adaptive) routing algorithms update the tables according to changes in network topology and traffic.

Routing protocols take the form of being distributed, isolated, or centralized.

Distributed routing

With distributed routing, each node (router) periodically identifies neighboring nodes, updates its routing table, and then, based on this information,

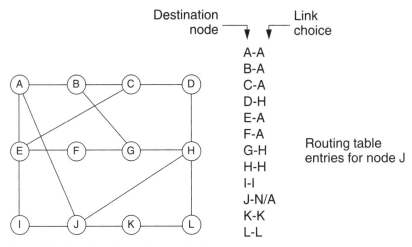

Figure 7.20   Sample routing table for node A

sends its routing table to all of its neighbors. Because each node follows the same process, complete network topology information propagates through the network and eventually reaches each node. Each node can then determine the best route by referring to its routing table, which contains topology information.

Distributed routing is the most common form of routing, and it has proven to be very robust and reliable with the Internet. Distributed routing is very survivable because there is no single point of failure. To decrease protocol overhead, routing information is normally "piggybacked" on normal information-carrying packets.

Isolated routing

In isolated routing, each node in the network independently determines its routing table entries by gathering routing information through nonobtrusive methods. That is, specialized routing control packets are not needed. Three classical approaches of isolated routing are flooding, hot potato, and backward learning.

With the pure flooding technique, each node within the network examines incoming packets and, if the packet has not reached its destination and a hop counter within the header of the packet has not expired, the node retransmits the packet on every outgoing line. In the case of a broadcast medium, the packet is simply retransmitted. Because every node follows this same process, the packet will eventually reach its destination.

The hop counter maintains the stability of the routing algorithm. The source node initially sets the hop count to some predetermined value (based on the maximum number of hops between source and destination), and intermediate nodes decrement the hop count by one before retransmiting the packet. If a node receives a packet with a hop count of zero, the node does not retransmit the packet.

To reduce the vast amount of overhead generated by flooding, each node can maintain a somewhat vague routing table so the node will at least put the packets on queues leading in the general direction of the destination. This is referred to as selective flooding.

Flooding is an effective routing technique with networks having rapidly changing connectivity. This reasoning stems from the fact that flooding does not require routing updates as the network changes. In addition, flooding, because of its nature, offers the least number of hops from source to destination.

The hot potato routing method bases routing decisions on the availability of outgoing queues within the current node. Pure hot potato will put an incoming packet in the outgoing queue having the least number of packets waiting for transmission. Thus, the current node treats the packet as a "hot potato" by getting rid of it as soon as possible, without regard to where the packet goes next. Eventually, the packet will reach its destination.

Static routing, which uses routing table entries that do not change, can effectively utilize hot potato by putting a packet on the second best (or lesser) choice output queue if the most favorable output queue has more than a certain number of packets waiting for transmission. As a result, congestion will be kept to a minimum on the best-choice lines.

With backward learning, each packet sent contains a source and a destination address, and a hop counter. The hop counter is initially set to zero and increments each time a node forwards a packet. The objective of backward learning is for each node to base its routing table entries on which port it notices packets coming in on, with the least number of hops, from the particular destinations. For updating routing tables, each node constantly monitors the incoming packets by noting their source addresses, hop counts, and addresses of the immediately preceding nodes. Using this information, a node can make educated decisions on which node to send outgoing packets to. A node, needing to send a packet to a particular destination, would transmit the packet to the node from which the most recent packets came with the smallest hop counts and originated from the destination node. Of course, this assumes network conditions are approximately the same in both directions.

Isolated routing is very survivable because it has no single point of failure. In addition, it maintains low network overhead because the routing algorithm does not require control packets in addition to the data packets. The protocol utilizes very few bits in each data packet. The concept of isolated routing seems desirable in packet radio networks, because of the low amount of overhead needed for adaptively updating routing tables.

Centralized routing

In centralized routing, a single entity (a Routing Control Center, or RCC) gathers connectivity information, determines the most efficient routes between all nodes, and distributes the routing table updates to all nodes. With centralized routing, each node monitors connectivity and delay metrics with its neighboring nodes and periodically sends this information to the RCC. The RCC, after using an algorithm that determines the best routes, sends each of the nodes new routing table entries depending on the current state of the network. Thus, with centralized routing, routing decisions are made by a physically centralized source (RCC) and distributed to all the nodes.

In the case of virtual circuits, a source node, needing to send a stream of packets, can notify the RCC of the source and destination. The RCC will respond with a special call request packet (called a needle packet) that contains the route that makes up the most efficient virtual circuit. The source node then sends the needle packet through the network to set up the virtual circuit, and then data packets can follow.

Although centralized routing offers a solution to adaptive routing, this technique has peculiar disadvantages worth discussing. For one, centralized routing requires a large amount of overhead due to the routing operations sent back and forth between the nodes and the RCC. As a result, centralized routing might not be suitable for some networks operating with limited bandwidth. Also, large networks having many nodes will require the RCC to grind through many calculations to determine the optimum routes for the network, thus taking a considerable amount of time. Therefore, the "optimum" table entries might not be valid if the network continually changes rapidly. In fact, the updates might even degrade the performance of the network.

Because of its centralized nature, the RCC becomes extremely vulnerable. Failure of the RCC will cease the adaptive operation of the routing algorithm, unless there are provisions for a backup RCC. Thus, the centralized technique normally also offers low survivability because of vulnerability of the RCC. In case of an RCC failure, the nodes in the network can revert back to some predetermined static routing table if no word has been received from the RCC (or its successor) after a certain period of time. In addition, all the nodes in the network periodically send connectivity information to the RCC; therefore, a great deal of traffic accumulates near the RCC. The heavy traffic burden near the RCC can cause congestion for legitimate data packets, thus increasing network delay.

Switching Design Considerations

If the modification encompasses a WAN, then the design team should define an appropriate switching technique, such as circuit switching or packet switching. As stated at the beginning of this section, LANs have predominately used nonswitched techniques, offering economical connections for local computers. However, newer applications demand a great deal of bandwidth, motivating many organizations to adopt LAN switches in place of traditional repeaters. For instance, ethernet LAN switches can provide all network devices with a dedicated 10-Mbps link. This tremendously increases network bandwidth and utilizes existing cabling and network interface cards.

Long-Haul Communications

Communications is the action of passing information from one point to another, which is a main function of the network. For LANs, the medium and medium access protocols facilitate communications. For example, an ethernet network utilizing twisted-pair wiring will support communications between network elements, such as clients, servers, and printers. WANs, however, typically utilize long-haul communications systems to support communications between network nodes. Most of these long-haul communication systems are available on a fee-for-service basis from Regional Bell Operating Companies (RBOCs). Figure 7.21 illustrates the concept of long-haul communications.

Plain Old Telephone System

The Plain Old Telephone System (POTS) is the common telephone system developed many years ago for voice communications. POTS can support low-speed (less than 50 Kbps) data communications between network devices through the use of modems. Modems interface digital computers to the analog telephone lines, making use of the widely available telephone system to provide communications between network elements on a worldwide basis. The main drawback of using modems is the limited bandwidth of the telephone system, which was designed to carry voice and not high-speed data traffic. A typical modem is capable of operating at 19.2 Kbps, but higher-speed modems are becoming more and more available.

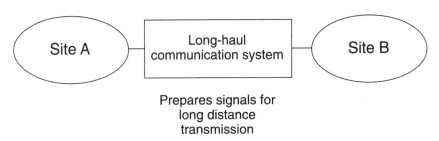

Figure 7.21 Illustration of a long-haul communications system

56-Kbps Digital Circuits

Most telephone companies offer leased circuits for the transmission of 56-Kbps digital signals. These circuits provide a fairly reliable link for data and digitized voice. However, organizations must pay for the use of the leased circuit whether they use it or not. Digital Service Units interface computers and network devices to a 56-Kbps digital line.

Integrated Services Digital Network

The Integrated Services Digital Network (ISDN) is a collection of CCITT standards specifying digital transmission service. The overall goal of ISDN is to provide a single physical network outlet and transport mechanism for the transmission of all types of information, including data, video, and voice. Figure 7.22 identifies the types of ISDN services. The current implementation of ISDN networks primarily supports fairly low speed data

The present ISDN networks are referred to as *Narrowband ISDN* (N-ISDN). To meet the growing need for bandwidth, CCITT is working on an upgrade to ISDN, called *Broadband ISDN* (B-ISDN). With B-ISDN, the maximum transfer rates will be 155.52 Mbps and 622.08 Mbps. B-ISDN will facilitate an effective integration of voice, video and data information.

X.25

X.25 operates in a connection-oriented mode at 64 Kbps. X.25 is a very robust packet switching protocol that was developed by CCITT in the 1970's, during a time when error rates on transmission media were relatively high. As a result, X.25 was developed to include excellent error control mechanisms, and to be capable of being used with many types of networks. Circuit establishment with X.25 is accomplished using in-band circuit control; that is, control and data packets travel across the same circuits. Thus, the advantage of X.25 is robustness. However, it operates at fairly low data rates.

Frame Relay

In the years since the development of X.25, error rates have dropped on most media, mainly because of the widespread use of optical fiber and the incorporation of better signaling methods. Frame relay, standardized by ANSI, is a streamlined version of X.25 offering a fast packet connection-oriented network interface with bit rates up to 2 Mbps. To achieve this higher data rate, frame relay uses out-of-band signaling and no error or flow control. With frame relay, higher layer protocols must provide error control. Typically, a frame relay service provider will supply a router that interfaces an organization between ethernet and the frame relay WAN.

A. Channel-4 KHz telephone channel

B. Channel-64 Kbps digital channel

C. Channel-8 or 16 Kbps digital channel

D. Channel-16 or 64 Kbps digital channel (out of band signaling)

E. Channel-64 Kbps digital channel (internal ISDN signaling)

Figure 7.22 Integrated services digital network (ISDN) services

The Frame Relay Forum, established in 1991, is an association of vendors, carriers, users, and consultants committed to the implementation of frame relay in accordance with national and international standards. The Forum's technical committees take existing standards, which are not sufficient for full interoperability, and create Implementation Agreements (IAs). These IAs represent the specific manner(s) in which standards will be applied, thus helping to ensure interoperability. The Forum's marketing committees are also chartered with worldwide market development, through education as to the benefits of frame relay technology.

Switched Multimegabit Digital Service

Switched Multimegabit Digital Service (SMDS) offers connectionless packet switching data service for WANs. As a result, SMDS does not require permanent relationships between end points of the network. SMDS currently supplies 56-Kbps connections; however, T1 speeds might be available in the future. SMDS defines a user interface based on the IEEE 802.6 Metropolitan Area Network (MAN) standard. Several carriers offer leased SMDS service.

The SMDS Interest Group (SIG), which started in 1990, is an industry association of service providers, equipment manufacturers, users, and others working cooperatively to speed the proliferation and interoperability of SMDS services, products, and applications. The SIG develops technical specifications, promotes awareness of SMDS, stimulates new applications for SMDS, and ensures worldwide service interoperability together with its international affiliates.

Asynchronous Transfer Mode

Asynchronous Transfer Mode (ATM) is cell-based and offers high-speed (up to Gbps range), connection-oriented data service. ATM integrates circuit and packet switching to handle both constant and burst information. Therefore, ATM can support the integration of voice, video, and data. Most ATM networks are owned and operated by the using organization. Many companies sell ATM switches and software.

The ATM Forum, which formed in 1991, is an international nonprofit organization formed with the objective of accelerating the use of ATM products and services through a rapid convergence of interoperability specifications. In addition, the Forum promotes industry cooperation and awareness. Currently, the ATM Forum consists of more than 500 member companies, and it remains open to any organization which is interested in speeding up the availability of ATM-based solutions.

T1

T1, originally developed by Bell Labs for digital telephone transmission, specifies a time division multiplexing scheme for transmission of digital signals. As shown in Figure 7.23, T1 consists of a continuous transmission of 193-bit data frames, each containing one synchronization bit and 8-bit samples of 24 separate communications channels. Based on original sampling requirements for digital voice communications, T1 can deliver data signals at a data rate of 1.544 Mbps. Telephone carriers in most areas will lease T1 services to organizations. Many organizations currently use T1 service for relatively high-speed data transmission between sites. Fractional T1 service offers independent 64 Kbps channels.

Satellite Transmission

By incorporating active radio repeaters in man-made, earth-orbiting satellites, it is possible to provide broadcast and point-to-point communications

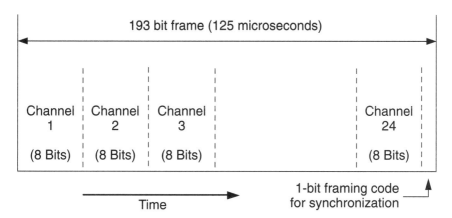

Figure 7.23 T1 frame structure

over large areas of the earth's surface. Figure 7.24 illustrates this concept. The broadcast capability of the satellite repeater is unique and, by suitable selection of satellite antenna patterns, it can be arranged to cover a well-defined area.

Satellites are located at various points in the geostationary orbit, depending on the system mission requirement. To obtain global coverage, a minimum of three satellites is required, but to obtain reasonably constant RF signal levels, four satellites are employed. The higher number also provides some freedom in positioning them.

With satellite communications, frequencies which are favorable in terms of power efficiency, minimal propagation distortions, and minimal susceptibility to noise and interference are used. Unfortunately, terrestrial systems tend to favor these frequencies as well. Space is an international domain; thus satellite frequencies are controlled by the ITU.

The band of frequencies between 450 MHz and 20 GHz is the most suitable for an earth-space-earth radio link. It is not practical to establish links to an earth terminal at frequencies higher than 20 GHz, when the terminal is located in a region that typically experiences heavy rainfall, if an availability better than 99.5% is required (unless some special provisions are provided).

For all operating bands, the lowest frequency spectrum is used for the downlink because it has the most severe power constraints. Lower frequencies are less sensitive to free space attenuation when compared to the

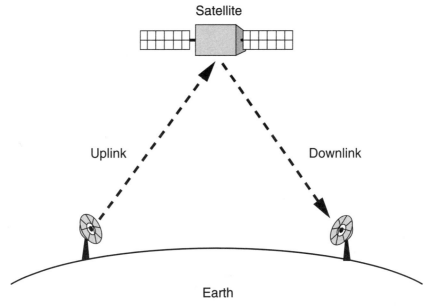

Figure 7.24 Satellite system

higher uplink frequencies. Losses are easier to overcome in the uplink with the higher transmit power available at the earth station.

The satellite acts as a signal repeater. Signals sent to it on the uplink are rebroadcast back to earth on the downlink. The device that handles this action is referred to as a *transponder*. The satellite transponder (receivers, translators, transmitters) is analogous to a repeater in a terrestrial communications link; it must receive, amplify, and retransmit signals from earth terminals. A satellite transponder is capable of acting as a transponder for one or more RF communications links.

Low-altitude satellites, which can have circular, polar or inclined orbits, have periods of less than twenty-four hours. These orbits are useful for surveillance purposes, and can be used to provide communications at extreme north and south latitudes.

One type of orbit of special interest to communications is the geostationary orbit. A satellite in such an orbit will have a twenty-four-hour period at an altitude of 22,300 miles, and will remain over a fixed location on the equator. As a result, the satellite will appear motionless to an observer on the earth. Actually, the satellite does not remain truly fixed. Even if the orbit were perfectly circular, perfectly placed in the equatorial plane, and at precisely the right altitude, natural perturbations due to low-level lunar and planetary gravitational fields and solar radiation pressure would induce slight drifts in the orbit. This slow and minor drift is corrected from time-to-time by small onboard thrusters activated by ground command.

A single geostationary satellite can illuminate in excess of one third of the earth's surface. As a result, a constellation of three satellites can provide global coverage except for a small area at extreme north and south latitudes. Antennas providing a coverage of one third of the earth's surface are (with considerable semantic inaccuracy) referred to as "earth" or "global-coverage" antennas. If communication is to be provided between areas serviced by the three satellites, a terrestrial repeater is provided at a location from which both satellites are visible.

The geostationary orbit has many desirable features. A major advantage is the simplification of tracking requirements. A "stationary" satellite permits continuous availability to all stations within its zone of coverage. A communication satellite in geostationary orbit provides a facility capable of instantaneous transmission of multichannel wide-band signals among widely dispersed ground stations. A relatively small number of such satellites can handle all commercial intercontinental traffic and satisfy the bulk of global military communication requirements. One disadvantage of this orbit is that it provides only minimum acceptable coverage at latitudes above or below approximately 71°.

Because of the long RF path involved (approximately 22,300 statute miles from an earth terminal to a satellite in geostationary orbit), a transmission delay of (typically) 119 milliseconds is experienced between an earth terminal and the satellite. This results in an approximate earth terminal to earth terminal delay of 238 ms. This causes the system to be very inefficient for use with protocols that require a response after each packet of information is transmitted before transmitting the next packet (it would take approximately 0.5 seconds to transmit each packet). Most networking protocols do not work efficiently over satellite sinks, because the protocols expect timely acknowledgments from the destination.

Line-of-Sight Microwave

Line of Sight (LOS) microwave transmission is an essential part of everyday communications. Almost every phone call, data transmission, and TV program eventually crosses a microwave system. Figure 7.25 illustrates the concept of microwave LOS.

LOS microwave signals follow what is known as a line-of-sight path. LOS characterizes a direct, open-air transmission path that is free of obstructions. Microwave links normally operate in the 1–15 GHz range, but can go as high as 30 GHz. The output power of the transmitter varies depending on several factors, but in most cases it is between 0.25 watts and 10 watts (typically, 2–5W). The output of the transmitter can be allowed to escape directly into free space, as is the case when it is mounted directly on the antenna, or more often, into a waveguide or coaxial cable, which is then connected to the antenna.

The purpose of the antenna is to couple the microwave energy produced by the transmitter to free space in the direction of the receiver's antenna. Microwave communications requires very high gain antennas. Several different antenna designs provide this gain requirement, but the parabolic reflector (dish) is most commonly used.

LOS repeaters fall into two basic categories: passive and regenerative. A passive repeater is used to redirect signals over or around path obstructions. There are two types of passive repeaters in use: two parabolic antennas back-to-back and a flat "billboard" type. The back-to-back type is seldom used because of its inefficiency. The flat type acts like a mirror for the transmitter and receiver, mainly to get around obstructions. However, noise is accumulative because the signals are not regenerated.

A regenerative repeater receives, reshapes, and reamplifies the signals before retransmitting them to the next repeater or receiver. Noise and distortion (for digital transmissions) are largely removed in the regeneration process. Repeaters are normally spaced 20–30 miles apart, but with proper conditions, 60-mile shots are feasible. It is common to see LOS microwave towers containing the repeaters scattered across the continental United States.

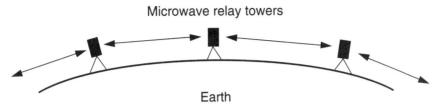

Microwave relay towers

Earth

Figure 7.25 Line of Sight microwave system

Meteor Burst Communications

Meteor burst communications can provide long-haul (1,500 mile), wireless data transmission links. The concept of meteor burst communications is shown in Figure 7.26. Every day, billions of tiny microscopic meteors enter the Earth's atmosphere. As these meteors penetrate the atmosphere at a very high altitude, they ionize into a gas. The idea of meteor burst communications is to direct a 40- to 50-MHz radio wave, modulated with a data signal, at this ionized gas. The radio signal then reflects off the gas and is directed back to Earth. Meteor burst equipment can receive the reflected signals up to a thousand miles away. Meteor burst communication supports mainly low data rates (300–2,400 bps), but it is relatively inexpensive.

Packet Radio

Packet radio offers long-haul data transmission capability through the utilization of radio waves. A typical packet radio system contains nodes consisting of a radio, an antenna, a terminal node controller (TNC), and an attached communication device. The radio and antenna provide connections with other stations through the atmosphere by broadcasting and receiving data packets. Thus, the radio acts as a transceiver. The concept of a packet radio node is shown in Figure 7.27. The broadcast frequency of the radio depends on the network design, as will be shown later, but frequencies typically fall in the HF, UHF, VHF, or SHF bands. Most packet radio systems operate at less than 50 Kbps.

   The TNC is the interface between a user's communication device (typically a personal computer) and the radio. The TNC acts as a buffer so that data packets, incoming from another station, can be stored without interrupting the attached communication device. In addition, the TNC normally has the ability to analyze a packet header to determine if the packet needs forwarding, or whether it has reached its destination.

   A typical packet radio network operates as follows. An attached communication device transfers data to the TNC, which partitions the data into packets and stores the packets in a queue. The TNC attempts to gain access

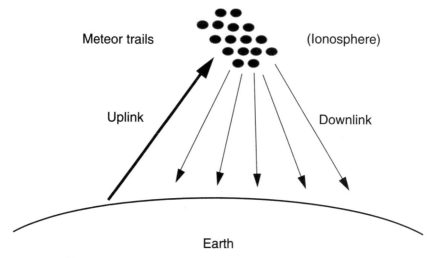

Figure 7.26 Meteor burst communications system

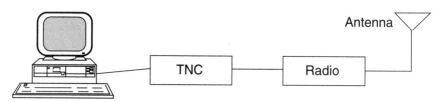

Figure 7.27 Concept of a packet radio node

to the media by using the radio and a carrier sense protocol. Once the TNC obtains media access, the TNC instructs the radio to broadcast a waiting packet. If the source station does not have direct connections with the destination, intermediate stations will receive and retransmit the packet until the packet reaches the destination.

Cellular Digital Packet Data (CDPD)

Cellular Digital Packet Data (CDPD) is a standard specifying how to send relatively low-speed data over analog cellular telephone networks. The CDPD standard was first released from the CDPD Forum in 1993. CDPD does not use primary voice channels to send data. It sends data over unused channels. However, voice traffic is given a higher priority. As a result, CDPD data signals switch to another unused channel if voice traffic becomes present. CDPD operates up to 19.2 Kbps and is best for bursty data signals.

Communications Software

Communications software allows users to connect to remote applications, directly supporting communications requirements and design specifications. Transmission Control Protocol/Internet Protocol (TCP/IP) is a very common communications protocol. Many vendors produce TCP/IP products that implement the TCP/IP protocol. TCP/IP products directly support communications specifications.

Long-Haul Communications Design Considerations

The design team should define a method to provide communications between remote sites. The selection of communication method depends on many factors, including distance, type of information, bandwidth needs, and security. In many cases, POTS provides an economical approach for communications if bandwidth needs are minimal (less than 50 Kbps) and telephone service is available.

When defining communications specifications, designers should focus on the following types of requirements and design specifications.

Topography

Be sure to consider the distances between network end devices, such as user workstations and databases. If covering a wide geographical area with more than four sites, it might be more economical to utilize frame relay instead of T1. The use of satellite communications can deliver high bandwidth transmissions over great distances without regard to rights-of-way. Meteor burst communications can provide economical low bandwidth (less than 20 Kbps) transmission to extremely remote areas.

Existing systems

Be sure to choose communications types that interoperate with existing systems.

Mobility

Communications must accommodate the need for movement of the end points of the communication circuit. Radio communications provide the best means to satisfy mobility requirements. The use of a satellite gives most effective worldwide coverage, but it is very expensive. Consider CDPD for wide area low data rate (less than 20 Kbps) applications.

Information flows

Ensure that the chosen communications adequately supports the required type and frequency of information flow.

Performance

Make certain that the communications approach operates at a rate that is able to send information within delay requirements.

Security

The communications must meet all needs to protect the information being sent.

Environmental

Make sure that the selection of communications will operate well through anticipated environmental disturbances, such as weather and atmospheric noise. In addition, for radio and laser communications, investigate other physical obstructions such as mountains.

Regulations

Abide by company policies to use specific long-haul communications types and protocols.

Remote Access

Remote access provides the ability for users to utilize network applications and services from a nonlocal place. This gives users who are traveling or working from home the ability to check their e-mail and share files with other users. Typically, remote access products are based on software which provides the functionality necessary to dial in to a computer located on the local network and use network services which could normally be utilized from that local computer. Thus, remote access software merely extends the keyboard and monitor of a networked computer to a remote location. Figure 7.28 illustrates the concept of remote access. Remote access products directly support communications requirements and preliminary design specifications.

Remote Node

Remote node products provide services similar to those of remote access. However, remote node software allows the remote computer to function as

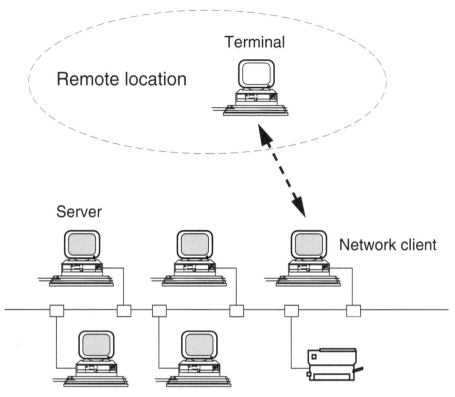

Figure 7.28 Illustration of remote access

an actual client; that is, it does not require access to a local networked computer. Figure 7.29 illustrates the concept of remote node. Remote node products directly support communications specifications.

Signal Distribution

Networks consist of many components, such as repeaters, bridges, modems, multiplexers, cabling, and connectors, which affect the distribution of information-carrying signals. Thus, it is important to specify the configuration and interconnectivity of these components. Some designers refer to signal distribution as the *cable plant design*. The signal distribution specifies where signals are allowed to go and how they will get there. The signal distribution is based largely on the topography and topology. Much of signal distribution is addressed through cabling and segmentation strategies.

The signal distribution might or might not be similar to the chosen topology. In some cases, the signal distribution will specify a layout very similar to the chosen topology. For example, the distribution of signals for an ethernet

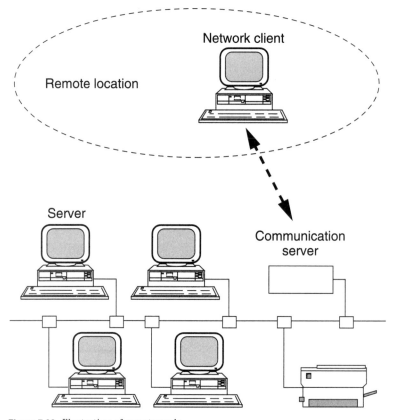

Figure 7.29 Illustration of remote node

network might fit the form of a bus. However, especially for larger ethernet networks, the signal distribution might follow the form of a star, as does EIA 568 building wiring standard. Figure 7.30 illustrates these differences.

Network Hubs

A network hub is a hardware device which acts as a chassis for multiple active network elements and contributes to the satisfaction of the signal distribution design specification. Figure 7.31 is an illustration of a network hub. The advantage of the hub is that it facilitates easier maintenance and management of active network components, especially those dealing with signal distribution. The hub provides electrical power via a backplane, physical mounting hardware for other network devices, and electronic management support.

Most network hubs have a modular design facilitating many combinations of network technologies. Hubs can facilitate multiple medium access technologies, such as ethernet and token ring, and can support signal distribution design specifications. Hubs also support different types of network components, such as repeaters, bridges, and routers. These components are typically available on circuit cards which plug directly into the hub.

Because of its centralized nature, a hub is an extremely critical component. As a result, hubs normally consist of a fault-tolerant design which supports very reliable operation. To accomplish this, most hubs utilize redundant power supplies to reduce the possibility of network downtime. Most hubs have very high MTBFs (typically 8,000,000 hours).

DSUs/CSUs

DSUs and CSUs (Data Service Units/Channel Service Units) are hardware devices that reshape data signals into a form that can be effectively transmitted over a digital transmission medium, typically a leased 56 Kbps or T1 line. DSUs and CSUs support point-to-point communications specifications. Figure 7.32 illustrates the use of DSUs/CSUs.

Modems

Modems convert digital signals into analog signals that can be transmitted through an analog telephone (POTS) line. As with CSUs/DSUs, modems di-

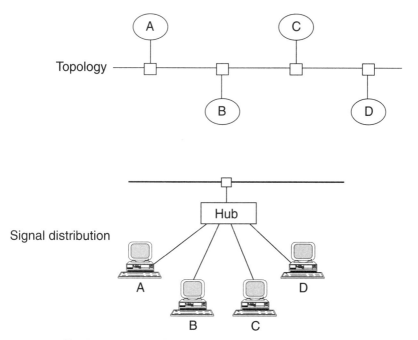

Figure 7.30 Topology versus signal distribution

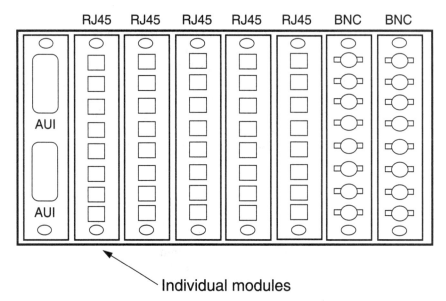

Individual modules

Figure 7.31 Illustration of a network hub

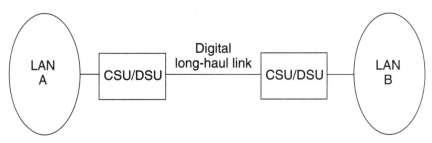

Figure 7.32 Illustration of the use of DSUs/CSUs

rectly support point-to-point communications specifications. Today, typical modems transmit data at 19.2 Kbps. Other specialized modems operate at higher speeds up to 50 Kbps.

Multiplexers

As shown in Figure 7.33, multiplexers are hardware devices that combine multiple signals into one composite signal in a form suitable for transmission over a long-haul connection, such as leased 56 Kbps or T1 circuits. Therefore, mulitplexers satisfy signal distribution and communications design specifications.

Patch Panels

Patch panels provide a centralized termination for all network cables, primarily twisted-pair wire. Figure 7.34 illustrates the configuration of a patch panel. Typically, network cables attach to the patch panel and span out to various network elements, such as user workstations, servers, and printers. The patch panels normally facilitate an easy connection to active signal distribution equipment, such as hubs, repeaters, and bridges. The patch panel satisfies the signal distribution design specification.

Equipment Racks

As shown in Figure 7.35, equipment racks house rack-mountable components, such as servers, bridges, and gateways, providing a maintainable and reliable component installation. Thus, the design team should maximize the mounting of network components in equipment racks. It is a good idea to designate an equipment room for the installation of equipment racks and associated network components. Equipment racks aid in satisfying signal distribution specifications.

Signal Distribution Design Considerations

The design team should define the architecture for signal distribution by focusing on the following types of requirements and design specifications.

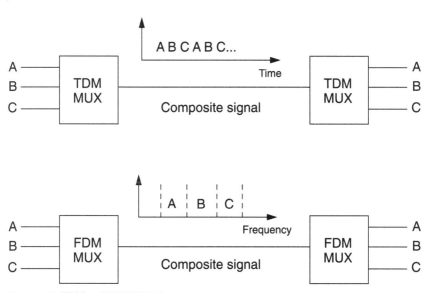

Figure 7.33 TDM and FDM Multiplexers

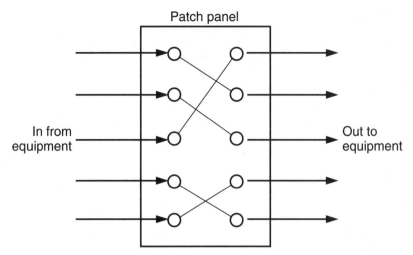

Figure 7.34 Patch panel configuration

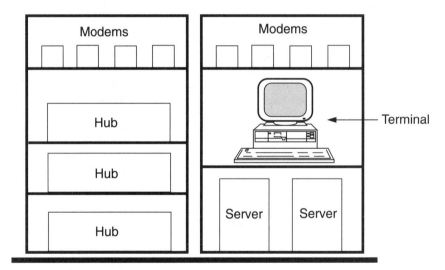

Figure 7.35 Illustration of equipment racks

Topography

Signal distribution depends a great deal on the location of users and network components. The EIA 568 building wiring standard, as described earlier in this chapter, provides a good architecture for the layout of most LANs. The use of a hub is a good general approach for LANs and offers flexibility in resizing the network if topography changes in the future.

Information flows

The signal distribution specification must support all flows of information.

Performance

Be sure the chosen set of components that comprise the signal distribution architecture provides adequate levels of availability and reliability.

Security

Designers must consider requirements for security. Be sure to designate secured communications rooms for locating active signal distribution components, such as switches, repeaters, bridges, and modems.

Environmental conditions

The facility structure and floor plan will affect the placement of cables and that locations of hubs, patch panels, and equipment racks.

Regulations

Be sure to abide by policies mandating the use of a particular building wiring standard.

Topology

Ensure that the signal distribution specifications accommodate the defined network topology.

Implementation

8

Preparing for Operational Support

The applications and services a network provides will normally not meet the users' expectations unless the project team fully defines the elements necessary for operation of the network. Operational support deficiencies equate to decreased user efficiency and higher operational costs. Most modifications will require preparations for operational support; therefore, the project team will need to identify proper network support that maximizes effectiveness of the network.

This chapter identifies how to determine and plan for various types of operational support. The emphasis in this chapter is on support preparation; that is, what needs to be in place before turning the modified network over to the users in a production environment. Not all modifications will require full development of the support mechanisms this chapter explains. In some cases, the project team will only need to revise existing levels of operational support and procedures.

Operational Support Preparation Concepts

Operational support makes sure that the network continues to operate effectively during its production phase, and that users are able to utilize the applications and services. The project team must fully prepare for operational support by planning what needs to be supported, and by determining "how to" and "who will" provide the necessary support. Figure 8.1 shows how preparations for operational support fit into the overall modification process.

- System administration planning
- Maintenance planning
- Security planning
- Configuration management procedures

Figure 8.1 Concept of preparing for operational support

Operational Support Preparation Elements

The operational support infrastructure will require many elements to properly support the network. The following paragraphs describe these items, and the project team should prepare them as part of this project phase.

Operational support plan

The operational support plan describes how the organization will support the operational network. This plan is necessary to ensure that provisions exist for supporting the network. At the conclusion of the detailed design, the team should have at least a draft of the support plan. The team can refine the support plan during the installation phase of the project, but the operational support plan should be finalized before switching the network into production mode.

The operational support plan should indicate which network elements require support, and which organizations are going to support them. This plan should address system administration, network monitoring and control, accounting and chargeback, maintenance, security, configuration management, training, and facilitation of system reengineering. The last section in this chapter further defines the contents of an operational support plan.

Specific operational plans

Specific operational plans describe how operations personnel should provide the operational support. The project team should update or prepare plans for system administration, maintenance, security, configuration management, and future reengineering. Later sections of this chapter define the content of each of these plans. The team can derive all information for the operations plans from the network requirements and design. Each operations plan should contain checklists for providing the applicable support. This will enable effective use by support personnel.

User manuals

The user manual provides user-level procedures on how to utilize the network, such as access network applications and services. The user manual should include descriptions of how to use the network and, most important, should also include checklists for quick reference. Users might need to read how to perform certain functions, then just refer to the checklists from time to time.

What makes a good user manual? A quick answer to this question is *clarity* and *efficiency*. It is really important that the manual be easy to read; otherwise, the users will not bother. As a result, the users will either spend a great deal of time trying to figure out how to operate the network or they will call the help desk with questions. Effective graphics in the manual will also help users understand the information faster. A picture really is worth a thousand words.

Training materials

The operational support plan identifies what training needs to be administered, when, and by whom. But the project team must also develop the training materials during support preparation. This is because the team should administer initial training to administrators and users before finishing the network installation. The training materials usually consist of overhead slides, student workbooks, and exercises. In a later section, this chapter describes how to develop and deliver training materials.

As part of preparing for operational support, the project team should guarantee that complete network design documentation is available. The team should not have to produce this documentation, assuming it was completed during the design phase. Support personnel will need accurate design documentation to adequately perform support functions, such as maintenance and future engineering efforts.

Operational Support Preparation Basis

The team should base operational support plans directly on network requirements and design. Design documentation should identify what to support, and network requirements can help the project team determine the appropriate level of support. For example, the materials list identifies all hardware and software the organization must support in terms of warranties, spares, and user help. The type of network operating system and cable type provides a basis for choosing the system administrator and maintenance team. In addition, the project team can utilize requirements dealing with availability and reliability to plan for disasters, and can utilize user profiles to develop training materials. The project team should base operational support plans on the requirements and design; however, knowledge of the factors influencing the network modification can provide insight into which support mechanisms to alter. Therefore, the team should review the factors causing the network changes and should determine how they affect operational support.

Operational Support Preparation Process

The project team should consider the following steps when preparing for operational support:

1. Identify support mechanisms requiring change.
2. Determine new levels of operational support.
3. Develop or revise support plans.
4. Develop or procure items that will facilitate the support.

Identifying Support Mechanisms Requiring Change

The network operational support structure might be very complex. Thus, the project team should identify support mechanisms requiring change before spending much time determining new levels of operational support. A network contains many components requiring varying degrees of operational support. These components include network interface cards, network operating systems, cabling, communications protocols, and users. These components and others contribute to the overall makeup of the network.

In general, network components commonly fall into one of the following three classifications: hardware, software, and people. Based on the modification, the project team must determine or refine a mechanism to support changes to these network elements.

Hardware Support

Hardware components, such as cabling, connectors, and disk assemblies, tend to malfunction. For example, someone could accidentally cut a network cable, causing downtime for that segment of the network. Or, a hard drive's head assembly could mechanically dysfunction, blocking the ability for users to store or receive data from the damaged disk drive. Other hardware components, such as network interface cards, PCs, and printers, could suffer from electronic malfunctions within the components themselves. For example, an integrated circuit residing on a circuit card could overheat, causing the card to malfunction. Therefore, maintenance support provides most support for hardware.

The following support mechanisms support hardware:

- **System administration** Installs hardware such as disk drives and monitors.

- **Network monitoring** Indicates hardware malfunctions.

- **Maintenance** Maintains warranties; repairs or replaces faulty hardware, such as cabling, repeaters, network interface cards, and bridges.

- **Network security** Employs anti-theft mechanisms.

- **Configuration management** Manages documentation (such as design specifications) which defines the hardware.

- **Training** Prepares and delivers training on how to perform preliminary tests on hardware.

- **Engineering** Assists in the troubleshooting of hardware problems; engineers solutions to counter hardware problems.

If the network modification involves changes in hardware, the team should identify applicable changes to the above support mechanisms.

Software Support

Software can malfunction by incorporating a virus or encountering defects introduced within the software during development. Therefore, the software should have support covering contingencies, maintenance, and configuration management.

These mechanisms normally support software:

- **System administration** Maintains software licenses; installs most applications and network operating systems.

- **Network monitoring** Detects problems in network communications.

- **Accounting and chargeback** Monitors the usage of software.

- **Maintenance** Assists in the troubleshooting of software.

- **Network security** Ensures proper handling of files.

- **Configuration management** Manages documentation (such as design specifications) which defines the software.

- **Training** Prepares and delivers training on how to use applications.

- **Engineering** Develops software.

If the network modification involves changes in software, the team should identify applicable changes to the above support mechanisms.

User Support

Users primarily need help in using applications, while other network functions are normally transparent to them. User support elements include training, network access, and periodic help. The team should present initial training to all users and system administrators during the system implementation. The system administrators need to incorporate a help desk to alleviate problems the users might eventually encounter.
These mechanisms help support users:

- **System administration** Assists users with questions dealing with the operation of applications.

- **Accounting and chargeback** Bills groups of users for utilizing applications and services.

- **Maintenance** Fixes problems the users encounter.

- **Network security** Educates users on effective security practices.

- **Training** Delivers training to the users on how to utilize applications

If the network modification involves changes in users, the team should identify applicable changes to the above support mechanisms.

Determining New Levels of Operational Support

The project team should determine new levels of operational support by determining what, when, and how to support the entire network. As a result, the team should create plans for each support element and should develop items necessary to facilitate the support.

The project team should follow these steps when determining levels of operational support for each support element:

1. Evaluate existing support plans.

2. Review network requirements and design documentation.

3. Revise existing support plans or create new ones to adequately support the network modification.

The team should evaluate existing support plans to determine their applicability to the modification, and should revise the plans to incorporate new levels of operational support. As mentioned before, the network requirements and design documentation identify what needs to be supported, and to what level. The main step in determining support for the network is to develop an applicable plan, which becomes part of the overall operational support plan.

The following paragraphs describe how to plan for each support mechanism. In some cases the project team can merely adjust the existing support elements, but in other cases the team will need to start from scratch.

System Administration Planning

The project team should plan for system administration to ensure that an effective interface exists between the users and the network, and to perform procedures to keep the network available for use. The team should develop a system administration plan addressing these elements:

- The system administration organizational structure
- Help desk procedures
- User accounts and access rights
- Directory structures
- Printer configurations
- Software licenses.

Figure 8.2 shows an outline of a system administration plan.

System administration organizational structure

The system administration organizational structure generally consists of one or more system administrators, assistant staff, and a help desk. Figure

---

System administration plan

I. Organizational structure
   A. Roles and responsibilities
   B. Staffing

II. Procedures
   A. User accounts
   B. Printing
   C. Applications
   D. Files
   E. Help desk

III. Attachments
   A. Hardware configurations
   B. Software configurations

Figure 8.2 Outline of a system administration plan

8.3 illustrates this organization. A system administrator performs activities, such as keeping the network in optimum running order, helping users, and protecting the network. As examples, the system administrator fine tunes network applications, answers questions of the users, opens network accounts for new users, and performs file backups. System administration plans describe how system administrators should perform their jobs. An organization should have a system administrator for each autonomous network, with an overall system administrator in charge of all others. If the individual network is large, the system administrator should have a staff of assistants.

The project team should plan on having a system administration staff with adequate knowledge of the network operating system, specialized network services, and applications. The system administrator and staff can accomplish most of their duties through an applicable system administration console for the particular network operating system.

Help desk

Roles of a system administrator include helping users with utilizing applications and solving network problems. However, if the network is large, then the system administrators alone might not be able to keep up with the number of user inquires. In this case, a help desk (which becomes an extension of the system administrator) can provide centralized assistance to users who encounter problems.

The central focus of the help desk should be user satisfaction. The project team should define a help desk which maximizes the effectiveness of

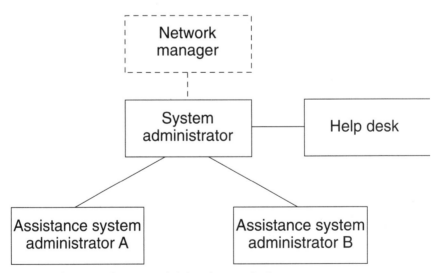

Figure 8.3 Structure of a system administration organization

the network. The help desk should attempt to help users utilize the network and should also fix minor problems, such as improperly installed software. The help desk should refer problems it cannot fix to the maintenance support organization.

Here are some suggestions in establishing or upgrading a help desk:

- Develop a set of help desk procedures outlining how the help desk operates.
- Ensure that all users know how to contact the help desk.
- Plan for increased call volume as the network grows.
- Incorporate a method to effectively track problems.
- Fully train the help desk team in network operations principles and, more important, in the users' applications.
- Automate as much of the help desk as possible after gaining some experience with manual methods.
- Use surveys to measure user satisfaction with the help desk.
- Incorporate methods to keep the help desk team from becoming too stressed.
- Review help desk usage statistics to determine optimum staffing.

User accounts and rights

The project team should identify who the initial users of the network will be, and should determine their account names, initial passwords, and rights to access servers, applications, and files. If user accounts and rights are properly planned in advance, the installation phase will go much more smoothly. The team should be able to obtain most user information from operator profile descriptions and security requirements, to determine user account names and access rights.

The team should standardize user account names to increase efficiency in assigning user names. This also simplifies the association between the user name and the actual user. For example, the project team could establish user names with first and second initial followed by last name. If two users have similar names, one of the user names could be followed by a number.

For example, user names could be assigned as follows:

Robert T. Smith becomes RTSMITH
John A. White becomes JAWHITE
Julie A. White becomes JAWHITE2

The project team should develop a plan for allocating and maintaining passwords. Users will need an initial password, then will need to be able to change the password periodically. The length and format of passwords should satisfy all security requirements and applicable regulations and policies. Typically, the length of the password should be at least six characters, and the format ought to consist of alphanumeric characters. The system administrator should make certain that users change their passwords periodically to avoid compromising passwords to others.

It might be effective to also associate sets of particular users as groups. System administrators might plan to develop group names for each department within the organization. For example, all users within the administration department could be given the group name ADMIN. This approach makes it easier to assign common rights to particular departments.

The project team should also assign names to servers and printers within the network. The team needs to allocate server names that address the server's function. For example, utilize names like APPS or APPLICATIONS as names for servers containing applications. Avoid using names that associate the server to its platform type and location, which is more likely to change than the server's function. This will decrease the need to change the name over the lifetime of the server.

The project team should identify the access rights of each group and user. The team should base the allocation of rights mainly on network security requirements. Users can be given rights to network resources if they have a need to utilize the resource or information contained within the associated files and databases. Users can normally be given any combination of the following rights to specific directories, subdirectories, and files:

- **Supervisory** Full rights and ability to assign rights
- **Read** Ability to read directories and files
- **Write** Ability to write to files
- **Create** Ability to create directories and files
- **Erase** Ability to erase directories and files
- **Modify** Ability to rename files and change file attributes
- **File scan** Ability to see directories and file names
- **Access control** Ability to assign rights for a particular directory

The proper issuance of these rights constrains users to the specific directories, files, and applications they need to access.

Directory structure

The directory structure provides a framework for the installation of applications and storage of files. Partly, the directory structure describes the mapping of logical drives on client workstations to network server directories. In addition, the directory structure identifies standard directory names and associated sub-directories. The project team should define a directory structure satisfying the needs of the applications and users.

Part of the directory structure design is to assign a mapping between the user and server drives. The following drive mappings normally work best for most networks:

Drive	Purpose
A–E	Local client drives (diskettes, hard drives, etc.)
F	User's home directory for storage of personal files
G–L	User-required directories
M–N	Program-specific directories
O–W	Program search directories
X	General network utilities
Y	DOS version applicable to the client
Z	Network operating system utilities directory

Directory structures should not be completely flat nor have more than four subdirectories. This facilitates simpler administration, backup, and file sharing. Here are some common subdirectory names:

\USERS\{user name}	Use for storing each user's home directory.
\WINAPPS\{application name}	Use for storing windows applications.
\DOSAPPS\{application name}	Use for storing DOS applications.
\WINUTILS\{utility name}	Use for storing windows utilities.
\DOSUTILS\{utility name}	Use for storing DOS utilities.
\COMMON\{user name}	Use for storing each user's common files.

Printer configurations

The project team should plan the allocation of printers to users. Each user should be assigned a primary printer, alternate printers, and any special printers. The primary printer should be within close proximity to the user and should meet everyday needs. Alternate printers should be the second-best printers in terms of distance and/or quality. A special service printer could be a high-quality color printer.

Software licenses

The team should define methods to manage all licenses associated with the network, especially software licenses. This is important in order to avoid exceeding the limited number of licenses and to keep track of which software versions the organization owns. The team can employ specialized metering software to keep tabs on software utilization, ensuring only the limited number of licenses are in use at any given time. The metering software can also help justify the purchase of additional licenses if usage for a particular application often hits the maximum.

Network Monitoring Planning

The project team should plan for the incorporation of network monitoring activities by defining a network monitoring and control center, as shown in Figure 8.4. This "center" could consist of one person, such as the system administrator, or a staff of people, depending on the size of the network. The project team should develop a network monitoring and control plan that covers network monitoring objectives, necessary equipment, and staffing.

Network monitoring objectives

Network monitoring offers rapid and effective fault isolation, which reduces network downtime. The team should first decide what network elements to monitor. Actually, this should be done during the design stage because it could affect the choice of network components having the ability to interact with network management protocols. The team should concentrate on monitoring central points of failure and any part(s) of the network reliant on mechanical devices. Central points of failure tend to be components such as servers, network backbones, and electricity. Mechanical devices, such as hard drives and cabling, often contribute to failures; therefore, the team should plan to monitor them as well.

Network monitoring equipment

The project team should establish and operate effective network monitoring equipment, which will maximize the detection of network problems before they affect the users. The network monitoring staff should provide

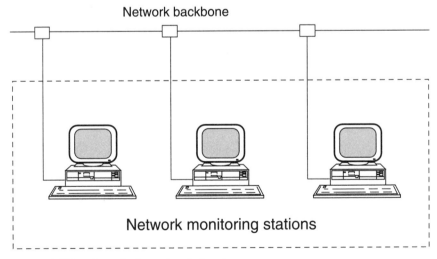

Network backbone

Network monitoring stations

Figure 8.4 Network monitoring and control center

quick resolutions to problems detected by monitoring equipment, by fixing the problems or by reporting them to maintenance personnel.

Network monitors can identify data traffic and can collect statistics from workstations, servers, and other active network devices. As mentioned before, this usually requires the implementation of network management protocols. Network monitors generally run in a passive mode, unable to disturb the normal operation of the network.

Network monitors consist of software residing on a hardware platform that is connected to the network via a network interface card. Network monitors usually have the following features:

- Graphical mapping of the network components and environment

- Event logging

- Alarms to be triggered when certain events occur

- Automatic fault isolation

- Statistics logging

- Report generation

The team should choose a network monitor with the features necessary to effectively satisfy the network monitoring objectives. Many active network components, such as servers and hubs, have vendor-specific network monitoring software available that does not rely on standard management protocols. This might be acceptable for smaller networks, but for larger networks having multivendor components the team should choose network monitoring equipment based on standard network management protocols, such as SNMP.

Staffing

For larger networks, the project team should define a network management center having a manager and staff. These people should be familiar with the architecture and operation of the organization's network and should know how to use network monitoring equipment.

Accounting and Chargeback Planning

The project team should plan an appropriate accounting and chargeback system to properly account and charge for the use of the network. This is critical to adequately funding operational support. The team should develop an accounting and chargeback plan that addresses accountable items, accountable groups, procedures, necessary equipment, and staffing. Figure 8.5 identifies an outline for an accounting and chargeback plan.

Accounting and chargeback plan

I. Organizational structure
   A. Roles and responsibilities
   B. Staffing

II. Accountability
   A. Accountability items
   B. Accountability groups

III. Items charges

IV. Billing procedures

Figure 8.5 Outline for an accounting and chargeback plan

Accountable items

The team should identify the accountable items that describe the network resources the organization needs to account for usage. Usage of these accountable items will help determine proper charging of resources and will help maintain statistics for future upgrade plans. Common items to account usage for are applications, user workstations, printers, communications circuits, CD drives, and fax machines.

The selection of accountable items depends on contracting methods, organizational structure, and procedures. For example, the organization might do business with another company and might have a contract specifying the ability to charge for nonlabor costs, such as computer usage. In this case, the organization would want to keep track of the amount of time each user utilizes his computer, in order to bill the customer. Or, a single organization might wish to have a centralized network operations center purchase and maintain internal applications and then, over time, charge each division or department for its share of applications and workstation usage.

The team should also consider accounting for items for gathering statistics for future decisions on modifying the network. For instance, heavy usage of one word processing application compared to another one might warrant an increase in the number of licenses for the heavily used application. Or, high utilization of a specific printer might support the decision to purchase another printer.

The team should determine the price, if any, of utilizing each of the network's resources. Overall, the team should strive to develop a pricing strategy covering all applicable expenses in supporting the network. The team, working with upper management, should decide on prices to charge the organizational groups.

Accountable groups

The project team will need to define the accountable groups that will be receiving a bill if a price applies for use of the network. The project team should plan to account for all users who will be utilizing chargeable network resources. In most organizations, though, it would not be practical (or appropriate) to bill each user independently. Thus, the project team should define suitable size groups that will pay the bills. Organizations often have sectors, divisions, and departments having separate budgets. Therefore, the team could designate the appropriate organizational levels to bill. To offer the most flexibility it is better to bill the lowest organizational level having an independent budget.

Accounting and chargeback procedures

The team should plan the implementation of the accounting and chargeback function. The main procedural items of this process are to periodically reconcile usage statistics from the accountable items and then to bill each accountable group for its share of usage. The procedures should call for at least the production of a monthly report identifying the usage level of each accountable item, who utilized the item, and how much each group will need to pay.

Accounting equipment

Accounting equipment consists of metering software running on the network and keeping track of the usage of accountable items. Other software can compute the bills for each organizational group. Many organizations customize accounting and chargeback software to best match their organizational structure and budgeting process.

Staffing

For smaller networks, the system administrator can handle accounting and chargeback procedures. Larger networks might require a dedicated person or staff to keep up with the larger number of accountable items and groups. These people should be familiar with the organization's network and should have knowledge of accounting principles.

Maintenance Planning

The project team should establish a maintenance plan ensuring that the network continues to provide quality service to its users. As a minimum, the plan should show how to maintain all network requirements, especially reliability and availability expectations. However, the team should include in the plan methods to maximize network effectiveness and minimize downtime. The team can achieve these goals by establishing effective maintenance techniques and procedures, and should document them in a maintenance plan. The plan should describe the maintenance organizational structure, scope of maintenance, maintenance procedures, warranties, the use of spares, and necessary test equipment. Figure 8.6 shows an outline for a maintenance plan.

Maintenance organizational structure

The project team should plan the structure of the maintenance organization, consisting of a maintenance manager and a field service team. Figure 8.7 illustrates the organizational structure of a maintenance organization. The maintenance manager directs the field service team, which includes technicians who can diagnose network problems and determine/implement solutions. The maintenance organization normally receives problem notifications from the system administrators, help desk, and network monitoring functions.

Maintenance plan

I. Organizational structure
    A. Roles and responsibilities
    B. Staffing
    C. Interfaces

II. Procedures
    A. Preliminary maintenance
    B. Corrective maintenance
    C. Sparing

Figure 8.6 Outline for a maintenance plan

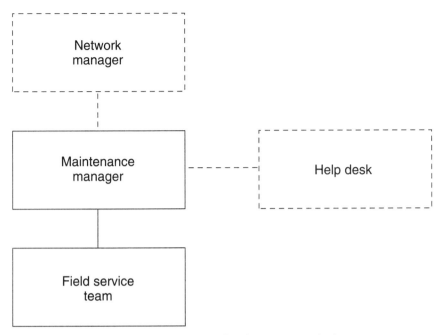

Figure 8.7 Organizational structure of a network maintenance organization

For smaller networks, as with other support functions, the system administrator might perform all maintenance functions. Larger networks will require a dedicated maintenance manager and technical staff to handle all problems that occur. The maintenance staff should be very familiar with the network and should have good skills in problem diagnosis and resolution.

Scope of maintenance

The project team should define the scope of maintenance; that is, what components the maintenance organization will support and to what level. Generally, the maintenance organization will support the entire local network, but the team should be specific in identifying network boundaries. As an example, the team could define the scope of maintenance to cover the local network, including the router connecting the local network to a wide area network. But, if the wide area network provider is responsible for maintaining the router, then the team would not include the router in the scope of maintenance.

The team should identify the level of support the maintenance organization will provide for each network component. To illustrate, the team should explain, for each component, whether the maintenance organization will locally repair faulty components or obtain replacements from the vendor. Generally, the most effective approach is to obtain warranties for most network components and replace components as they fail.

Maintenance procedures

The maintenance staff should have procedures explaining how to perform preventive maintenance, how to respond to problems, and how to track problem resolution. This will improve the efficiency of the maintenance staff, resulting in less downtime.

The goal of preventive maintenance is to find network faults and defects before they become problems to users. The following preventive maintenance actions will help keep the network in good working order:

- Perform visual inspections of network cabling and connectors to spot erosion or destruction.

- Execute time-domain reflectometry testing of network cabling to detect impedance mismatches, cable opens, and improper cable splices.

- Monitor traffic flows and component behavior to detect bottlenecks.

The maintenance organization should have a field service team ready at all times to respond quickly to network problems. Thus, most maintenance technicians should be easily accessible and should remain relatively close to potential problem spots. After learning of a network problem, the maintenance manager should open a "trouble ticket" by recording the date, time, and problem description. The maintenance manager can then assign the "trouble" to a particular technician or set of technicians, to find the cause of the problem and counter it.

In many cases the problem will be a faulty hardware component, such as a hard drive, a network interface card, or a cable connector. Normally, the best approach for fixing these problems is to replace the faulty component with a spare, and then to fix or replace the faulty component. To allow effective maintenance, the project team should determine appropriate levels of sparing for critical or failure-prone network components. Sparing can increase the availability of the network, because the spares will allow technicians to quickly replace faulty network components, resulting in less downtime.

Other network problems could be caused by software malfunctions, resulting from improperly installed applications, lack of interoperability, or software having defects incorporated by the manufacturer. With these examples, the maintenance crew might need to reinstall the applications correctly, work out the interoperability issues, or upgrade (or downgrade) the application to a less-defective version.

Technicians should track the progress of the problem resolution by periodically updating the trouble ticket. The trouble ticket should remain open until the technicians resolve the problem and implement a solution. After correcting the problem, the maintenance manager can close the trouble ticket and, if appropriate, announce that the problem is fixed.

Test equipment

The project team should identify any test equipment the maintenance technicians will need to fulfill their duties. As part of the project, the team should also procure the equipment as well. The main types of network test equipment are protocol analyzers and cable testers.

A protocol analyzer is a valuable network test tool which allows technicians to visualize network characteristics. Protocol analyzers capture (record) data traffic, decode and display protocol headers and information, trap specific protocol functions, generate and transmit test data traffic, and trigger programmed alarms. These features enable maintenance staff to efficiently troubleshoot network problems.

Another effective testing tool is the cable tester. The heart of most cable testers is a time-domain reflectometer (TDR), which tests the effectiveness of network cabling. Figure 8.8 illustrates the concepts of a TDR. The TDR is an intrusive tool which connects to an end of a cable the technician wishes to test and sends a test signal throughout the cable. The test signal reflects off any change in cable impedance, such as opens, splices, and connectors. The amplitude of the reflected wave designates the amount of impedance mismatch, and the length of time for the reflection to return to the TDR tool identifies the distance at which the impedance mismatch occurred. Thus, the TDR can help technicians find the location of impedance mismatches.

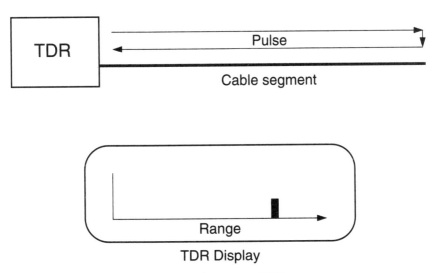

Figure 8.8 Illustration of a time-domain reflectometer (TDR)

Network Security Planning

The project team should establish a network security plan to guarantee that the network will continue to provide proper levels of required availability and information protection. The team should base the security plan on requirements, design specifications, and any existing security regulations or policies. The security plan should provide a security role for everyone within the company, including users, operators, and maintenance people. The project team should develop a security plan for the security organization structure, potential network disasters, and information security.

Security organization structure

The project team should plan the structure of a network security organization, consisting of a network security manager and security representatives. The structure of a network security organization is shown in Figure 8.9. Other functional groups, such as system administration, will implement network security techniques, such as file backups, maintenance of passwords, and data encryption, but the security organization provides oversight to ensure the proper implementation of the security practices. The network security manager is responsible for developing and maintaining security plans and for directing the security representatives. The security representatives ensure that security requirements are met through effective security practices.

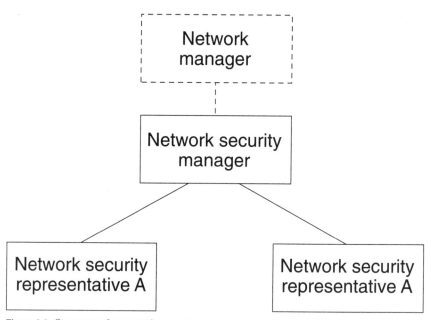

Figure 8.9 Structure of a network security organization

The project team should identify who will act as the network security manager. For larger networks, the team should identify security representatives as well. In every case, though, all people within the organization should be part of the security organization. The network security manager should have a background in general security concepts and a good understanding of the network's architecture, security requirements, and security techniques. The representatives should have at least a basic background in security concepts and a detailed understanding of chosen security techniques.

Disaster planning

A disaster situation is anything which disrupts or has great potential for disrupting the use of the network. As shown in Figure 8.10, disasters have varying levels of severity, based on their potential impact on the organization and users of the network. The lowest level of severity is a network crisis situation, which has a high-risk potential for interrupting applications and services. For example, the detection of a virus on a PC would constitute a crisis situation, because the virus might spread to other PCs and network devices, crippling network operations. The highest level of disaster severity are those disasters that cause an interruption in the operations of the organization. For example, equipment failures, accidental file deletion, and widespread virus attacks constitute high-level disasters.

The most common reasons for network disasters are user and system administrator mistakes. Users might inadvertently delete documents or fail to check files for viruses. System administrators might accidentally delete files or, more seriously, accidentally shut down communications devices or servers. Maintenance technicians could also cause network downtime by accidentally cutting active network cabling. Fire, flooding, and earthquakes can definitely cause disasters as well, but they do not occur very often.

The design team should incorporate methods to effectively accommodate possible disasters. The disaster plan, also known as a contingency plan, describes how the organization should minimize and recover from inadvertent loss of their computing resources. Disaster planning is serious business because most organizations suffer significant losses if they lose their computing resources for as few as two days. The team should write a disaster plan that identifies the type and scope of anticipated disasters, business impacts of each disaster, methods to minimize disaster impact, and methods to recover from disasters. Figure 8.11 shows an outline of a disaster plan.

Organizations should consider running "fire drills" to test the disaster plan; however, network managers should coordinate the drills with upper management and should choose a time and date for the drill which would provide minimal negative impact on the business and users.

Crisis situation ⟹ High potential of interrupted operations

Disaster ⟹ Loss of operations

Figure 8.10 Varying degrees of network disasters

Disaster plan

I. Loss impact analysis
   A. Potential loss
   B. Cost of loss

II. Major threats
   A. Power loss
   B. Disk crash
   C. Information compromise

III. Recovery procedures
   A. Power backup
   B. File backup

Figure 8.11 Outline of a disaster plan

Information security planning

The project team should plan security for stored and transmitted information, depending on requirements for information security. The team should identify the level of protection each type of information requires. For example, some information could be of public use and would not require any encryption or special handling. Other information might be classified as "secret" and might require a higher degree of protection. The team should also identify how the security organization will implement necessary levels of security. For instance, the information plan would identify the type of encryption and methods of handling sensitive information. Figure 8.12 illustrates an outline of an information security plan.

Configuration Management Planning

The project team should develop a configuration management plan (if none already exists), identifying procedures the organization should follow to maintain a complete network baseline. The network baseline identifies the makeup of the network, which includes hardware, software, documentation, and the people who use and maintain the system. Thus, the baseline is a snapshot of the current system configuration. Effective configuration management procedures make certain that the organization will effectively plan and complete network changes. The team should develop a configuration management plan that covers the configuration management organizational structure, configuration items, and processes and procedures. Figure 8.13 shows an outline of a configuration management plan.

Configuration management organizational structure

The configuration management organizational structure should consist mainly of a configuration manager and a library. The configuration manager administers the configuration management process, and other managers and technical staff implement the process. This person must ensure that unauthorized changes to the network do not occur. The library maintains current network documentation originals and provide copies of documen-

Information security plan

I. Type information

II. Security requirements

III. Security procedures

IV. Security mechanisms

Figure 8.12 Outline of an information security plan

Configuration management plan

I. Organizational structure
   A. Roles and responsibilities
   B. Staffing
   C. Interfaces

II. Accountability items

III. Procedures
   A. Change request
   B. Technical review panel
   C. Configuration control board
   D. Documentation update

Figure 8.13 Outline of a configuration management plan

tation to the remaining organization. The library should contain the entire set of network documentation.

The configuration manager should be very familiar with the contents of network documentation and general library principles. The library should include a librarian, who is knowledgeable about the operation of a library. The librarian should maintain a database containing a list and status of all official network documentation.

Configuration items

A configuration item is anything the organization wants to include in the baseline of the system. This usually includes every network hardware and software component, such as network operating systems, network interface cards, and applications. In addition, the team could define other network elements as configuration items, such as the following:

- Requirements
- Design specifications
- Schematics
- Cabling drawings
- Component configurations

- Installation plans
- Support plans

Configuration management process

The configuration management process should describe how the configuration management organization will maintain an accurate and descriptive network baseline. Figure 8.14 illustrates a configuration management process. The overall goals of this process are to consider and approve requested network changes by providing proper technical and managerial review.

The Technical Review Panel (TRP) reviews and approves the technical nature of requested changes. This panel ensures that any changes are technically possible and that they will coexist with existing systems. The TRP consists of the following positions:

TRP chairperson

The TRP chairperson has the authority to approve the technical aspects of a requested change. This person is typically an engineering manager having a broad technical background in network technologies and architectures.

TRP secretary

The TRP secretary accepts change requests from project managers, schedules TRP meetings, prepares meeting minutes, and tracks the progress of requested changes.

TRP reviewers

TRP reviewers analyze the requested changes and provide opinions on whether the changes are technically sound. Reviewers should consist of design engineers and operational support staff having strong technical backgrounds in the subject area(s) of the requested changes.

The Configuration Control Board (CCB) reviews and approves requested changes that will significantly affect the organization. Members of the CCB

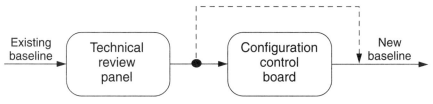

Figure 8.14 Illustration of the configuration management process

evaluate changes based on the availability of funding and the impact the changes have on the entire corporate infrastructure. The CCB consists of the following positions:

CCB chairperson

The CCB chairperson approves changes that will significantly affect the organization. This person must have knowledge of the company's budget and the authority to guarantee the availability of funds.

CCB secretary

The CCB secretary accepts technically approved change requests from the TRP secretary, schedules CCB meetings, and prepares meeting minutes.

CCB reviewers

CCB reviewers determine how the requested change will affect the company's budget and resources. These people normally consist of managers and business analysts.

The general procedures for configuration management should be as follows:

1. The configuration management organization maintains a library containing documents addressing all configuration items.

2. The project manager of a network modification submits a change request to the TRP secretary. This change should be submitted after a project has completed the preliminary design phase. The TRP secretary, in turn, sends the request to the TRP chairperson and applicable reviewers. The TRP chairperson indicates which reviewers should receive the specific request and whether a review meeting needs to be scheduled. Figure 8.15 shows an example of a change request.

3. The TRP reviewers analyze the technical content of each requested change and recommend whether it should be approved or not.

4. Based on the technical review, the TRP chairperson should either approve or disapprove each change, or should recommend CCB review. As mentioned before, the CCB should review requested changes if they significantly affect the company. For example, the addition of one or two users to the network will not usually have serious impacts and should be reviewed by the TRP only. However, switching from one long-haul communications system to another might affect the company enough to warrant a CCB review. The TRP chairperson should consult with the configuration manager if it is unclear whether to obtain CCB review.

Change request
_____

I.   Type change

II. Projected cost of change

III. Projected schedule

IV. Projected impacts

V.   Approval
     A. Technical review panel
     B. Configuration control board

Figure 8.15 Example of a change request

5. If the TRP approves the change, the project manager should proceed with implementing it.

6. In the case of CCB review, the TRP secretary submits the change request to the CCB secretary. The CCB secretary ensures that all CCB participants review the requested change and, if necessary, convene a CCB meeting. As with the TRP, the CCB chairperson should indicate which reviewers should receive a specific change request, and whether a review meeting needs to be scheduled.

7. Based on the CCB review, the CCB chairperson either approves or disapproves the requested change. If the change is approved, the project manager can proceed with implementing it.

8. The configuration manager ensures that the project team submitting the change updates all applicable documentation.

Training Planning

The project team should plan a training curriculum and should develop materials to properly train network users and operators. The curriculum depends mostly on application requirements and network operating system design specifications. It also depends on the level of understanding and background of each user and operator. For example, training should cover how to utilize the chosen electronic mail system. If most users have no background in using electronic mail, the training should cover the basics. If the modification is to merely upgrade the current software, then training would probably need to cover only the new upgrade features. The incorporation of an initial network would probably require a great deal of training, because few users might have experience in using network resources and services.

In general, users and system administrators will need initial and continuous training to utilize the network system effectively. System administrators need to know how to perform their duties, such as how to add and delete users from the network, how to tune the network operating system, and how to backup system resources. Users need to know how to log on to the network, as well as how to access and use applications. If the network modification incorporates new applications, be sure to properly train the system administrators and users. Not doing so usually forces a heavy learning curve on users, discouraging them from utilizing the network. The project team should develop a training plan that highlights the training organizational structure, course development, delivery schedule, and necessary equipment. Figure 8.16 illustrates an outline of a training plan.

Training organizational structure

As shown in Figure 8.17, the training organization should consist of a network training manager, course developers, and trainers. The training man-

---

Training plan

I. Organizational structure
    A. Roles and responsibilities
    B. Staffing
    C. Interfaces

II. Training requirements
    A. Users
    B. Support staff

III. Development procedures

IV. Schedule
    A. Initial training
    B. Periodic training

Figure 8.16 Outline of a training plan

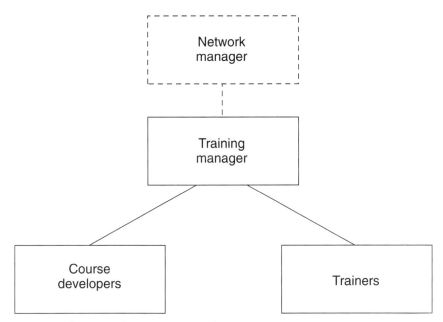

Figure 8.17 Structure of a training organization

ager directs the training organization and ensures that users and operators receive adequate training. Course developers determine training objectives and prepare course materials, such as overhead slides, exercises, and student manuals. Trainers deliver the training through classroom or one-on-one instruction, using the training materials.

The training manager should have knowledge of training principles, including course development and delivery. It is not necessary that the training manager have extensive background in networking. The course developers should fully understand training development techniques and, preferably, should have detailed knowledge and background in the particular training they are developing. Trainers should be proficient in delivering training and should fully understand the material they are delivering. It is especially efficient to have the course developer and the trainer be the same person, because the process of developing the course will help prepare the trainer for delivering the training. However, it is important that course developers be good at preparing effective course materials and that trainers be good at instructing.

Training development

The project team should plan to develop and deliver initial training before transitioning the network to production mode. This will ensure that users and operational support staff will have the skills necessary to utilize the network. Training development includes the creation of learning objectives, teaching plans, and training materials.

Learning objectives specify what the student is expected to do after receiving instruction. Course developers should first define all learning objectives before proceeding with course development. Learning objectives should be action-oriented, should meet a standard for satisfying objectives, should state any conditions, and should be measurable. Therefore, each learning objective should state conditions, actions, and standards. For example, consider the following sample learning objective for sending an electronic mail message attachment:

Given a text-only file needing transmission, the student will be able to send the file as an attachment to a remote network without encountering errors.

The statement *given a text-only file needing transmission* is the condition, *send the file as an attachment to a remote network* is the action, and *without encountering errors* is the standard. Clearly stated learning objectives will lead to the development of effective training.

Teaching plans describe definable lessons that comprise the entire course. Figure 8.18 illustrates the structure of a teaching plan. Teaching plans explain what to teach and what the trainers will need to properly deliver the lessons. For each lesson, the teaching plan should consist of a les-

```
Teaching plan
_____


  I.   Instructional staff

 II.   Lesson objectives

III.   Instructional methods

IV.   Lesson plans
       A. Time allocations
       B. Lesson content
       C. Instructional notes
```

Figure 8.18 Structure of a teaching plan

son overview identifying the overall course objectives, lesson objectives, instructional methods, learning objectives, and the level of skill the students should be expected to acquire.

The teaching plan should also identify the method of instruction trainers should use when delivering the training. Common instructional methods are lecture, discussion, and exercises. The following explains attributes of each:

- **Lecture** Primarily one-way information flow from instructor to students; efficient for conveying common information to large groups; involves a great deal of preplanning.

- **Discussion** Uniform information flow among students and the instructor; good for exchanging ideas within a small group, especially if some students have experience in the subject area; requires the instructor to facilitate the discussion to maintain focus.

- **Exercises** Learning by doing; students will retain the information longer; involves preplanning.

The teaching plan should specify a combination of these methods to effectively train the users and the technical staff. Most network user training explains how to use applications. Therefore, exercises should be a significant part of the training.

Before delivering the training, course developers should create materials to increase the effectiveness of the training. Training materials usually consist of overhead slides, exercise instructions, and student manuals. When developing overhead slides, use concise bullet statements (preferably of five words or less), avoid more than four or five bullets per slide, use a font style and size which is easy to read when projected on the screen, and maximize the use of graphics to convey ideas.

Exercises can add much value to the training session, because students always remember more if they have a chance to actually perform what they are supposed to learn. When developing exercises, write very clear instructions, create all worksheets and answer sheets, and practice the exercises before administering them to the students. Student manuals should be kept and used by the students as references after receiving the training. Student manuals should identify all learning objectives, should include all essential detailed information, should identify reading material applicable to the learning objectives, and should have a glossary if applicable.

Delivery schedule

The training plan should include details on when to deliver the training. The plan should include dates for both initial and follow-up training. The team should ensure that most users will be able to attend at least initial introductory training before completion of the installation phase. In most cases, follow-up training can cover more details and should be scheduled after users gain some experience in using the operational network. The delivery schedule should also be flexible to accommodate initial training for future new hires.

Training equipment

The training plan should indicate necessary training equipment. Training equipment might consist of an overhead projector and screen, a white board, a VCR, an audio system, and computers with applicable applications. The project team should investigate and recommend the purchase or lease of necessary training equipment.

Engineering Support Planning

In most cases, the system administrator or maintenance staff will correct network problems. However, some operational problems might require engineering support. Therefore, the project team should make certain that there is an adequate engineering support organization which can respond to complex problems and reengineer the network, if necessary. Figure 8.19 illustrates an engineering support organization.

The engineering support organization should implement network reengineering concepts and should utilize a structured methodology, as described in this book, if it is necessary to modify the network.

The Operational Support Plan

The project team should finalize operational support preparations by producing an overall support plan document, which covers or references each

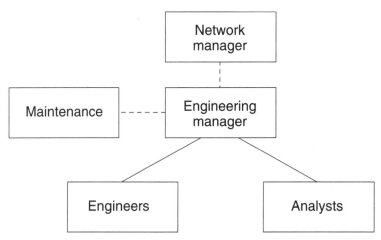

Figure 8.19 Illustration of an engineering support organization

type of support. This document fully describe how the operational support staff will support all aspects of the modification.

Specifically, the operational support plan should include:

- Structure of the operational support organization
- Which organizations are responsible for supporting the network
- System administration plan
- Network monitoring and control plan
- Accounting and chargeback plan
- Maintenance plan
- Security plans
- Configuration management plan
- Training plan
- Engineering support plan

The support plan should also appoint an overall network manager, who will manage the overall support organization. It should also and identify individual functional support managers, such as system administrators and maintenance manager. Figure 8.20 shows an outline for an operational support plan document.

With a support plan in place, the team can begin the installation phase of the network project.

Operational support plan

I.   Items requiring support

II. Support organizations
     A. Roles and responsibilities
     B. Staffing
     C. Interfaces

III. Attachments
     A. System administration plan
     B. Security plan
     C. Maintenance plan
     D. Accounting/chargeback plan
     E. Training plan

Figure 8.20 Outline for an operational support plan

Chapter

9

Network Installation

After receiving network components, the project team should be ready to install the components and complete the modification. Many organizations install the entire network modification, then use the "big bang" concept of testing. The problem with this approach is that it is very expensive to correct defects in the design or installation during the final stages of installation. A well-planned installation contributes to a network installation that is completed on time and within budget. This chapter covers applicable preparations and execution procedures for network installations that minimize defects, installation time, and user disturbances.

Network Installation Concepts

The main objective of the network installation is to produce a completely installed network satisfying all requirements. As shown in Figure 9.1, the installation phase consists of installing the network components and running a series of tests to guarantee the proper functioning of the network. The installation is accomplished by technicians, testers, and possibly engineers who, together, comprise an installation crew. The installation crew should develop a plan to complete all activities that will contribute to a successful installation.

Network Installation Elements

The installation phase will identify items the project team and operational support staff will need to adequately complete the installation and provide

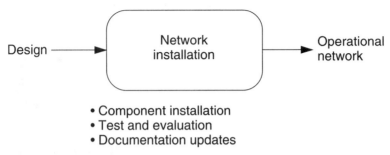

Design ⟶ | Network installation | ⟶ Operational network

- Component installation
- Test and evaluation
- Documentation updates

Figure 9.1 Concept of network installation

maintenance. As with all other phases of the modification, it is extremely important to fully document all aspects of the installation. The process of installing the network should result in these items:

Installation plan

The installation plan describes procedures for installing components and testing the resulting network. The procedures should be written at a level the installation crew can understand. This plan should also identify any other information the crew should know before, during, and after the installation. For instance, the plan should indicate who the installation crew should contact to gain access to restricted parts of the facility or to ask questions concerning the installation. Of course, this plan should be written before installation begins, and the installation crew should follow the plan during all stages of installation.

Test results

Network testing will produce test results, providing a measurement of how well the network performs under specified conditions. The project team utilizes the test results to evaluate results and determine whether corrective actions are necessary.

Evaluation comments

During the installation, the project team should document the evaluation of the test results, especially if some test results do not meet expectations. The evaluation analyzes inadequate test results and offers solutions to problems. The project team will base corrective actions on the evaluation comments. In some cases, the solution could be to replace a defective component or reinstall some faulty cabling. However, testing could reveal defects in the design as well. For this situation, the team would need to reengineer the faulty part of the design before completing the installation.

Corrective actions

Corrective actions explain what was accomplished to fix the installation problems. These corrective actions might result from defects found in the installation of the network. For example, testing could have shown a discontinuity in a cable running between a workstation and the network hub. In this case, the installation crew might fix the problem by replacing the cable. The installation crew should then document this corrective action.

Revised network documentation

It is important that the project team update any documentation based on changes made during the installation phase. For instance, a company might have remodeled part of its facility since the project team developed the requirements and design, forcing the installation team to cable the facility differently than was shown in the design. Therefore, the team should then update the cabling drawings.

Network Installation Basis

The project team should mainly base the installation of a network on the design, policies, and regulations, and experience. The network design provides an installation crew with enough details to plan the installation and test the network. The network design identifies what components the installers should install and shows how to cable the system. For example, the network schematic and cabling drawings show how to interconnect the components. Other plans, such as the operational support plan, show the configurations of servers, workstations, and directories. Policies and regulations might identify installation requirements. As an example, fire safety regulations might specify the need for plenum cable or installation within conduit. Policies might describe required aesthetics for network outlets. Experience is also an important basis for installation, mainly because it is not feasible to provide minute details in the installation plan. The installation crew should have "common sense" experience related to network installation. This will highly decrease the number of defects and resulting network problems.

Network Installation Process

The installation phase of the network modification might have more impact on users than other phases of the modification, because the installation process might disturb users, causing them to be less productive. Some modifications completely disrupt the operations of the network while the installation takes place, forcing users to rely on secondary means, decreasing their ability to accomplish day-to-day tasks. Through effective planning and execution of the network installation, the project team should be able to install the network in minimal time and should therefore decrease loss in user productivity.

The project team should consider the following actions to install a network:

1. Prepare for the installation.
2. Install (and test) components.
3. Perform system and integration testing.
4. Update network documentation.

The remainder of this chapter will focus on each one of these steps.

Preparing for Installation

The project team should dedicate the necessary time to properly prepare for the installation of the network or modification. An unplanned installation has the potential to cause cost and schedule overruns, upset users, and cause personal injuries. The project team should give the installation crew enough details to install the network while minimizing both user disturbances and total installation time.

The project team should accomplish these activities when preparing for installation:

1. Develop installation procedures.
2. Develop test procedures.
3. Identify tool requirements.
4. Develop a schedule.
5. Prepare an installation plan.
6. Conduct a preinstallation meeting.

Installation Procedures

The installation procedures should, as a minimum, identify what components the installation crew needs to install and in what order. Procedures should also accommodate a strategy that minimizes installation time. Typically, networks are designed from the top down; however, it is most efficient to perform the installation from the bottom up. Figure 9.2 illustrates this concept.

The team should plan a bottom-up installation strategy but should attempt to install as many components in parallel as possible. In other words, the installation crew could be installing the cabling while other team members configure the servers and workstations. For this effort, the installation team will be ready to connect the servers and workstations to the network cabling at about the same time the cable installation is complete.

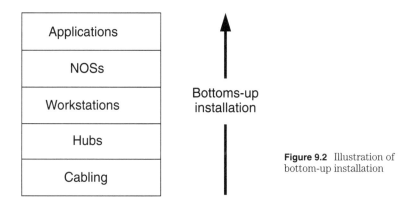

Figure 9.2 Illustration of bottom-up installation

The procedures should also describe how to install certain components, if necessary. The level of description depends greatly on the experience of the installation crew and the level of criticality of the components being installed. If the installation crew has installed or modified many similar networks, then the procedures can be written at a high level. Otherwise, the team should identify more detailed procedures. If the components being installed are extremely critical, such as the replacement of a server or hub, then the team should specify more installation details to avoid severe problems.

The installation procedures should also reference the design and support documentation that apply to the installation. As examples, the procedures explaining the installation of cabling should reference the installation crew to the network cabling diagrams and schematic. Or, the server installation procedures could reference applicable support plans identifying directory structures and security plans.

Test Plan Development

The test plan explains how to perform specific tests designed to guarantee that the network is installed correctly and meets all user requirements. Thus, the test plan identifies tests and applicable evaluation criteria. The evaluation criteria are expected results. The key to successfully testing the network installation is to catch and correct defects as soon as possible during the course of installation. This is very important, because defects usually take more time and money to correct during the later stages of installation. The project team should develop a test plan covering test execution, test result evaluation, and corrective action implementation.

Test execution planning

Testers will need to know how to run checks based on an effective test strategy. This strategy should ensure that testing is applied throughout the installation process and should not follow the "big bang" approach of test-ing at the end of installation. If the testers wait until the end of installation to test, defects discovered then might require tremendous amounts of rein-stallation and repair time. Thus, testers should incrementally test the net-work installation to catch any defects as soon as possible. The most effective approach is to utilize four types of tests: unit testing, integration testing, system testing, and acceptance testing.

Unit testing. Unit testing, which is sometimes referred to as whitebox test-ing, verifies the accuracy of each network component, such as servers, ca-bles, hubs, and bridges. The goal of unit testing is to make certain that the component works properly by running checks that fully exercise the inter-nal workings of the component. Figure 9.3 illustrates the concept of unit testing.

It is important that the installation crew perform unit testing on most components, especially servers and other critical components, before inte-grating them into the existing network. This allows the installation crew to counter any defects in isolation and to preclude other components from masking the defect. Examples of network unit tests include the verification of the following: the server will boot with no errors; the hub will initialize with no errors; each cable can transfer data.

Integration testing. Integration testing verifies the interfaces between net-work components as the components are installed. The installation crew should integrate components into the network one by one, and should per-

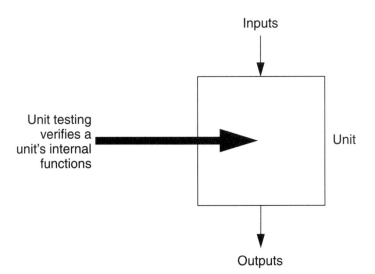

Figure 9.3 Concept of unit testing

Integration testing verifies the interfaces between units, as the units are integrated into the overall system

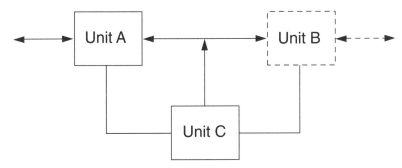

Figure 9.4 Concept of integration testing

form integration testing when necessary to ensure proper, gradual integration of components. Figure 9.4 illustrates the concept of integration testing.

Integration testing enables testers to find defects before completing the installation. As mentioned before, defects are much easier to find and correct before the installation nears completion. Examples of integration tests include: verification that each workstation installed will properly communicate with the server via the hub; confirmation that a bridge filters traffic properly; checks to see whether each installed printer will respond to print commands received from the server; proof that the UPS will support the server in case of power failure.

System testing. As illustrated in Figure 9.5, system testing verifies the installation of the entire network. Testers complete system testing in a simulated production environment, simulating actual users to make sure that the network meets all stated requirements. Examples of network system tests include verifications that server logins can occur from all client workstations, that the tape backup system works correctly, and that remote servers are accessible from all client workstations.

Acceptance testing. Acceptance testing determines whether the network is acceptable to the actual users. The tests are similar to one done in system testing, but in this case the users themselves perform the tests. It is important that these users participate in developing acceptance criteria and running the tests. If this is not done, the customer (or users) might reject the system if it does not work the way they feel it should during production mode.

A common question when developing a test plan is, "How much of the network do we test when making a modification?" There is no simple answer

System testing verifies the complete system meets requirements

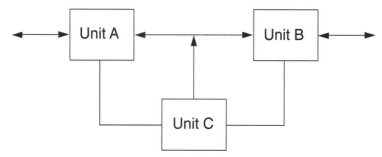

Figure 9.5 Illustration of system testing

to this question. The amount of test coverage depends on how likely it is that users will utilize the network modification and the risks associated with having potential defects. One approach is to concentrate on testing functions users operate most often; then, if time permits, check the functions the users very seldom use. However, the team should fully test modifications that introduce a high degree of risk if defects remain undiscovered, especially if they could cause personal injury.

The main task in identifying test procedures is to develop appropriate test cases for each type of testing. A test case is an executable test with a specific set of input values and a corresponding expected result. Figure 9.6 shows the structure of a test case.

The following identifies attributes of a good test case:

- It has a good chance of uncovering a defect.
- It is easily performed, preferably automatically.
- It delivers an unambiguous result.
- It has an expected result, which is easily verified.

The team should plan effective test cases to verify that all network requirements and design specifications are met.

Test result evaluation planning

The team should plan to evaluate test results. The concept of test evaluation is to compare the expected test results with actual results of the tests. If the test produces a result unacceptable in terms of the expected values, the testers should attempt to identify the defect(s) causing the problem. The team should plan to have the testers record all defects found and coordinate corrective action with the project team.

Corrective action planning

The project team should plan the procedures for implementing corrective actions for defects which are found. After completing the test and evaluation, the project team can produce a document specifying test results and necessary corrective actions. The project team should implement corrective measures to counter any unsatisfactory results.

Installation Tool Requirements

The project team should identify all tools the installation team will need to install and test the network. The team should also ensure that the tools will be available when the installation team will need them. This simple planning might avoid unnecessary time needed to locate special tools during the installation.

Here is a list of tools the installation crew might need:

- Flashlights, which assist in inspecting and installing cabling above ceilings.
- Ladders, which provide access to ceilings.
- Screwdrivers, which facilitate component installation/removal.
- Wire cutters/strippers, which are necessary for preparing cables.
- Wire crimping tools, which assist in the installation of connectors.
- Electric or hand drills, which might be needed to assist in the installation of cabling.
- Saws, which are necessary for the installation of wall plates.
- Two-way radios, which can be helpful with large installations in which the team is spread out over large areas.
- Test equipment, which is needed to test the network installation.

Installation Schedule

The project team should develop an installation schedule identifying when and where the installation will take place. Figure 9.7 identifies a generic in-

Test case = Test input + Expected output

Figure 9.6 Structure of a test case

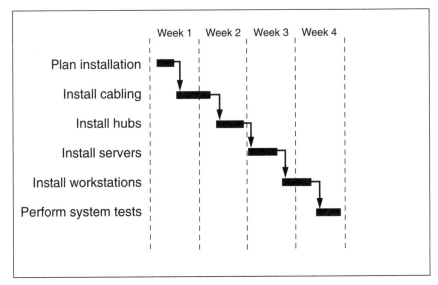

Figure 9.7 Generic installation schedule

stallation schedule. The schedule should indicate milestones that explain when certain parts of the network will be completed. For example, the cable installation might take place during days two, three, and four, and the server installation make take place during days five and six. The installation plan should allow enough time to test the installation; therefore, the schedule should identify when the team will perform testing. For example, on day six the team could accomplish server unit testing and on day eight the team could do system testing.

The team should coordinate development of the installation schedule with the customer representative and the installation crew. As mentioned before, the goals of installation and testing are to minimize both user disturbances and total installation time. This is important because the users might be utilizing the existing network. Installers can highly minimize user disturbances by performing installations during times when the users are not using the network. This will avoid causing work flow disruptions. If the organization utilizes the network twenty-four hours per day, then the crew should schedule the installation to occur during non-peak periods, if possible.

Installation Plan Development

The project team should develop an installation plan containing all the procedures associated with installing and testing the network. The installation crew will use this document as guidance to install and test the network. The installation plan should consist of the following elements: installation procedures, test procedures, tool requirements, schedule, points-of-contact, installation locations, and names of installers. Figure 9.8 shows an outline of an installation plan.

The Preinstallation Meeting

The project team should hold a preinstallation meeting before executing the installation procedures. The entire installation crew should attend this meeting to ensure that they are aware of all procedures associated with the installation. During the preinstallation meeting, the project team should review the installation plan and should focus on the procedures and schedule. The team should also discuss safety practices.

Installing the Components

The installation crew should install the network according to the installation plan the project team prepared during installation preparations. Most of these installation tasks can occur simultaneously to decrease installation time, but it is effective to at least concentrate on each of the component categories separately. Be sure to perform unit testing after the installation of each component. The team should also carry out integration testing as the components

```
Installation plan
───────────────────────

I.   Modification overview

II.  Installation procedures
     A. Cabling
     B. Hubs
     C. Servers
     D. Workstations

III. Test procedures

IV.  Schedule
```

Figure 9.8 Outline of an installation plan

are combined to form the complete network. After completing the entire installation, the team should accomplish system and acceptance testing.

The succeeding sections cover important aspects of completing the installation.

Cable installation

Before installing the cabling, the installation team should ensure that no changes have occurred since previous plans were made, such as new construction, design changes, or changes in hub locations. It is very important to ensure that the planned locations of network components, especially hubs and workstations, will not have to change because the length of cable depends on these locations. Therefore, the installation crew should visually inspect the installation site and review the schematics and cable layout drawings. The team should also distribute the cabling and applicable tools, such as wire cutters, crimpers, flashlights and ladders, to the installation site.

The following are tips for installing cable:

- Pull cable from the hub outward to workstation locations to ease the installation.
- Leave extra cable length at the hubs and cable outlets to facilitate future changes.
- To improve aesthetics, install wall plates for cable outlets and run the cabling above ceilings and behind walls, if possible.
- For solid walls, use elevated cable trays to improve aesthetics and increase safety.
- Secure wires to beams and other structures.
- Label all wires to facilitate easier maintenance.

After installing the cabling, the installation crew should verify a quality installation by utilizing a cable tester capable of performing TDR tests. This will identify cable discontinuities and other imperfections. The team should correct any defective installations by reinstalling the faulty cable segments.

Distribution component installation

Distribution components consist of the components necessary to disperse information throughout the network, such as hubs, repeaters, bridges, and routers. The installation team should move the components to their proper installation location(s) and should gather necessary tools.

The following are tips for installing distribution components:

- Install distribution components in equipment racks or set them on sturdy raised platforms, to ensure that the components do not easily move after installation.

- Make sure all connectors are well marked and keyed to schematics and cable layout diagrams to facilitate easier maintenance.

- Ensure that there are no unsafe conditions in the room that could lead to electrical hazards, such as leaky air conditioners on roofs or water drains located nearby.

- Install locks on the doors leading to the rooms housing the distribution rooms, to prevent curious people or intruders from disrupting the components.

After installing each distribution component, the team should run self-checks supplied with the unit. If tests fail, correct the problems by fixing or replacing the faulty component(s).

Server installation

For server installations, the installation team should gather all components comprising the server, such as the hardware platform, network operating system software, and network interface cards. In addition to following the installation plan, the installation team should refer to applicable support plans identifying directory structures and user account information. The following is a checklist for installing servers:

1. Assemble and test the hardware platform, if necessary.

2. Install the network interface card(s).

3. Install server software.

4. Run server self-diagnostics.

5. Create applicable directory structures.

6. Set up printer queues.

7. Install applications.

8. Establish user accounts.

9. Connect the server to the network.

As shown in the above procedures, the installation crew should test the server hardware platform before installing the server software. If the hardware platform is defective, the team can correct the faulty platform before spending a great deal of time installing the server software.

User workstation installation

The workstations include any devices the users need to interface to the network. If the workstations are new, it is more efficient to set up the workstations before distributing them to the users' locations. This minimizes user disturbances. For these new workstations, establish a staging area from which to perform most of the workstation installation, then distribute the workstations to the user locations. If the workstations already reside at the users' locations, then it is usually best to perform the installation on-site. However, the installation team should coordinate on-site workstation installations with affected users to minimize disruptions.

The following is a checklist for installing each workstation:

1. Assemble and test the hardware platform, if necessary.

2. Install the network interface card.

3. Install the server client software.

4. Run client self-diagnostics.

5. Connect the workstation to the network.

6. Test server access.

As part of the user workstation installation, the installers will need to locate available interrupts and base addresses. This is relatively simple in the case of all new workstations because the team can standardize the configuration of the workstations, including interrupt assignments. However, organizations having several types of previously installed workstations will challenge the installer, because the configuration of each workstation is likely to be different. Thus it is often helpful for the installer to have a software tool which quickly determines the configuration of the workstations.

Peripheral installation

Peripherals consist of printers, fax machines, optical drives, and similar equipment. As with workstation installation, the team should utilize a staging area, if possible, to set up the peripherals.

The following is a checklist for installing each peripheral:

1. Assemble the peripheral, if necessary.

2. Run peripheral self tests.

3. Install the network interface card, if applicable.

4. Install the peripheral interface components, such as print-sharing devices, if applicable.

5. Connect the peripheral to the network.

Most peripherals installations are fairly simple; however, the installation crew should review any vendor-supplied installation procedures before completing the installation.

System and acceptance testing

After the team finishes installing the network, they should run overall system tests to make sure the network is fully functional and satisfies all network requirements. The team should maintain a checklist of all requirements and should keep good records of which requirements have been tested. If a test fails, the team should identify the responsible defect and fix the problem.

Before transferring the network to production mode, the users should perform acceptance tests to ensure that the network meets user needs as outlined in the network requirements. The project team should monitor acceptance tests, and the users should actually perform the tests. The team should strive for heavy user participation in acceptance testing, to maximize the validity of the tests.

Under certain circumstances, it might be more effective to pilot the network with a selected set of users. A pilot installation tests the network operation in production mode for a small group of users. It is normally beneficial to pilot the installation when there will be multiple deployment locations or highly critical operations. If there are multiple sites, the team should deploy the network to the pilot site, run appropriate acceptance tests, then deploy it to other sites after correcting all faults. For highly critical operations in which large losses are possible, the team should consider piloting a part of the network first, or limiting the number and type of users at first. Again, after fixing any problems the team can complete the network installation.

Periodic walk-throughs

During the course of installation, the project team should periodically perform walk-throughs to ensure a quality installation. If possible, the team should complete walk-throughs every day.

Here is a checklist for completing walk-throughs:

1. Are the installers following installation plans?
2. Have any tests failed?
3. Have there been any problems requiring design changes?
4. Are the installers using safe installation practices?
5. Do the installers have any questions?

The evaluators should review responses to these questions and should take actions to resolve any problems.

Network documentation updates

After completing the installation, the installation team should update drawings and other design documentation with any changes incurred while installing the network. This will enable the project team to produce an accurate set of documentation for the support organizations, ensuring that the support staff will have accurate documentation for maintaining the network.

Before claiming the network as operational, the project team must first properly transfer the project over to supporting organizations. The next chapter covers this crucial step.

10

Transferring the Network to Operational Mode

After completing the installation and testing of network components, the project team should transfer the network modification to operational mode. An official transfer avoids common misunderstandings relating to network functionality and operational responsibilities. This chapter explains how to prepare for the proper transfer to operational mode, how to close the project, and how to evaluate the project outcome.

Concepts of Transferring the Network to Operational Mode

As shown in Figure 10.1, the concept of transferring the network to operational mode involves the transition of the network development project to users and operational support organizations. This transfer marks the official end of the project. At this point, users will begin operating the network. In addition, operational support staff will begin supporting the network.

The transfer to operational mode is very important and applies to all types of network modifications. It is especially significant for major modifications, such as initial network creations, organizational moves, and technology migrations. For example, the creation of an initial 200-user network would require a careful transfer to operational mode to avoid a tremendous drop in employee productivity.

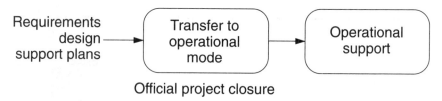

Official project closure

Figure 10.1 Concept of transferring the network to operational mode

The following identifies the benefits of officially transferring the network to operational mode:

- It clearly marks the end of development and the beginning of the operational phase.

- It ensures that proper support is in place before users begin operating the network.

- It facilitates better control over resources and future changes.

- It avoids decreases in employee productivity.

To efficiently transfer the network to operational mode, the project team should complete each of the following steps:

1. Prepare for the transfer to operational support.

2. Announce the new network capability.

3. Officially close the project.

4. Evaluate the outcome of the project.

5. Monitor the network modification.

Operational Mode Transfer Preparations

The project team should prepare for the transfer to operational mode to ensure that the network is ready for use. The project team should accomplish the following preparations:

- Review network documentation

- Ensure that the network is ready for operational mode

- Develop a support turnover agreement

Network documentation is the key to communicating aspects of the design and installation of the network to operational support staff. Therefore, the project team should perform a final review of network documentation, especially operational support plans and design documents, to ensure completeness. The operational support staff will need this documentation to efficiently maintain and manage the network.

If the network is ready for operational status, the team should be able to answer "Yes" to the following questions:

- Does the modified network deliver anticipated tangible and intangible benefits?

- Does the modified network meet stated requirements?

- Is network performance acceptable?

- Have all open issues and tasks been accomplished?

- Has the network been adequately documented?

- Do support plans clearly state required support and indicate who will provide the support?

- Are all users and support staff properly trained?

- Has the team prepared a turnover agreement?

For some modifications, such as the incorporation of new applications, initial network creations, and special services, the users will require training to adequately utilize the network and its applications. For these cases, lack of user training is a common reason for low interest in using the network. Thus, the project team should ensure that all applicable users and support staff have received proper levels of training.

The network project will have led project members through the determination of user requirements, design of a solution, and installation of the network. During this process, particularly during installation, the project team assumes unofficial operational support roles. For example, the team might install a 100-user network as a pilot. If problems were encountered during installation, the installation crew would normally fix the problems instead of utilizing existing support staff. As a result, users and management might begin viewing the project team unofficially as operational support staff. Therefore, to avoid continual calls to fix problems after the network is in operational mode, the project team must make it clear when the project is completed and operational support begins.

One method of clearly identifying the demarcation between installation of the project and operational support is to develop a support turnover agreement describing the modification and who is going to support it. Figure 10.2 shows a typical outline of a turnover agreement. The project team should complete a turnover agreement before officially announcing the operational status of the modification.

Turn over agreement

I.   Modification overview

II. Support requirements

III. Support org. acceptance

IV. Customer acceptance

V.   Attachments
     A. Support plans
     B. Design documentation

Figure 10.2 Typical outline of a turnover agreement

Announcing Operational Status

The users should receive an advance notice of what the new network capabilities are and when they will be available. If the team does not properly advertise the new capabilities, there might be considerable delay until users learn that the capabilities exist.

Here are some methods to announce new network capabilities:

- Place an announcement in the company newsletter.
- Send a memo to affected users via physical distribution or e-mail.
- Make announcements at staff meetings.
- Add the new network capabilities to user training programs.

Project Closure

The close of the project marks the official beginning of operational mode and operational support. To close the project, the team should:

1. Deliver applicable network documents to operational support organizations.
2. Conduct a project closure meeting, if necessary.

The project team must guarantee that all applicable operational support organizations receive copies of network documentation, such as operational support plans, design specifications, test results, and the support turnover agreement. As mentioned previously, the network documentation is critical in the proper delivery of operational support. The project team should conduct a project closure meeting to officially end the project and transfer responsibility of the network to operational support organizations. At the meeting the project team can make certain that all operational support organizations, as identified in the support turnover agreement, have accepted the responsibility of supporting the network.

Post Project Activities

At the conclusion of the project, the team should accomplish these activities:

1. Evaluate the outcome of the project.
2. Monitor how well the modification works.

After the turnover of the network to operational support, the project team should evaluate the outcome of the project. The team should do this soon, before forgetting project details. The evaluation can consist of reviewing and documenting lessons learned during the completion of the project. This will protect future teams from having to "reinvent the wheel" or from encountering similar problems. The knowledge of past problems and how they were dealt with can help future project teams determine better solutions.

The project team can evaluate the outcome of the project by answering these questions:

- What were the major lessons learned during the project?
- Have the lessons learned been documented?
- Was the project completed on time and within budget?
- How accurate were the cost and schedule estimates?
- Was user involvement high, medium, or low?
- How did user involvement affect the outcome of the project?
- If requirements changed during the network design or installation, how well were the changes incorporated?
- Were project team member roles clearly defined?
- How did upper management and users perceive the project outcome?
- What future enhancements could improve the system?

Make certain that answers to the above questions are incorporated into future projects.

Someone from the project team, possibly the project manager, should monitor the network modification to make sure it continues to meet expectations. The project manager can periodically check its status by remaining in contact with the operational support staff. If the network does not continue to meet requirements, the team should reconvene to alleviate the problems.

Network Component Vendors

3Com Corporation

P.O. Box 58145
5400 Bayfront Plaza
Santa Clara, CA 95052-8145
800-638-3266
408-764-5000
408-764-5001 (F)

Year established: 1979
Number employees: 2,000
Gross annual sales: $620M
Ownership: Publicly traded
  NASDAQ (COMS)

Product types:

- Bridges/routers/gateways
- Hubs
- Repeaters
- Network interface cards
- Network management
- Communications software
- Networking software

Abacus Controls, Inc.

80 Readington Rd.
Somerville, NJ 08876
908-526-6010
908-526-6866 (F)

Year established: 1974
Number employees: 25
Gross annual sales: $3M
Ownership: Privately held

Product Types:

- UPS

Abbott Systems, Inc.

62 Mountain Rd.
Pleasantville, NY 10570
800-552-9157
914-747-4171
914-747-9115 (F)

Year established: 1989
Ownership: Privately held

Product Types:

- Graphics software
- GUI software
- Personal information managers

Able Communications, Inc.

2823 McGaw Ave.
Irvine, CA 92714
800-654-1223
714-553-8825
714-553-1320 (F)

Year established: 1991
Number employees: 50
Gross annual sales: $15M
Ownership: Privately held

Product types:

- Modems
- Multiplexors
- Network management

Absolute Software Corporation

1212 W. Broadway
Suite 304
Vancouver, BC, CD V6H 3B1
800-220-0733
604-730-9851
604-730-9581 (F)

Product types:

- Security and auditing software

ACC Systems, Inc.

8320 Guilford Rd.
Suite G
Columbia, MD 21046-1280
800-242-0739
410-290-8100
410-290-8106 (F)

Year established: 1991
Number employees: 75
Gross annual sales: $8M
Ownership: Privately held

Product types:

- Network interface cards
- Network management
- Communications software

ACCEL Technologies, Inc.

6825 Flanders Dr.
San Diego, CA 92121-2986
800-488-0690 (Includes tech support)
619-554-1000
619-554-1019 (F)
800-488-0680 (Direct sales)
619-554-1018 (Tech support BBS)

Year established: 1983
Number employees: 35
Ownership: Privately held

Product types:

- Engineering/scientific applications

Accent Data Solutions, Inc.

3270 Seldon Court
Bldg. 1
Fremont, CA 94538
510-490-6299
510-490-2546 (F)

Year established: 1991
Number employees: 6
Ownership: Privately held

Product types:

- Scanners
- Accounting applications
- Terminals

Accounting Systems, Inc.

2950 W. Square Lake Rd.
Suite 207
Troy, MI 48098
800-968-8305
810-641-5150
810-641-5947 (F)

Year established: 1968
Ownership: Privately held

Product types:

- Accounting, inventory, and purchasing applications

AccuSoft Corporation

Two Westborough Business Park
P.O. Box 1261
Westborough, MA 01581
800-525-3577
508-898-2770
508-898-9662 (F)

Year established: 1988
Number employees: 20
Gross annual sales: $3M
Ownership: Privately held

Product types:

- Graphics software
- GUI software

Ace Software Corporation

1708 McCarthy Blvd.
Milpitas, CA 95035-7417
800-345-3223
408-232-0300
408-451-0118 (F)

Year established: 1991
Number employees: 20
Ownership: Privately held

Product types:

- Home use and entertainment software

Acme Electric Corporation

9962 Rt. 446
Cuba, NY 14727
800-325-5848
716-968-2400
716-968-1420 (F)

Year established: 1917
Number employees: 900
Gross annual sales: $75,812,000
Ownership: Parent company stock traded on NYSE (ACE)

Product types:

- UPS

Action Image Systems Technology, Inc.

42 Chestnut Hill Dr.
Murray Hill, NJ 07974
908-508-0596
908-771-0140 (F)

Product types:

- Graphics software
- GUI software

Adaptec, Inc.

691 S. Milpitas Blvd.
Milpitas, CA 95035
800-934-2766
408-945-8600
408-262-2533 (F)

Year established: 1981
Number employees: 1,700
Gross annual sales: $466M

Ownership: Publicly traded
NASDAQ (ADPT)

Product types:

- Network interface cards
- Sound boards
- Networking software
- Peripheral device drivers

Adianta, Inc.

2 N. Santa Cruz Ave.
Suite 201
Los Gatos, CA 95030
408-354-9569
408-354-4292 (F)

Year established: 1990
Number employees: 2
Gross annual sales: $1M
Ownership: Privately held

Product types:

- Design and testing software

Adobe Systems, Inc.

1585 Charleston Rd.
P.O. Box 7900
Mountain View, CA 94039-7900
800-833-6687
415-961-4400
415-961-3769 (F)

Year established: 1982
Number employees: 1,600
Gross annual sales: $598M
Ownership: Publicly traded
NASDAQ (ADBE)

Product types:

- Desktop publishing applications
- Peripheral device drivers
- Printer utilities

Advance Multimedia Corporation

603 11th Ave., SW
Suite 300
Calgary, AB, CD T2R 0E1
800-465-3641
403-237-0426
403-237-0457 (F)

Year established: 1987
Number employees: 6
Gross annual sales: $15M
Ownership: Publicly traded Alberta
Stock Exchange (AMM)

Product types:

- Education and training software

Advanced Computer Communications

10261 Bubb Rd.
Cupertino, CA 95014
800-444-7854
408-864-0600
408-446-5234 (F)

Year established: 1991
Number employees: 100
Ownership: Privately held

Product types:

- Bridges/routers/gateways
- Networking software

Aironet Wireless Communications, Inc.

47358 Fremont Blvd.
Fremont, CA 94538-6501
510-249-6930
510-249-6920 (F)

Year established: 1969
(Corporation)

Number employees: 1,100
(Corporation)
Gross annual sales: $296M
(Corporation)
Ownership: Parent company stock
traded on NASDAQ (TLXN)

Product types:

- Networking software

Alliance Computer Services

301 E. Wallace
Suite 110
San Saba, TX 76877
800-256-1786
915-372-5715
915-372-5716 (F)

Year established: 1986
Ownership: Privately held

Product types:

- Accounting applications

Altair Computing, Inc.

1757 Maplelawn Dr.
Troy, MI 48084
810-614-2400
810-614-2411 (F)

Year established: 1985
Number employees: 170
Ownership: Privately held

Product types:

- Engineering applications

Amdahl Corporation

1250 E. Arques Ave.
P.O. Box 3470
Sunnyvale, CA 94088-3470
800-538-8460
408-746-6000
408-773-0833 (F)

Year established: 1970
Number employees: 5,600
Gross annual sales: $1,700M
Ownership: Publicly traded AMEX
(AMH)

Product types:

- Mainframes and supercomputers
- Compilers and languages
- Networking software

America Online, Inc.

8619 Westwood Center Dr.
Vienna, VA 22182
800-827-6364
703-448-8700
800-827-4595 (F)

Year established: 1985
Ownership: Publicly traded
NASDAQ (AMER)

Product types:

- Communications services
- PC Communications utilities

AMP, Inc.

P.O. Box 3608
Harrisburg, PA 17105
800-488-8459
717-564-0100
717-986-7575 (F)

Year established: 1941
Number employees: 29,000
Gross annual sales: $3,000M
Ownership: Publicly traded NYSE
(AMP)

Product types:

- Modems
- Multiplexors

- Test equipment
- Network interface cards
- Fax boards
- Soundboards/MIDI

Ancor Communications, Inc.

6130 Blue Circle Dr.
Minnetonka, MN 55343
612-932-4000
612-932-4037 (F)

Year established: 1986
Number employees: 55
Gross annual sales: $4,000M
Ownership: Publicly traded
  NASDAQ (ANCR)

Product types:

- Bridges/routers/gateways
- Network interface cards
- Hubs

Apple Computer, Inc.

20525 Mariani Ave.
Cupertino, CA 95014
800-776-2333
408-996-1010
408-996-0275 (F)

Year established: 1977
Number employees: 12,000
Gross annual sales: $9,000M
Ownership: Publicly traded
  NASDAQ (AAPL)
Publicly traded Tokyo Stock
  Exchange

Product types:

- Hardware platforms
- Modems
- Multiplexers

- Hubs
- Network interface cards
- Network management
- Printers
- Communications software
- Electronic mail

Artisoft, Inc.

2202 N. Forbes Blvd.
Tucson, AZ 85745
800-233-5564
602-670-7100
602-670-7101 (F)

Year established: 1982
Number employees: 500
Gross annual sales: $108M
Ownership: Publicly traded
  NASDAQ (ASFT)

Product types:

- Hubs
- Network interface cards
- Server/sharing units
- Printer spoolers

Ascend Communications, Inc.

1275 Harbor Bay Pkwy.
Alameda, CA 94502
800-ASCEND-4
510-769-6001
510-814-2300 (F)

Year established: 1989
Number employees: 87
Gross annual sales: $40M
Ownership: Publicly traded
  NASDAQ (ASND)

Product types:

- Bridges/routers/gateways

AT&T Global Information Solutions (formerly NCR Corporation)

1700 S. Patterson Blvd.
Dayton, OH 45479-0001
800-225-5627
513-445-5000
513-445-4184 (F)

Year established: 1885
Number employees: 309,000
Gross annual sales: $67,000M
Ownership: Parent company stock
traded on NYSE (T)

Product types:

- Hardware platforms
- Bridges/routers/gateways
- Hubs
- Network interface cards
- Network management
- Power equipment
- Printers
- Graphics and GUI software
- Office automation software

Autodesk, Inc.

111 McGuinness Pkwy.
San Rafael, CA 94903
800-879-4233
415-507-5000
415-507-5100 (F)

Year established: 1982
Number employees: 1,425
Gross annual sales: $450M
Ownership: Publicly traded
NASDAQ (ACAD)

Product types:

- CAD software

Banyan Systems Inc.

120 Flanders Rd.
Westborough, MA 01581-1033
800-222-6926
508-898-1000
508-898-1755 (F)

Year established: 1983
Number employees: 625
Gross annual sales: $150M
Ownership: Publicly traded
NASDAQ (BNYN)
Product types:

- Network management
- Electronic mail
- Network server software

BBN Enterprise Networks

10 Moulton St.
Cambridge, MA 02138
800-765-4441
617-873-3970
617-873-5421 (F)

Year established: 1948
(Corporation)
Number employees: 1,600
(Corporation)
Gross annual sales: $197M
(Corporation)
Ownership: Parent company stock
traded on NYSE (BBN)
Product types:

- Bridges/routers/gateways

Bechtel Corporation

3000 Post Oak Blvd.
P.O. Box 2166
Houston, TX 77252-2166
713-235-2741

713-235-4075 (F)

Year established: 1985

Ownership: Privately held

Product types:

- Manufacturing software

Black Box Corporation

P.O. Box 12800
Pittsburgh, PA 15241-0800
412-746-5500
412-746-0746 (F)

Year established: 1976
Number employees: 600
Gross annual sales: $142M
Ownership: Publicly traded
  NASDAQ (BBOX)

Product types:

- Modems
- Multiplexers
- Test equipment
- Bridges/routers/gateways
- Hubs
- Network interface cards
- Network management
- Fax boards
- ISDN adapters

Bolt Beranek and Newman Inc.

10 Moulton St.
Cambridge, MA 02138
800-422-2359
617-873-3000
617-873-3315 (F)

Year established: 1948
Number employees: 1,600
Gross annual sales: $197M

Ownership: Publicly traded NYSE
  (BBN)

Product types:

- Compilers and languages
- Design and testing software

Borland International, Inc.

100 Borland Way
Scotts Valley, CA 95066-3249
800-233-2444
408-431-1000
408-431-4122 (F)

Year established: 1983
Number employees: 1,200
Gross annual sales: $254M
Ownership: Publicly traded
  NASDAQ (BORL)

Product types:

- Communications software
- Compilers and languages
- Design and testing software

Cable & Wireless, Inc.

8219 Leesburg Pike
Vienna, VA 22182
800-486-8686
703-790-5300
703-905-7099 (F)

Year established: 1975
Number employees: 2,200
Gross annual sales: $578M
Ownership: Parent company stock
  traded on NYSE (CWP)

Product types:

- Modems
- Multiplexors
- Communications services

Cabletron Systems, Inc.

35 Industrial Way
Rochester, NH 03866-5005
800-332-9401
603-332-9400
603-337-2211 (F)

Year established: 1983
Number employees: 4,900
Gross annual sales: $820M
Ownership: Publicly traded
  NYSE (CS)

Product types:

- Bridges/routers/gateways
- Hubs
- Repeaters
- Network interface cards

Castelle, Inc.

3255-3 Scott Blvd.
Santa Clara, CA 95054
800-289-7555
408-496-0474
408-492-1964 (F)

Year established: 1987
Number employees: 70
Ownership: Privately held

Product types:

- Server/sharing units

CBIS, Inc.

5875 Peachtree Industrial Blvd.
Bldg. 100, Suite 170
Norcross, GA 30092
800-344-8426
404-446-1332
404-446-9164 (F)

Year established: 1978

Number employees: 50
Ownership: Privately held

Product types:

- LAN/WAN products
- Networking software

Chipcom Corporation

118 Turnpike Rd., Southborough
  Office Park
Southborough, MA 01772-1886
800-228-9930
508-460-8900
508-490-5696 (F)

Year established: 1983
Number employees: 850
Gross annual sales: $270M
Ownership: Publicly traded
  NASDAQ (CHPM)

Product types:

- Modems
- Multiplexers
- Bridges/routers/gateways
- Hubs
- Terminal servers
- Networking software

Cisco Systems, Inc.

170 W. Tasman Dr.
San Jose, CA 95134-1706
800-553-6387
408-526-4000
408-526-4100 (F)

Year established: 1984
Number employees: 2,000
Gross annual sales: $1,200M
Ownership: Publicly traded
  NASDAQ (CSCO)

Product types:

- Bridges/routers/gateways
- Hubs
- Network interface cards
- Networking software

Citel, Inc.

1111 Park Centre Blvd.
Suite 474
Miami, FL 33169
800-CITEL4-U
305-621-0022
305-621-0766 (F)

Year established: 1983
Number employees: 4
Gross annual sales: $1M
Ownership: Privately held

Product types:

- Power equipment
- Surge suppressors

Compaq Computer Corporation

20555 State Hwy. 249
Houston, TX 77070-2698
800-345-1518
713-374-0484
713-374-4583 (F)

Year established: 1982
Number employees: 11,900
Gross annual sales: $11,000M
Ownership: Publicly traded NYSE (CPQ)
Product types:

- Hardware platforms
- Networking software

CompuServe, Inc.

5000 Arlington Centre Blvd.
P.O. Box 20212
Columbus, OH 43220
800-848-8199
614-457-8600
614-457-0348 (F)

Year established: 1969
Number employees: 2,200 (Corporation)
Gross annual sales: $430M
Ownership: Parent company stock traded on NYSE (HRB)

Product types:

- Communications services

Digital Equipment Corporation

146 Main St.
Maynard, MA 01754-2571
800-344-4825
508-493-5111
508-493-8780 (F)

Year established: 1957
Number employees: 78,000
Gross annual sales: $13,000M
Ownership: Publicly traded NYSE (DEC)
Publicly traded PSE
Publicly traded Midwest Stock Exchange

Product types:

- Hardware platforms
- Modems
- Test equipment
- Bridges/routers/gateways
- Hubs
- Network interface cards

- Network management
- Terminal servers
- Printers
- Electronic mail
- Networking software

DTK Computer, Inc.

770 Epperson Dr.
Los Angeles, CA 91748
818-810-8880
818-810-0090 (F)

Year established: 1981
Number employees: 1,500
Gross annual sales: $200M
Ownership: Privately held

Product types:

- Hardware platforms

Dupont Printing and Publishing

Barley Mill Plaza
Rts. 141 & 48
Wilmington, DE 19805
800-538-7668
302-892-1966
302-892-7245 (F)

Year established: 1802
(Corporation)
Number employees: 140,000
(Corporation)
Gross annual sales: $40,000M
(Corporation)
Ownership: Parent company stock
traded on NYSE (DD)

Product types:

- Digitizers
- Scanners equipment

Dynacomp, Inc.

178 Phillips Rd.
Dynacomp Office Bldg.
Webster, NY 14580
800-828-6772
716-265-4040

Year established: 1978
Ownership: Privately held

Product types:

- Software applications

Eastman Kodak Co.

343 State St.
Rochester, NY 14650-0519
800-242-2424
716-724-4000
716-724-0663 (F)

Year established: 1880
Number employees: 133,000
Gross annual sales: $19,500M
Ownership: Publicly traded NYSE
(EK)

Product types:

- CD-recordable drives
- Optical jukeboxes
- Digitizers
- Graphics systems
- Printers
- Scanners
- GUI software

Eicon Technology Corporation

2196 32nd Ave.
Montreal, QC, CD H8T 3H7
800-803-4266

514-631-2592
514-631-3092 (F)

Year established: 1984
Number employees: 500
Gross annual sales: $72M
Ownership: Publicly traded Toronto
Stock Exchange (EIC)

Product types:

- Network management
- GUI software
- Networking software
- ISDN terminal adapters

Elgar Corporation

9250 Brown Deer Rd.
San Diego, CA 92121
800-733-5427
619-450-0085
619-458-0267 (F)

Year established: 1965
Number employees: 350
Ownership: Privately held

Product types:

- Power equipment

Epson America, Inc.

20770 Madrona Ave.
P.O. Box 2842
Torrance, CA 90503
800-289-3776
310-782-0770
310-782-4455 (F)

Year established: 1975
Number employees: 700
Gross annual sales: $1,000M
Ownership: Privately held

Product types:

- Hardware platforms
- Network interface cards

- Fax boards
- Printers

Everex Systems, Inc.

5020 Brandin Court
Fremont, CA 94538
800-821-0806
510-498-1111
510-683-2186 (F)

Year established: 1983
Number employees: 300
Gross annual sales: $250M
Ownership: Privately held

Product types:

- Hardware platforms

Exide Electronics Corporation

8521 Six Forks Rd.
Raleigh, NC 27615
800-554-3448
919-872-3020
800-75-EXIDE (F)

Year established: 1962
Number employees: 1,300
Gross annual sales: $350M
Ownership: Publicly traded
NASDAQ (XUPS)

Product types:

- UPS
- Networking software

Fairchild Data Corporation

350 N. Hayden Rd.
Scottsdale, AZ 85257
800-247-9489
602-949-1155
602-941-0023 (F)

Year established: 1978
Number employees: 85

Ownership: Parent company stock traded on NYSE (FA)

Product types:

- Networking software

Farallon Computing, Inc.

2470 Mariner Square Loop
Alameda, CA 94501-1010
800-425-4141
510-814-5100
510-814-5023 (F)

Year established: 1986
Number employees: 250

Product types:

- Bridges/routers/gateways
- Hubs
- Network interface cards
- Networking software

Fibermux Corporation

21415 Plummer St.
Chatsworth, CA 91311
800-800-4624
818-709-6000
818-709-1556 (F)

Year established: 1984
Number employees: 300
Gross annual sales: $400M
Ownership: Parent company stock traded on NASDAQ (ADCT)

Product types:

- Modems
- Multiplexers
- Bridges/routers/gateways
- Hubs
- Networking software

Fibronics International, Inc.

16 Esquire Rd.
North Billerica, MA 01862-2590
800-327-9526
508-671-9440
508-667-7262 (F)

Year established: 1977
Number employees: 400
Gross annual sales: $54M
Ownership: Publicly traded
NASDAQ (FBRX)

Product types:

- Bridges/routers/gateways
- Hubs
- Network management
- Networking software

Fujitsu Networks Industry, Inc.

1266 E. Main St.
Soundview Plaza
Stamford, CT 06902-3546
800-446-4736
203-326-2700
203-964-1007 (F)

Year established: 1991
Number employees: 75
Gross annual sales: $32,000M
(Corporation)
Ownership: Parent company stock traded on Tokyo Stock Exchange (FJT)

Product types:

- Help desk applications
- Video/teleconferencing software

Gandalf Systems Corporation

501 Delran Pkwy.
Delran, NJ 08075-1249

800-426-3253
609-461-8100
609-461-4074 (F)

Year established: 1970
Number employees: 1,450
Gross annual sales: $160M
Ownership: Parent company stock
  traded on NASDAQ (GANDF)
Chairman: Desmond Cunningham

Product types:

- Modems
- Bridges/routers/gateways
- Hubs
- Networking software
- ISDN adapters

Gateway 2000, Inc.

610 Gateway Dr.
P.O. Box 2000
North Sioux City, SD 57049-2000
800-846-2000
605-232-2000
605-232-2023 (F)

Year established: 1985
Number employees: 5,000
Gross annual sales: $2,700M
Ownership: Publicly traded
  NASDAQ (GATE)

Product types:

- Hardware Platforms

Grand Junction Networks, Inc.

47281 Bayside Pkwy.
Fremont, CA 94538
800-747-FAST
510-252-0726
510-252-0915 (F)

Year established: 1987

Number employees: 50
Ownership: Privately held

Product types:

- Hubs

Hayes Microcomputer Products, Inc.

5835 Peachtree Corners East
Norcross, GA 30092-3405
800-96-HAYES
800-665-1259 (CD)
404-840-9200
404-441-1213 (F)

Year established: 1977
Number employees: 1,000
Gross annual sales: $250M
Ownership: Privately held

Product types:

- Modems
- Bridges/routers/gateways
- Network management
- Fax boards
- Electronic mail
- Networking software
- ISDN adapters

Hewlett-Packard Company

3000 Hanover St.
Palo Alto, CA 94304-1181
800-752-0900
415-857-1501
800-333-1917 (F)

Year established: 1939
Number employees: 98,000
Gross annual sales: $25,000M
Ownership: Publicly traded NYSE
  (HWP)

Product types:

- Hardware platforms
- Test equipment
- Bridges/routers/gateways
- Hubs
- Network interface cards
- Network management
- UPS
- Printers
- Electronic mail
- Networking software
- ISDN adapters

Hitachi America, Ltd.

3617 Parkway Lane
Norcross, GA 30092
800-446-8820
404-446-8821
404-242-1414 (F)

Year established: 1984
Number employees: 4,000
Gross annual sales: $71,000M
Ownership: Parent company stock
  traded on NYSE (HIT)

Product types:

- Network management

Hughes LAN Systems, Inc.

1225 Charleston Rd.
Mountain View, CA 94043
800-395-LANS
415-966-7300
415-966-6161 (F)

Year established: 1979
Number employees: 350
Gross annual sales: $75M

Ownership: Parent company stock
traded on NYSE (GMH)

Product types:

- Bridges/routers/gateways
- Hubs
- Terminal servers
- Networking software

IBM

Old Orchard Rd.
Armonk, NY 10504
800-426-3333
914-765-1900

Year established: 1914
Number employees: 250,000
Gross annual sales: $63,000M
Ownership: Publicly traded NYSE
  (IBM)

Product types:

- Hardware platforms
- Multiplexers
- Bridges/routers/gateways
- Hubs
- Network interface cards
- Network management
- Fax boards
- Software applications

Immersion Corporation

3350 Scott Blvd.
Bldg. 30
Santa Clara, CA 95054
408-653-1160
408-654-9360 (F)

Year established: 1992

Number employees: 15
Gross annual sales: $1,000,000
Ownership: Privately held

Product types:

- Digitizers

InSoft, Inc.

4718 Old Gettysburg Rd.
Suite 307, Executive Park West I
Mechanicsburg, PA 17055
717-730-9501
717-730-9504 (F)

Year established: 1991
Number employees: 50
Ownership: Privately held

Product types:

- Video/teleconferencing software

Intel Corporation

5200 N.E. Elam Young Pkwy.
Hillsboro, OR 97124-6497
800-538-3373
503-629-7354
503-629-7580 (F)

Year established: 1968
Number employees: 27,000
Gross annual sales: $8,000M
Ownership: Parent company stock
  traded on NASDAQ (INTC)

Product types:

- Test equipment
- Network interface cards
- Fax boards
- Modems
- Software applications
- Fax software

- Networking software
- ISDN adapters

ISDN Systems Corporation

8320 Old Courthouse Rd.
Suite 200
Vienna, VA 22182
800-KNOW-ISC
703-883-0933
703-883-8043 (F)

Year established: 1990
Ownership: Privately held

Product types:

- Bridges/routers/gateways
- Network management
- ISDN adapters

Lantronix

15353 Barranca Pkwy.
Irvine, CA 92718-2216
800-422-7055
714-453-3990
714-453-3995 (F)

Year established: 1988
Ownership: Privately held

Product types:

- Bridges/routers/gateways
- Terminal servers

Laser Communications, Inc.

1848 Charter Lane
Suite F
P.O. Box 10066
Lancaster, PA 17605-0066
800-527-3740
717-394-8634
717-396-9831 (F)

Year established: 1983
Number employees: 12
Gross annual sales: $3,000,000
Ownership: Privately held

Product types:

- Laser transmission equipment

Lotus Development Corporation

55 Cambridge Pkwy.
Cambridge, MA 02142-1295
800-343-5414
617-577-8500
617-693-3512 (F)

Year established: 1982
Number employees: 4,980
Gross annual sales: $970M
Ownership: Publicly traded
  NASDAQ (LOTS)

Product types:

- Office automation software
- Spreadsheets
- Electronic mail software
- Networking software

LSI Logic Corporation

1551 McCarthy Blvd.
Milpitas, CA 95035
800-433-8778
408-433-8000
408-434-6457 (F)

Year established: 1981
Number employees: 3,400
Gross annual sales: $719M

Product types:

- Engineering applications

Mass Optical Storage Technologies, Inc.

11205 Knott Ave.
Suite B
Cypress, CA 90630
714-898-9400
714-373-9960 (F)

Year established: 1987
Number employees: 120
Ownership: Privately held

Product types:

- Optical disk drives

McDATA Corporation

310 Interlocken Pkwy.
Broomfield, CO 80021-3464
800-545-5773
303-460-9200
303-465-4996 (F)

Year established: 1982
Number employees: 140
Ownership: Privately held

Product types:

- Modems
- Multiplexers
- Network management

MCI Communications Corporation

3 Ravinia Dr.
Atlanta, GA 30346
800-825-9675
404-668-6000

Year established: 1968
  (Corporation)
Number employees: 30,964
  (Corporation)

Gross annual sales: $12,000M
(Corporation)
Ownership: Parent company stock
traded on NASDAQ (MCIC)

Product types:

- Communications Services

Memorex Telex Corporation

545 E. John Carpenter Frwy., LB 6
Irving, TX 75062-3931
800-944-4455, ext. 7788
214-444-3500
214-444-3501 (F)

Year established: 1987
Number employees: 4,000
Gross annual sales: $1,000M
Ownership: Publicly traded
  NASDAQ (MEMXY)

Product types:

- Hardware platforms
- Hubs
- Network management
- Printers

MICOM Communications Corporation

4100 Los Angeles Ave.
Simi Valley, CA 93063-3397
800-642-6687
805-583-8600
805-583-1997 (F)

Year established: 1973
Number employees: 400
Gross annual sales: $81M
Ownership: Publicly traded
  NASDAQ (MICM)

Product types:

- Modems
- Multiplexers
- Terminal servers
- Networking software

MicroTest, Inc.

4747 North 22nd St.
Phoenix, AZ 85016-4700
800-526-9675
602-952-6400
602-952-6401 (F)

Year established: 1984
Number employees: 160
Gross annual sales: $22M
Ownership: Publicly traded
  NASDAQ (MTST)

Product types:

- Test equipment
- Networking software

Micro Computer Systems, Inc.

2300 Valley View Lane
Suite 800
Irving, TX 75062
214-659-1514
214-659-1624 (F)

Year established: 1981
Ownership: Privately held

Product types:

- Networking Software

Microsoft Corporation

One Microsoft Way
Redmond, WA 98052-6399

800-426-9400
206-882-8080
206-93-MSFAX (F)

Year established: 1975
Number employees: 10,000
Gross annual sales: $5,000M
Ownership: Publicly traded
  NASDAQ (MSFT)

Product types:

- Software applications
- Electronic mail Software
- Networking software

Motorola Codex

20 Cabot Blvd.
Mansfield, MA 02048-1193
800-446-6336
508-261-4000
508-337-8004 (F)

Year established: 1962
Number employees: 3,000
Gross annual sales: $500M
Ownership: Parent company stock
  traded on NYSE (MOT)

Product types:

- Modems
- Multiplexers
- Bridges/routers/gateways
- Network management
- Networking software

Motorola

2900 S. Diablo Way
Tempe, AZ 85282
800-759-1107
602-438-3000
602-438-3370 (F)

Year established: 1969
Number employees: 110,000
Gross annual sales: $5,000M
Ownership: Parent company stock
  traded on NYSE (MOT)

Product types:

- Hardware platforms
- Network interface cards
- Network management
- Testing software

Newbridge Networks, Inc.

593 Herndon Pkwy.
Herndon, VA 22070-5241
800-343-3600
703-834-3600
703-471-7080 (F)

Year established: 1986
Number employees: 1,000
Gross annual sales: $250M
Ownership: Publicly traded
  NASDAQ (NNCXF)
Publicly traded Toronto Stock
  Exchange (NNC)

Product types:

- Multiplexers
- Bridges/routers/gateways
- Network management
- Networking software
- ISDN adapters

Novell, Inc.

122 East 1700 South
Provo, UT 84606-6194
800-453-1267
801-429-7000
801-429-5155 (F)

Year established: 1983
Number employees: 10,000
Gross annual sales: $2,000M
Ownership: Publicly traded
  NASDAQ (NOVL)

Product types:

- Network operating systems
- Software applications
- Electronic mail

On-Line Power Corporation

5701 Smithway St.
Commerce, CA 90040
213-721-5017
213-721-3929 (F)

Year established: 1975
Number employees: 200
Gross annual sales: $30M
Ownership: Privately held

Product types:

- UPS

Racal-Datacom, Inc.

1601 N. Harrison Pkwy.
Sunrise, FL 33323-2802
800-RACAL-55
305-846-4811
305-846-4942 (F)

Year established: 1955
Number employees: 2,000
Gross annual sales: $550M
Ownership: Parent company stock
  traded on London Stock Exchange

Product types:

- Modems
- Multiplexers

- Bridges/routers/gateways
- Hubs
- Network management
- Terminal servers
- Networking software

Retix

2401 Colorado Ave.
Suite 200
Santa Monica, CA 90404-3563
800-255-2333
310-828-3400
310-828-2255 (F)

Year established: 1985
Number employees: 400
Gross annual sales: $60M
Ownership: Publicly traded
  NASDAQ (RETX)

Product types:

- Multiplexors
- Bridges/routers/gateways
- Hubs
- Software applications
- Electronic mail
- Networking software

Siemens Stromberg-Carlson

900 Broken Sound Blvd.
Boca Raton, FL 33487
407-955-5000
407-955-8771 (F)

Year established: 1990
Number employees: 40,000
Gross annual sales: $51,000M
Ownership: Parent company stock
  traded on Frankfurt Stock
  Exchange

Product types:

- Network management

SMS Data Products Group, Inc.

1501 Farm Credit Dr.
McLean, VA 22102-5004
800-331-1767
703-709-9898
703-356-4831 (F)

Year established: 1975
Number employees: 100
Gross annual sales: $50M
Ownership: Privately held

Product types:

- Server/Sharing Units

StrataCom, Inc.

1400 Parkmoor Ave.
San Jose, CA 95126
800-767-4479
408-294-7600
408-999-0115 (F)

Year established: 1986
Number employees: 700
Gross annual sales: $20M
Ownership: Publicly traded
  NASDAQ (STRM)
Product types:

- Multiplexers

- Network management

- Routers

Sun Microsystems Computer Corporation

2550 Garcia Ave.
Mountain View, CA 94043-1100
800-821-4643

415-960-1300
415-969-9131 (F)

Year established: 1982
Number employees: 14,000
Gross annual sales: $5,000M
Ownership: Parent company stock
  traded on NASDAQ (SUNW)

Product types:

- Hardware platforms

- Network interface cards

- Software applications

- Networking software

SynOptics Communications, Inc.

4401 Great America Pkwy.
P.O. Box 58185
Santa Clara, CA 95054-8185
800-PRO-NTWK
408-988-2400
408-988-5525 (F)

Year established: 1989
Number employees: 45
Gross annual sales: $700M
Ownership: Parent company stock
  traded on NASDAQ (SNPX)

Product types:

- Bridges/routers/gateways

TASC, Inc.

55 Walkers Brook Dr.
Reading, MA 01867-3297
617-942-2000
513-426-1040 (OH)
617-942-7100 (F)

Year established: 1966
Number employees: 2,000

Gross annual sales: $300M

Ownership: Parent company stock traded on NYSE (PMK)

Product types:

- Software Applications
- Document Management

TDK Systems

136 New Mohawk Rd.
Nevada City, CA 95959
800-999-4TDK
916-265-5395
916-478-8290 (F)

Year established: 1992
Ownership: Privately held

Product types:

- Network interface cards
- Fax boards
- Modems

Thomas-Conrad Corporation

1908-R Kramer Lane
Austin, TX 78758
800-332-8683
800-654-3822 (CD)
512-836-1935
512-836-2840 (F)

Year established: 1985
Number employees: 300
Gross annual sales: $55M
Ownership: Privately held

Product types:

- Hubs
- Network interface cards
- Networking software

Toshiba America Information Systems, Inc.

9740 Irvine Blvd.
P.O. Box 19724
Irvine, CA 92713-9724
800-334-3445
714-583-3000
714-583-3645 (F)

Year established: 1988
Number employees: 7,500
Gross annual sales: $45,000M
Ownership: Parent company stock traded on Tokyo Stock Exchange

Product types:

- Hardware platforms
- Network interface cards
- Fax Boards
- Modems

TRW, Inc.

1760 Glenn Curtiss St.
Bldg. DH6, Rm. 2271
Carson, CA 90746
800-795-4TRW
310-764-9464
310-764-9491 (F)

Year established: 1985
Number employees: 50
Gross annual sales: $20M
Ownership: Parent company stock traded on NYSE (TRW)

Product types:

- Bridges/routers/gateways
- Network interface cards
- Terminal servers

UB Networks, Inc.

P.O. Box 58030
3900 Freedom Circle
Santa Clara, CA 95052-8030
800-777-4LAN
408-496-0111
408-970-7300 (F)

Year established: 1979
Number employees: 1,000
Gross annual sales: $300M
Ownership: Parent company stock
  traded on NYSE (TDM)

Product types:

- Bridges/routers/gateways
- Hubs
- Network interface cards
- Network management
- Terminal servers
- Networking software

Unisys Corporation

P.O. Box 500
Blue Bell, PA 19424-0001
800-874-8647
215-986-4011
215-986-3170 (F)

Year established: 1986
Number employees: 50,000
Gross annual sales: $7,500M
Ownership: Publicly traded NYSE
  (UIS)

Product types:

- Hardware platforms
- Software applications
- Communications software

U.S. Robotics, Inc.

8100 N. McCormick Blvd.
Skokie, IL 60076-2999
800-USR-CORP
708-982-5010
708-933-5800 (F)

Year established: 1976
Number employees: 1,000
Gross annual sales: $400M
Ownership: Publicly traded
  NASDAQ (USRX)

Product types:

- Modems
- Network management
- Fax Boards
- Modems
- Networking software

Wang Laboratories, Inc.

600 Technology Park Dr.
Billerica, MA 01821-4130
800-225-0654
508-967-5000
508-967-0828 (F)

Year established: 1951
Number employees: 7,200
Gross annual sales: $1,940,000,000
Ownership: Publicly traded
  NASDAQ (WANG)

Product types:

- Hardware platforms

Wyse Technology, Inc.

3471 N. First St.
San Jose, CA 95134-1803
800-438-9973

408-473-1200
408-473-1222 (F)

Year established: 1981
Number employees: 2,000
Ownership: Privately held

Product types:

- Hardware platforms
- Terminal servers

Xircom, Inc.

2300 Corporate Center Dr.
Thousand Oaks, CA 91320-1420
800-438-9472
805-376-9300
805-376-9311 (F)

Year established: 1988
Number employees: 300
Gross annual sales: $130M
Ownership: Publicly traded
  NASDAQ (XIRC)

Product types:

- Network interface cards
- Server/sharing units

Zenith Electronics Corporation

1000 Milwaukee Ave.
Glenview, IL 60025-2493
800-788-7244
708-391-8000
708-391-8919 (F)

Year established: 1918
Number employees: 22,000
Gross annual sales: $1,000M
Ownership: Publicly traded NYSE
  (ZE)

Product types:

- Bridges/routers/gateways
- Hubs

B

Network Standards

100Base-T Proposed IEEE standard for a 100 Mbps LAN.

100VG-ANYLAN Proposed IEEE standard for a 100 Mbps LAN using four pairs of Category 5 cabling.

10Base-2 IEEE standard (known as "thin ethernet") for 10 Mbps baseband ethernet over coaxial cable at a maximum distance of 185 meters.

10Base-5 IEEE standard (known as "thick ethernet") for 10 Mbps baseband ethernet over coaxial cable at a maximum distance of 500 meters.

10Base-F IEEE standard for 10 Mbps baseband ethernet over optical fiber.

10Broad-36 IEEE standard for 10 Mbps broadband ethernet over broadband cable at a maximum distance of 3,600 meters.

ANSI FDDI (Fiber Distributed Data Interface) An ANSI standard for token passing networks. FDDI uses optical fiber and operates at 100 Mbps.

ANSI X.12 An ANSI standard for EDI.

ASN.1 (Abstract Syntax Notation One) OSI standard language describing data types.

Bell 103 AT&T specification for a modem providing asynchronous originate/answer transmission at speeds up to 300 bps.

Bell 113 AT&T standard for asynchronous 300 bps full-duplex modems using FSK modulation on dial-up lines.

Bell 201 AT&T standard for synchronous 2,400 bps full-duplex modems sing DPSK modulation.

Bell 202 AT&T standard for asynchronous 1,800 bps full-duplex modems using DPSK modulation over four-wire leased lines.

Bell 208   AT&T standard for synchronous 4,800 bps modems.

Bell 209   AT&T standard for synchronous 9,600 bps full-duplex modems using QAM modulation.

Bell 212   AT&T standard for asynchronous 1,200 bps full-duplex modems using DPSK modulation on dial-up lines.

EIA 568   An EIA standard for commercial building wiring.

EIA 569   An EIA standard for telecommunications pathways and spaces, such as conduit, equipment rooms, etc.

EIA 606   An EIA standard for telecommunications administration.

HiPPI (High Performance Parallel Interface channel)   An ANSI-standard for high-speed (100–200 Mbps) point-to-point transmission between supercomputers or high-speed LANs.

HSSI (High-Speed Serial Interface)   A standard for up to 52 Mbps serial connections, often used to connect T3 lines.

IEEE 802.1   IEEE standard for network management.

IEEE 802.1D   IEEE standard for inter-LAN bridges.

IEEE 802.2   IEEE standard for Logical Link Control (LLC).

IEEE 802.3   IEEE standard for CSMA/CD (ethernet) LAN access.

IEEE 802.4   IEEE standard for token bus LAN multiple access.

IEEE 802.5   IEEE standard for token ring LAN multiple access.

IEEE 802.6   IEEE standard for DQDB metropolitan area network multiple access.

IEEE 802.7   IEEE standard for broadband LANs.

IEEE 802.9   IEEE standard for integrated digital and video networking.

IEEE 802.10   IEEE standard for network security.

IEEE 802.11   IEEE standard for wireless LANs.

IEEE 802.12   IEEE standard for a demand priority LAN access (also called "Fast Ethernet").

IEEE 1284   IEEE standard for an enhanced parallel port compatible with the Centronics parallel port.

IEEE 488   IEEE standard for computer-to-electronic instrument communication.

ISO 7498   ISO standard for the Open System Interconnection (OSI) basic reference model.

ISO 9001   ISO standards for quality design, development, production, installation and service procedures.

JPEG (Joint Photographic Experts Group)   An ISO standard for lossy compression.

LAP (Link Access Procedure)   An ITU error correction protocol derived from the HDLC standard.

LAP-B (LAP-Balanced) LAP protocol used in X.25 networks.

LAP-D (LAP-D channel) LAP protocol used in the data channel of ISDN networks.

LAP-X (LAP-Half-dupleX) LAP protocol used for ship-to-shore transmission.

MPEG (Moving Pictures Experts Group) An ISO standard for lossless compression of full-motion video.

PCMCIA (Personal Computer Memory Card International Association) A standard set of physical interfaces for portable computers. PCMCIA specifies three interface sizes, Type I (3.3 millimeters), Type II (5.0 millimeters), and Type III (10.5 millimeters).

PPP (Point-to-Point Protocol) A router-to-router and host-to-network protocol for connections over both synchronous and asynchronous circuits. PPP is the successor to SLIP.

RJ-45 An 8-pin connector used for data transmission over standard telephone wire.

RS-232 An EIA standard for up to 20 Kbps, 50 foot, serial transmission between computers and peripheral devices.

RS-422 An EIA standard specifying electrical characteristics for balanced circuits. RS-422 is used in conjunction with RS-449.

RS-423 An EIA standard specifying electrical characteristics for unbalanced circuits. RS-423 is used in conjunction with RS-449.

RS-449 An EIA standard specifying a 37-pin connector for high-speed transmission.

RS-485 An EIA standard for multipoint communications lines.

S-100 bus An IEEE 696, 100-pin, bus standard.

SCI (Scaleable Coherent Interface) An IEEE standard for a high-speed (up to 1 Gbps) bus.

SLIP (Serial Line IP) A protocol superseding PPP, allowing a computer to use the Internet protocols.

SONET (Synchronous Optical NETwork) A fiber optic transmission system for high-speed digital traffic. SONET is part of the B-ISDN standard.

T1 Originally developed by Bell Labs for digital telephone transmission, specifies a time division multiplexing scheme for transmission of digital signals.

V.21 An ITU standard for asynchronous 0–300 bps full-duplex modems.

V.21 FAX An ITU standard for facsimile operations at 300 bps.

V.22 An ITU standard for asynchronous and synchronous 600 and 1,200 bps full-duplex modems.

V.22 bis An ITU standard for 2,400 bps duplex modems.

V.23 An ITU standard for asynchronous and synchronous 0–600 and 0–1,200 bps half-duplex modems.

V.32 An ITU standard for asynchronous and synchronous 4,800 and 9,600 bps full-duplex modems

V.32 bis   An ITU standard for 14,400 bps modems.

V.32terbo   An AT&T standard for 19,200 bps modems.

V.33   An ITU standard for synchronous 12,000 and 14,400 bps full-duplex modems.

V.34   An ITU standard for 28,800 bps modems.

V.35   An ITU standard for group band modems combining several telephone circuits to achieve high data rates.

V.42   An ITU standard for modem error checking.

X.21   An ITU standard for a circuit switching network.

X.25   An ITU standard for an interface between a terminal and a packet switching network.

X.75   An ITU standard for packet switching between public networks.

X.121   An ITU standard for international address numbering.

X.400   An ITU standard for OSI messaging.

X.500   An ITU standard for OSI directory services.

Glossary

acceptance testing Type of testing that determines whether the network is acceptable to the actual users. The users of the network should participate in developing acceptance criteria and running the tests.

accounting and chargeback A mechanism that keeps track of network utilization and determines charges for resources users utilize. Users, departments, or divisions can then be charged for the resources.

adaptive routing A form of network routing in which the path data packets traverse from a source to a destination node depends on the current state of the network. Normally, with adaptive routing, routing information stored at each node changes according to an algorithm that calculates the best paths through the network.

ADCCP (Advanced Data Communications Control Procedures) ANSI standard bit-oriented communications protocol.

algorithm A finite process for the solution to a problem.

alpha test Product testing done by the vendor

analog signal An electrical signal with an amplitude that varies continuously as time progresses.

ANSI (American National Standards Institute) The primary standards-forming body in the United States.

APD (Avalanche Photodiode) A high-performance device used in an optical communication system, which converts light into electrical signals. Normally, the APD is used in conjunction with an injection laser diode light source.

application process An entity, either human or software, that uses the services offered by the Application Layer of the OSI Reference Model.

ARP (Address Resolution Protocol) A TCP/IP protocol that binds logical (IP) addresses to physical addresses.

ARPANET (Advanced Research Project Agency Network) A Department of Defense network that provided the groundwork for development of the Internet.

ARQ (Automatic Repeat-Request) A method of error correction wherein the receiving node detects errors and uses a feedback path to the sender for requesting the retransmission of incorrect frames.

asynchronous transmission A type of synchronization in which there is no defined time relationship between transmission of frames.

AT Bus A PC bus that supports 16-bit data.

ATM (Asynchronous Transfer Mode) A cell-based, connection-oriented data service offering high speed (up to Gbps range) data transfer. ATM integrates circuit and packet switching to handle both constant and burst information.

AUI (Attachment Unit Interface) A 15-pin interface between an ethernet network interface card and a transceiver.

autonomous computer A computer that can function on its own; that is, it has its own processor, keyboard, storage and applications.

bandwidth The amount of the frequency spectrum that is usable for data transfer. It identifies the maximum rate a signal can fluctuate without encountering significant attenuation (loss of power).

baseband signal A signal that has not undergone any shift in frequency. Normally, with LANs, a baseband signal is purely digital.

baud rate The unit of signaling speed derived from the duration of the shortest code element of the digital signal. In other words, baud rate is the speed the digital signal pulses travel.

beta testing Product testing done by potential users.

bit rate The transmission rate of binary digits. Bit rate is equal to the total number of bits transmitted in relation to the time it takes to send them.

boot virus A virus resident in the boot sectors of a floppy disk that infects the system when a floppy is booted. An example of a boot virus is Michelangelo that destroys data on Michelangelo's birthday, which is March 6th.

bridge A network component that provides internetworking functionality at the data link or medium access layer of a network's architecture. Bridges can provide segmentation of data frames.

bus topology A type of topology in which all nodes share a common transmission medium.

cabling diagram Part of a design specification, which illustrates the location of network hardware and layout of cabling throughout the facility.

CAD (Computer Aided Design) software Applications that utilize vector graphics to create complex drawings.

carrier currents Type of medium utilizing electrical power wires within facilities to transport data.

Category 1 twisted-pair wire Old-style phone wire, which is not suitable for most data transmission. This includes most telephone wire installed before 1983, in addition to most current residential telephone wiring.

Category 2 twisted-pair wire Certified for data rates up to 4 Mbps, which facilitates IEEE 802.5 Token Ring networks (4 Mbps version).

Category 3 twisted-pair wire Certified for data rates up to 10 Mbps, which facilitates IEEE 802.3 10baseT (ethernet) networks.

Category 4 twisted-pair wire Certified for data rates up to 16 Mbps, which facilitates IEEE 802.5 Token Ring networks (16 Mbps version).

Category 5 twisted-pair wire Certified for data rates up to 100 Mbps, which facilitates ANSI FDDI Token Ring networks.

CCITT (International Telegraph and Telephone Consultative Committee) An international standards organization that is part of the ITU and is dedicated to establishing effective, compatible telecommunications among members of the United Nations. CCITT develops the widely used V-series and X-series standards and protocols.

CDDI (Copper Data Distributed Interface) A version of FDDI specifying the use of unshielded twisted pair wiring (Category 5).

CDLC (Cellular Data Link Control) Public domain data communications protocol used in cellular telephone systems.

CDPD (Cellular Digital Packet Data) A standard specifying how to send relatively low speed data over analog cellular telephone networks.

Centronics A de facto standard, 36-pin, parallel, 200-Kbps, asynchronous interface for connecting printers and other devices to a computer.

CGA (Color/Graphics Adapter) An IBM video display standard providing low-resolution text and graphics.

CGM (Computer Graphics Metafile) A standard format for interchanging graphics images.

CLNP (Connectionless Network Protocol) An OSI protocol for providing the OSI Connectionless Network Service (datagram service). CLNP is similar to IP.

CMIP (Common Management Information Protocol) An ISO network monitoring and control standard.

CMIS (Common Management Information Services) An OSI standard defining functions for network monitoring and control.

CMOL (CMIP over LLC) A version of CMIP that runs on IEEE 802 LANs.

CMOT (CMIP over TCP) A version of CMIP that runs on TCP/IP networks.

coaxial cable Type of medium having a solid metallic core with a shielding as a return path for current flow. The shielding within the coaxial cable reduces the amount of electrical noise interference within the core wire; therefore, coaxial cable can extend to much greater lengths than twisted pair wiring.

constraints Requirements that are not possible or feasible to change. Examples of constraints are money, geographical layout, regulations, and politics.

communications cabinet drawings Illustrates the placement of network components that require mounting within communications cabinets.

computer network   Part of an information system that disseminates information between autonomous computers and peripherals. An autonomous computer is one that can function on its own; that is, it has its own processor, keyboard, storage, and applications. Peripherals are items such as printers, fax machines, and modems. Computer networks provide electronic transfer of information, which enables timely information dissemination, collection, and storage capabilities. The network allows its users to have seamless access to a variety of resources, such as printers, applications, and other networks. In the strictest sense, a mainframe system containing a centralized processor and terminals whereby users can gain access is not really a computer network. However, mainframe computers are commonly attached to computer networks. Traditionally, most computer networks transfer textual information; however, networks today need to support a greater number of applications requiring the dissemination of video, voice, and imagery. This challenges network engineers to utilize the most effective technologies to support the growing need for network bandwidth.

concept of operations   Defines system-level functionality, operational environment, and implementation priorities of an information system. Project team members use the concept of operations as a basis for planning the development and determining the requirements of the information system.

configuration management   A process that ensures that there is a complete description of the network components and that proper control exists for making network changes. Configuration management typically requires that anyone wanting to change the network must first request the change by having a technical and managerial review of the recommended change.

connectivity   A path for communications signals to flow through. Connectivity exists between a pair of nodes if the destination node can correctly receive data from the source node at a specified minimum data rate.

contact managers   Applications that make it easy to keep track of clients and sales activities.

customer representative   A project team member representing the interests of the users who will be receiving the network modification.

data link layer — Layer 2 of the OSI Reference Model   The data link layer that provides synchronization and error control mechanisms.

datagram service   A connectionless form of packet switching in which the source does not need to establish a connection with the destination before sending data packets.

DB-9   A standard 9-pin connector commonly used with RS-232 serial interfaces on portable computers. The DB-9 connector will not support all RS-232 functions.

DB-15   A standard 15-pin connector commonly used with RS-232 serial interfaces, ethernet transceivers and computer monitors.

DB-25   A standard 25-pin connector commonly used with RS-232 serial interfaces. The DB-25 connector will support all RS-232 functions.

DES (Data Encryption Standard)   A cryptographic algorithm that protects unclassified computer data. DES is a National Institute of Standards and Technology (NIST) standard and is for both public and Government use.

design   Process that determines how the network will meet requirements. Design involves the selection of technologies, standards, and products that provide a solution to the stated requirements.

design specifications   Describes the technologies, standards, components, and configurations of hardware and software comprising the network.

desktop conferencing   An application allowing users to have televideo conferences directly from PCs located in their offices. Users who participate in a desktop conference can hear and see a video image of each participant. Desktop conferences also allow participants to jointly edit documents and facilitate electronic white boards.

desktop publishing software   Applications that provide the capability to effectively merge text and graphics and maintain precise control of the layout of each page of the document.

Detailed Design   The final phase of network design that selects components and finalizes network configurations and documentation.

Diffused laser light   Type of laser transmission in which the light is reflected off a wall or ceiling.

directive antenna   Type of antenna that sends radio waves primarily in one direction.

distributed routing   A form of routing in which each node (router) in the network periodically identifies neighboring nodes, updates its routing table, and with this information then sends its routing table to all its neighbors. Because each node follows the same process, complete network topology information propagates through the network and eventually reaches each node.

document management   An application allowing users to effectively manage and access information contained within different file types. Most document management software allows users to manipulate both data and images, as well as easily manage files through indexing, search and query functions.

DQDB (Distributed Queue Dual Bus)   A technology that provides full duplex 155 Mbps operation between nodes of a metropolitan area network. The IEEE 802.6 standard is based on DQDB.

DSU/CSU (Data Service Unit/Channel Service Unit)   A network component that reshapes data signals into a form that can be effectively transmitted over a digital transmission medium, typically a leased 56 Kbps or T1 line.

EGA (Enhanced Graphics Adapter)   An IBM video display standard providing medium-resolution text and graphics.

EIA (Electronics Industry Association)   A domestic standards forming organization which represents a vast number of United States electronics firms.

EISA (Extended ISA)   A PC bus standard that extends the 16-bit ISA bus to 32 bits and runs at 8 MHz.

electronic data interchange (EDI)   A service that provides standardized intercompany computer communications for business transactions. ANSI standard X.12 defines the data format for business transactions for EDI.

electronic mail   A service that provides the capability to compose electronic letters that may be sent through the network to other computers. Most electronic mail applications allow the inclusion of attachments, read receipts and recipient replies. Many companies sell proprietary electronic mail packages. These products are vendor specific; that is, they only work with products from the same vendor.

ethernet   A 10-Mbps LAN medium access method that uses CSMA to allow the sharing of a bus-type network. IEEE 802.3 is a standard that specifies ethernet.

FDDI (Fiber Distributed Data Interface)   An ANSI standard for token passing networks. FDDI uses optical fiber and operates at 100 Mbps.

FEC (Forward Error Correction)   A method of error control where the receiving node automatically corrects as many channel errors as it can without referring to the sending node.

file transfer   Capability to send files from one computer to another. File transfer mechanisms allow you to move a file from a disk directory on one computer to that of another. The File Transfer Protocol (FTP), a de facto standard, is a popular protocol for transferring files. Issues involved with file transfer include file size and type. Of course, the larger the file the more bandwidth it takes to deliver, possibly making it not feasible to send very large files. Some networks will support only the transfer of text-only files, but other networks are capable of sending binary files as well.

firewall   A device that interfaces the network to the outside world and shields the network from unauthorized users. The firewall does this by blocking certain types of traffic. For example, some firewalls permit only electronic mail traffic to enter the network from elsewhere. This helps protect the network against attacks made to other network resources, such as sensitive files, databases, and applications.

fractional T2D1   A 64-Kbps increment of a T1 frame.

frame relay   A type of WAN that is a streamlined version of X.25, offering a fast packet-connection-oriented network interface with bit rates up to 2 Mbps.

FTAM (File Transfer, Access, and Management)   An OSI remote file service protocol.

FTP (File Transfer Protocol)   A TCP/IP protocol for file transfer.

fully connected topology   A topology in which every node is directly connected to every other node in the network.

gateway   A network component that provides interconnectivity at higher network layers. For example, electronic mail gateways can interconnect dissimilar electronic mail systems.

hardware   Physical elements containing the electronics necessary to move, store, and display information on the network. The hardware provides connectivity between the users and information stored in memory devices. Hardware, such as monitors and printers, provides a means to view the information. Other examples of network hardware elements include network interface cards, server and client platforms, cabling, bridges, and routers.

hardware configuration plan   Identifies how the team should configure hardware the network utilizes.

hardware platform   A computer which provides necessary processors and file storage. The processors execute the program code, enabling the software to run. The file storage facilitates the storage of software programs and data files. With a network, applications and network operating systems normally reside on some type of hardware platform.

HDLC (High-level Data Link Control)   An ISO bit-oriented protocol for link synchronization and error control.

hierarchical topology   A topology in which nodes in the same geographical area are joined together, then these groups are tied to the remaining network. The idea of a hierarchical topology is to install more links within high-density areas and fewer links between these populations.

HSSI (High-Speed Serial Interface)   A standard for up to 52 Mbps serial connections, often used to connect T3 lines.

HTML (HyperText Markup Language)   A standard used on the Internet World Wide Web for defining hypertext links between documents.

IEEE (Institute of Electrical and Electronic Engineers)   A United States-based standards organization participating in the development of standards for data transmission systems. IEEE has made significant progress in the establishment of standards for LANs, namely the IEEE 802 series of standards.

Infoware   Applications that provide online encyclopedias, magazines, and other references.

installation plan   A plan that describes the tools and procedures necessary for an installation team to install and test network hardware and software components.

integration testing   A type of testing that verifies the interfaces between network components as the components are installed. The installation crew should integrate components into the network one by one, and should perform integration testing when necessary to ensure proper gradual integration of components.

internetwork   A collection of interconnected networks. Often it is necessary to connect networks together, and an internetwork provides the connection between different networks. One organization having a network may want to share information with another organization having a different network. The internetwork provides functionality needed to share information between these two networks.

ISA (Industry Standard Architecture)   A widely used PC expansion bus that accepts plug-in boards, such as ethernet cards, video display boards, and disk controllers. ISA was originally called the AT bus, because it was first used in the IBM AT, extending the original bus from 8 to 16 bits. Most ISA PCs provide a mix of 8-bit and 16-bit expansion slots. Contrast with EISA and Micro Channel. See also, local bus.

ISDN (Integrated Services Digital Network)   A collection of CCITT standards specifying WAN digital transmission service. The overall goal of ISDN is to provide a single physical network outlet and transport mechanism for the transmission of all types of information, including data, video, and voice.

IS-IS (Intermediate System to Intermediate System) protocol   An OSI protocol for intermediate systems exchange routing information.

ISM (Industrial, Scientific, and Medicine)　Radio frequency bands which the Federal Communications Commission (FCC) authorized for wireless LANs. The ISM bands are located at 902 MHz, 2.400 GHz, and 5.7 GHz.

ISO (International Standards Organization)　A nontreaty standards organization active in the development of international standards, such as the Open System Interconnection (OSI) network architecture.

isochronous transmission　Type of synchronization in which information frames are sent at specific times.

installation plan　Describes procedures for installing components and testing the resulting network.

Internetworking　A mechanism defining the communications process necessary to connect two dissimilar autonomous networks.

ITU (International Telecommunications Union)　An agency of the United States providing coordination for the development of international standards.

JPEG (Joint Photographic Experts Group)　An ISO standard for lossy compression.

Lantastic　A peer-to-peer network operating system by Artisoft, Inc.

LAP (Link Access Procedure)　An ITU error-correction protocol derived from the HDLC standard.

learning objectives　A training development element specifying what students are expected to do after receiving instruction.

LED (Light Emitting Diode)　A diode, used in conjunction with optical fiber, which emits incoherent light when current is passed through it. Advantages of LEDs include low cost and long lifetime, and they are capable of operating in the Mbps range.

Local Area Network (LAN)　A computer network confined to a local area, such as a building. The specific uses of a LAN mainly include interoffice communications and peripheral sharing. Usually, a LAN is owned by a single funding organization. That is, a single department, division or organization will normally independently purchase and install the LAN hardware and software.

local bridge　A bridge that connects two LANs within close proximity.

mail gateway　A type of gateway that interconnects dissimilar electronic mail systems.

Maintenance　A mechanism that corrects problems that may occur on the network. Maintenance includes functions such as fault isolation (troubleshooting), repair, and testing.

MAP (Manufacturing Automation Protocol)　A protocol used extensively by General Motors for automated factory floor equipment.

MAU (Multistation Access Unit)　A multiport wiring hub for token ring networks.

MCA (Micro Channel Architecture)　An internal 32-bit bus originally introduced by IBM.

medium   A physical link that provides a basic building block to support the transmission of information signals. Most media are composed of either metal, glass, plastic, or air.

medium access   A data-link function that controls the use of a common network medium.

meteor burst communications   A type of communication system that provides long-haul (1,500-mile) wireless data transmission links. The idea of meteor burst communications is to direct a 40 to 50 MHz radio wave, modulated with a data signal, at ionized gas in the atmosphere. The radio signal then reflects off the gas and is directed back to Earth.

MHS (Message Handling Service)   A Novell messaging system that supports multiple operating systems and messaging protocols.

MIB (Management Information Base)   A collection of objects that can be accessed via a network management protocol.

MIPS (Million Instructions Per Second)   Identifies the number of instructions a computer processes over time. High-speed personal computers, such as pentiums, are usually capable of operating at 100 MIPS or faster. A 386 PC usually runs between 3 to 5 MIPS. However, MIPS rates are not uniform because some vendors utilize the best-case value of the platform while others utilize average rates.

MIDI (Musical Instrument Digital Interface)   A standard protocol for the interchange of musical information between musical instruments and computers.

mobility   Ability to continually move from one location to another.

Motif   A standard GUI for UNIX. Motif is endorsed by the Open Software Foundation.

MPEG (Moving Pictures Experts Group)   An ISO standard for lossless compression of full-motion video.

multimedia   The integration of graphics, text, and sound into a single application.

multimedia software   Applications that add graphics, sound, and video for use in education and specialized applications.

multiplexer   A network component that combines multiple signals into one composite signal in a form suitable for transmission over a long-haul connection, such as leased 56 Kbps or T1 circuits.

NetBIOS (Network Basic Input Output System)   A standard interface between networks and PCs.

NetBEUI   A protocol that governs data exchange and network access. NetBEUI is Microsoft's version of NetBIOS.

NetWare   A server-based network operating system by Novell, Inc.

NetWare Loadable Module (NLM)   An application coexisting with the core NetWare network operating system.

network documentation   Documentation which provides a description of a network. This description identifies and describes all hardware, software, protocols, people, and the operating environment. Complete documentation identifies a baseline, which describes the current makeup of the system. Documentation is very important because it allows people to effectively use and maintain the system.

Network Interface Card (NIC)   A network component that provides the interface between network elements and a medium. NICs typically employ the medium access technique.

Network Layer   Layer 3 of the OSI Reference Model. The network layer controls the major operation of the subnet; that is, the routing of packets from source to destination.

network monitoring   A form of operational support allowing network management people to view the inner workings of the network. Most network monitoring equipment is nonobtrusive and can determine the network's utilization and locate faults.

Network Operating System (NOS)   A network component that provides a platform for network applications to operate. A NOS normally offers communications, printing, and file services for applications residing on the network.

network reengineering   A structured process that can help an organization proactively control the evolution of its network. Network reengineering consists of continually identifying factors influencing network changes, analyzing network modification feasibility, and performing network modifications as necessary.

network requirements   Defines detailed functional and system requirements, operational environment, and constraints of the network.

network security   A form of operational support which attempts to protect the network from compromise and destruction, as well as to make sure the network will be available when needed. Network security includes elements such as access control, data encryption, and data backup.

NFS (Network File System)   A distributed file system allowing a set of dissimilar computers to access each other's files in a transparent manner.

Node   Any network addressable device on the network, such as a router or network interface card.

NSAP (Network Service Access Point)   A point in the network at which OSI network services are available to a transport entity.

ODI (Open Data2DLink Interface)   Novell's specification for network interface card device drivers, allowing simultaneous operation of multiple protocol stacks.

office software   Applications that typical office personnel use, such as word processing, database, spreadsheet, graphics, and electronic mail.

omnidirectional antenna   Type of antenna that sends radio waves in all directions.

operating environment   The physical location in which the network will operate. Thus, the environment contains the system. The environment plays a significant role in a network. Lack of ventilation can allow room temperatures to reach a level that causes electronic devices to overheat, which can cause the system to fail. Weather affects networks in many ways. For instance, lightning can cause serious damage to sensitive equipment such as memory, radio receivers, and transponders, often causing down time. Rain can affect networks in several ways. For example, rain can cause water intrusion in outdoor equipment and can seriously degrade certain types of radio and infrared transmission. It is very important that the system be able to operate effectively within its environment.

operational support plan   A plan that describes how the organization will support the operational network in terms of system administration, network monitoring and control, accounting and chargeback, maintenance, security, configuration management, training, and system reengineering.

operator profiles   Profiles that identify and describe attributes of each person who will be operating the system.

optical fiber   A type of medium that uses changes in light intensity to carry information through glass or plastic fibers.

OSI (Open System Interconnection)   An ISO standard specifying an open system capable of enabling the communications between diverse systems. OSI has seven layers of distinction. These layers provide the necessary functions to allow standardized communications between two application processes.

OSPF (Open Shortest Path First)   Routing protocol for TCP/IP routers.

packet radio   A type of communications system offering long-haul data transmission capability through the utilization of omni-directional radio waves and carrier sense medium access.

PCM (Pulse Code Modulation)   A common method for converting analog voice signals into a digital bit stream.

PCMCIA (Personal Computer Memory Card International Association)   A standard set of physical interfaces for portable computers. PCMCIA specifies three interface sizes, Type I (3.3 millimeters), Type II (5.0 millimeters), and Type III (10.5 millimeters).

peer-to-peer network   A network that enables communications between a group of equal devices. A peer-to-peer LAN docs not depend upon a dedicated server but allows any node to be installed as a nondedicated server and then allows it to share its files and peripherals across the network. Peer-to-peer LANs are normally less expensive because they do not require a dedicated computer to store applications and data, but they do not perform well in place of larger networks.

peripherals   Items external to the computing hardware itself, such as printers, fax machines, and modems.

physical layer   Layer 1 of the OSI Reference Model. The physical layer is concerned with transmitting raw bits over a communications channel. Functions within the physical layer ensure that, when a transmitter sends a bit the receiver gets it. Various types of circuitry within the network, and physical connections between pieces of equipment, guarantee this criterion. The processes that occur within a digital communication system, such as encoding, link encryption, and error control, are examples of functions within the physical layer.

polymorphic virus   A virus that, to avoid identification, changes its binary pattern each time it infects a new file.

portability   Defines network connectivity that can be easily established, used, then dismantled.

POSIX (Portable Operating System Interface for UNIX)   An IEEE 1003.1 standard defining the interface between application programs and the UNIX operating system.

POTS (Plain Old Telephone System)   The common analog telephone system developed many years ago for voice communications.

PPP (Point-to-Point Protocol)   A protocol that provides router-to-router and host-to-network connections over both synchronous and asynchronous circuits. PPP is the successor to SLIP.

preliminary design   The first phase of network design that produces a conceptual solution, by identifying technologies and standards necessary to facilitate the selection of components. Preliminary design allows the team to experiment and compare different solutions before spending a great deal of time and money specifying design details and purchasing products.

project management   Oversight needed to make sure actions are planned and executed in a structured manner.

project management software   Applications that provide the ability to efficiently track a project and analyze the impact of changes.

protocols   Rules which the system must follow to operate correctly. Most network protocols are based on technology and describe rules for communications among system hardware and software elements. These rules govern format, timing, sequencing, and error control. Without protocols, system elements would not be able to make sense out of communications from other elements. Most systems have sets of protocols, often referred to as protocol stacks. Many protocols have been established as standards and approved by various national or international organizations. Examples of protocols include ethernet, token ring, and X.400.

prototyping   A method of determining or verifying requirements and design specifications. The prototype normally consists of network hardware and software that supports a proposed solution. The approach to prototyping is typically a trial-and-error experimental process.

red book   A document of the United States National Security Agency (NSA) that defines criteria for secure networks.

remote bridge   A bridge that connects networks separated by longer distances. Organizations use leased 56-Kbps circuits, T1 digital circuits, and radio waves to provide long-distance connections between remote bridges.

repeater   A network component that provides internetworking functionality at the physical layer of a network's architecture. A repeater regenerates digital signals.

requirements   Identify what the network is supposed to do, not how. Requirements should be easily verified and unambiguous.

requirements analysis   A process of defining what the network is supposed to do, providing a basis for the network design.

requirements satisfaction matrix A documentational method that identifies which requirements the chosen technologies and standards satisfy. This matrix helps designers identify an overall solution that covers all requirements.

resource requirements Specifications that identify people and equipment the project will need to accomplish the project's goals.

resource sharing Allows users of the network to share network resources, such as printers, disk drives, applications, modems, and fax machines.

ring topology A topology in which a set of nodes are joined together in a closed loop.

router A network component that provides internetworking at the network layer of a network's architecture, by allowing individual networks to become part of a WAN.

SAP (Service Access Point) A point at which the services of an OSI layer are made available to the next higher layer.

Schematic A drawing that is normally part of a design specification and illustrates the electrical connections between network hardware components. The schematic serves two main purposes: (1) the installation team uses the schematic to properly install the network; (2) maintenance technicians use the schematic to facilitate effective troubleshooting.

SCI (Scalable Coherent Interface) An IEEE standard for a high-speed (up to 1 Gbps) bus.

scientific applications Applications that provide the analysis of real-world events by simulating them with mathematics.

server-oriented network A network architecture in which the network software is split into two pieces, one each for the client and the server. The server component provides services for the client software. The client component interacts with the user. The client and server components run on different computers. Usually the server is more powerful than the client. The main advantage of a server-oriented network is less network traffic. Therefore, networks having a large number of users will normally perform better with server-oriented networks.

SIMM (Single In-line Memory Module) Standard packaging for PC memory.

simulation A method of determining or verifying requirements and design specifications. Simulation includes the development of a simulation model consisting of a software program written in a simulation language. Simulation allows designers to fabricate a logical software model of the network and try out different solutions by reconfiguring the model and testing its performance.

SLIP (Serial Line Internet Protocol) An Internet protocol used to run IP over serial lines.

SMDS (Switched Multimegabit Digital Service) A packet switching connectionless data service for WANs.

SMTP (Simple Mail Transfer Protocol) The Internet electronic mail protocol.

SNA (Systems Network Architecture) IBM's proprietary network architecture.

SNMP (Simple Network Monitoring Protocol)   A network management protocol that defines the transfer of information between Management Information Bases (MIBs). Most high-end network monitoring stations require the implementation of SNMP on each of the components the organization wishes to monitor.

software   A set of instructions that run on a computer and tell the hardware what to do. Software provides an interface for people to use the system and facilitates various network services and functionality, such as printing and sharing applications. Examples of network software elements include applications, drivers, network operating systems, and communications software.

software configuration plan   A plan that identifies how the team should configure software the network utilizes.

SONET (Synchronous Optical NETwork)   A fiber optic transmission system for high-speed digital traffic. SONET is part of the B-ISDN standard.

spread spectrum   A modulation technique that spreads a signal's power over a wide band of frequencies. The main reasons for spreading is that the signal then becomes much less susceptible to electrical noise and is less interfering with other radio-based systems.

SQL (Structured Query Language)   An international standard for defining and accessing relational databases.

SST connector   An optical fiber connector that uses a bayonet plug and socket.

star topology   A topology in which each node is connected to a common central switch or hub.

Statement Of Work (SOW)   A documents that describes what needs to be done to accomplish the network modification.

stealth virus   A virus that is undetectable.

strategic information systems plan   A plan that provides long-term vision and general procedures necessary to manage the efficient evolution of a quality information system. The organization can use this plan for technical guidance and as a basis for budgeting and allocating resources. The strategic information system plan identifies a clear set of milestones, avoids stovepiping and the evolution of legacy systems, identifies long-term and short-term technical goals and tells how to reach the goals, identifies realistic constraints, supports all projected business objectives, identifies a complete strategy for engineering the information system, and specifies general technologies and standards.

synchronous transmission   Type of synchronization in which information frames are sent within certain time periods.

system administration   Type of operational support that provides a human interface between the system and its users. A system administrator assigns user addresses and log-in passwords, allocates network resources, and performs some network security functions.

system analysts   Technicians who determine the requirements for the network.

system testing   Type of testing that verifies the installation of the entire network. Testers normally complete system testing in a simulated production environment, simulating actual users to ensure that the network meets all stated requirements.

T1   A standard specifying a time division multiplexing scheme for point-to-point transmission of digital signals at 1.544 Mbps.

TCP (Transmission Control Protocol)   A very common de facto standard transport layer protocol.

TDR (Time-Domain Reflectometer)   A device that tests the effectiveness of network cabling.

technology comparison matrix   A documentation method that compares similar technologies, based on attributes such as functionality, performance, cost and maturity.

telecommuting   Off-site working via the electronic stretching of an office to (for example) a person's home.

telnet   A virtual terminal protocol used in the Internet, allowing users to log into a remote host.

test case   An executable test with a specific set of input values and a corresponding expected result.

token ring   A medium access method that provides multiple access to a ring-type network through the use of a token. FDDI and IEEE 802.5 are token ring standards.

TOP (Technical and Office Protocol)   A protocol used extensively by General Motors to exchange information between the factory floor and engineering offices.

topography   A description of the network's physical surface spots. In other words, it specifies the type and location of nodes with respect to one another.

topology   A description of the network's geographical layout of nodes and links.

TP0 — OSI Transport Protocol Class 0 (Simple Class)   A protocol that is useful only with very reliable networks.

TP4 — OSI Transport Protocol Class 4 (Error Detection and Recovery Class)   A protocol that is useful with any type of network. The functionality of TP4 is similar to that of TCP.

transceiver   A device for transmitting and receiving packets between the computer and the medium.

transport layer   Layer 4 of the OSI Reference Model. The transport layer's job is to provide the most efficient and reliable end-to-end communication between two users (or hosts).

twisted pair   Type of medium using metallic-type conductors twisted together to provide a path for current flow. The wire in this medium is twisted in pairs to minimize the electromagnetic interference between one pair and another.

unit testing   Type of testing that verifies the accuracy of each network component, such as servers, cables, hubs and bridges. The goal of unit testing is to make certain the component works properly by running tests that fully exercise the internal workings of the component. Unit testing is sometimes referred to as whitebox testing.

UNIX A multiuser and multitasking operating system originally developed by AT&T.

UPS (Uninterruptible Power Supply) A network component that provides a short supply of power to servers and other critical devices if power discontinues.

user interface A mechanism that allows users to access network services.

user manual A document providing user-level procedures on how to log in and utilize network services and applications.

vertical market applications Applications that provide customized data entry, query, and report functions for various industries, such as insurance and banking.

VGA (Video Graphics Array) An IBM video display standard.

VINES A server-oriented network operating system by Banyan, Inc.

virus Software that infects a computer and causes it to malfunction and destroy data.

Wide Area Network (WAN) A type of network that makes long-haul, interoffice communications possible. WANs provide information transport between LANs and users, often over a wide geographical area. A WAN's diameter is typically greater than the size of a building. In addition, separate funding organizations normally own the WAN. For example, a WAN connecting two organizations might not be owned by either organization. Or, the WAN might be owned by a part of the organization that does not own either LAN. The basic structure of a WAN is that of a collection of nodes and links. Nodes are normally switching elements that route data through the network, and links connect nodes together to form at least one or more communication paths or circuits between each user. Each node normally maintains a routing table that the node can use to determine whether data it receives has reached its destination or which link the data should be sent to next to get closer to its destination. Most WANs provide a mechanism that automatically updates the routing tables as the WAN's topology changes.

Work Breakdown Structure (WBS) Shows how the team will accomplish the project by listing all tasks the team will need to perform and the products they must deliver.

World Wide Web, or "Web" An interconnection of privately owned and operated servers. Each server stores a set of hypertext pages that users, or "Web Surfers," can easily search for and view from their workstations through a Web browser, via an Internet connection.

X Windows A windowing system which runs under UNIX.

Index

Illustrations are in **boldface**.

ABOUT THE AUTHOR

Jim Geier has seventeen years of experience in analyzing, developing, and managing information systems. Currently, Jim is a senior systems consultant at TASC, where he provides information system management and engineering consultation to commercial companies and government organizations. In addition, he develops and instructs short courses internationally on project management, network technologies, reengineering methodologies, and software development.

Some of Jim's past projects include the management of development and operational support of a 15,000-user corporate network; design of numerous large-scale local area networks; evaluation of the effectiveness of wireless LAN technology for use in mobile and portable office environments; principal investigator for a Small Business Innovative Research (SBIR) grant that led to the development of an automated software tool that assists engineers in planning, upgrading, and maintaining computer networks; lead analyst in the research and development of a tool to aid engineers in the installation of wireless networks; evaluation of network technologies for use in mobile sensor systems; development and implementation of an adaptive automatic routing algorithm for a worldwide packet radio network; lead engineer for a test team that performed system tests on global networks; development and instruction of an eight-week course that instructed engineers and technicians on the theory and testing of networks; and lead test engineer in the acceptance testing of an automatic tracking radar system.

Mr. Geier has served as chairman of the Institute of Electrical and Electronic Engineers (IEEE) Computer Society, Dayton Section, and chairman of the IEEE International Conference on Wireless LAN Implementation. He is an active member of the IEEE 802.11 Working Group, responsible for developing international standards for wireless LANs. He is an adjunct instructor for Wright State University, Department of Computer Science and Engineering, where he teaches graduate level courses in computer communications. He has published numerous articles in magazines and conference proceedings and has given many presentations at conferences and workshops. He holds a B.S. and an M.S. in electrical engineering, with emphasis in computer communications.

Jim resides with his family in Yellow Springs, Ohio. You can reach him via e-mail at 71165.2045@compuserve.com.